VOLUNTEER WORK
SIXTH EDITION
THE COMPLETE GUIDE TO VOLUNTARY SERVICE

CENTRAL BUREAU
FOR EDUCATIONAL VISITS & EXCHANGES

LONDON   EDINBURGH   BELFAST

Every effort has been made to ensure the accuracy of the information contained in **Volunteer Work**, but the Central Bureau for Educational Visits & Exchanges cannot accept responsibility for any errors which may exist, or for changes made after publication. The Central Bureau and officers accept no responsibility collectively or individually for the services offered by agencies or persons advertised or announced in the pages of this book or any misdescriptions, defaults or failures by any of them. Although publishing in good faith, the Central Bureau gives no express or implied warranty in relation to such matters. All rights reserved throughout the world. No part of this publication may be reproduced, stored in a retrieval system, or transmitted, in any form or by any means, electronic, mechanical or otherwise, without the prior permission in writing of the publishers.

Sixth edition   April 1995
© Central Bureau for Educational Visits & Exchanges

ISBN 1 898601 05 4

Published by the Central Bureau for Educational Visits & Exchanges, Seymour Mews, London W1H 9PE

Head of Publications/Editor Thom Sewell
Contributing Editor Moira Jenkins
Editorial support Rebecca Sewell

Cover illustration © Hans Neleman/Image Bank

Compiled, edited and produced for print by the Information, Print & Design Unit, Central Bureau for Educational Visits & Exchanges, London

Printed and bound in Britain by BPC Hazell Books Ltd

CONTENTS

Section I
TO BE A VOLUNTEER
9 - 24

VOICES OF EXPERIENCE
25 - 32

Section II
UNDERSTANDING DEVELOPMENT
33 - 39

INFORMATION RESOURCES
40 - 47

Section III
PREPARATION & TRAINING
49 - 53

RETURNING HOME
54 - 58

TRAVEL ADVICE
59-64

Section IV
OVERSEAS SERVICE

66 Action Health
67 Africa Inland Mission
68 APSO
69 Associate Missionaries of the Assumption
70 Associates of Mill Hill Missionaries
71 ATD Fourth World
72 Baptist Missionary Society
73 Brethren Volunteer Service
74 Bristol Link with Nicaragua
75 Britain-Nepal Medical Trust
76 Britain-Vietnam Friendship Society
77 British Executive Service Overseas
78 Calcutta Rescue
79 Camphill am Bodensee
80 Camphill Special Schools (Beaver Run)
81 Camphill Village Kimberton Hills
82 Camphill Village USA Inc
83 Centro Studi Terzo Mondo
84 Christian Appalachian Project
85 Christian Foundation for Children & Aging
86 Christian Medical Fellowship
87 Christian Outreach
88 Christian Welfare & Social Relief Organisation
89 Christians Abroad
90 Church Missionary Society
91 Community for Creative Non-Violence
92 Concern/Concern Worldwide
94 Crosslinks
95 Dienst Over Grenzen
96 East European Partnership
98 Education for Development
99 Food for the Hungry
100 Föreningen Staffansgården
101 Frontiers Foundation/ Operation Beaver
102 Future in Our Hands Movement
103 German Leprosy Relief Association
104 Guide Association (UK)
105 Health Projects Abroad
106 Health Volunteers Overseas
107 Help International
108 India Development Group
109 Innisfree Village
110 International Cooperation for Development
111 International Health Exchange
112 Interserve
113 Irish Missionary Union
114 Jacob's Well Appeal
115 Jesuit Volunteer Corps (United States-Southwest)
116 Joint Assistance Centre
117 Lanka Jathika Sarvodaya Sangamaya
118 Latin Link

119	Link Africa	161	World Vision UK
120	Médecins Sans Frontières		
121	Medical Aid for Palestinians		*Section VI*
122	Mennonite Central Committee		**SERVICE IN BRITAIN &**
123	Mission Aviation Fellowship		**IRELAND**
124	Missions to Seamen		
125	Neve Shalom/Wahat Al-Salam	164	ATD Fourth World
126	Options	165	Beannachar Ltd
127	Overseas Service Bureau	166	Camphill Rudolf Steiner Schools
128	Peace Brigades International	167	Camphill Village Trust
130	Peace Corps	168	Careforce
132	Richmond Fellowship International	169	Community Service Volunteers
133	St Joseph's Indian School	170	Corrymeela Community
134	Scottish Churches World Exchange	171	Cotswold Community
135	Services for Open Learning	172	Crypt Foundation
136	SHATIL: Support Project for Voluntary Organizations	173	Edinburgh Cyrenians
		174	Glasgow Simon Community
137	Skillshare Africa	175	Great George's Project
138	South American Missionary Society	176	Homes for Homeless People
139	Southern Africa Resource Centre	177	Independent Living Schemes
140	United Nations Association International Service	178	Jesuit Volunteer Community (Britain)
		179	L'Arche Limited
141	United Nations Volunteers (UNV)	180	Land Use Volunteers
142	United Reformed Church in the United Kingdom	181	Leonard Cheshire Foundation
		182	Loch Arthur Village Community
143	United Society for the Propagation of the Gospel	183	Lothlorien (Rokpa Trust)
		184	Nansen Society (UK) Ltd
144	Universities' Educational Fund for Palestinians (UNIPAL)	185	Paradise Community
		186	St Christopher's Hospice
145	VADHU	187	Share Discovery 80 Ltd
146	Viatores Christi	188	Simon Community
147	Vincentian Service Corps	189	Simon Community (Ireland)
148	Visions in Action	190	Stallcombe House Ltd
149	Volunteer Missionary Movement	191	Sue Ryder Foundation
151	Volunteers for Latvia	192	Time for God Scheme
152	VSO	193	Vincentian Service Corps
154	World Assembly of Youth		

Section V
**PROFESSIONAL
RECRUITMENT**

Section VII
**NON-RESIDENTIAL
SERVICE**

**SHORT-TERM
VOLUNTARY WORK**

156	British Red Cross		
157	Health Unlimited		
158	HelpAge International	196	ACET
159	Overseas Development Administration	197	ADFAM National
		198	Book Aid International
160	Oxfam	199	British Dyslexia Association

200	British Limbless Ex-Service Men's Association
201	Cat Survival Trust/The Earth
202	Christian Aid
203	Council for Education in World Citizenship
204	CRISIS
205	Daycare Trust
206	DIAL UK
207	FARM-Africa
208	Friends of the Earth
209	Greenpeace UK
210	Guideposts Trust
211	Imperial Cancer Research Fund
212	Manic Depression Fellowship
213	National Society for the Prevention of Cruelty to Children (NSPCC)
214	Oxfam
215	QUIT
216	REACH
217	Richmond Fellowship
218	Survival International
219	Terrence Higgins Trust
220	Tourism Concern
221	Victim Support
222	War on Want
223	Womankind Worldwide
224	Woodland Trust
225	World Development Movement
226	Short-term voluntary work

Section VIII
INDEX
REPORT FORM

232	Countries index
235	Projects index
236	Organisations index
239	Report form

VOLUNTEER WORK is published by the Central Bureau for Educational Visits & Exchanges, the UK national office for the provision of advice and information on all forms of educational visits and exchanges; the development and administration of a wide range of curriculum-related pre-service and in-service exchange programmes; the linking of educational establishments and local education authorities with counterparts abroad; and the organisation of meetings, workshops and conferences related to professional international experience.

Its information and advisory services extend throughout the educational field, and in addition over 30,000 individual enquiries are answered each year. Its range of publications cater for the needs of people of all ages seeking information on the opportunities available for educational contacts and travel abroad.

The Central Bureau was established in 1948 by the British Government and now forms part of the British Council. It is a registered charity, number 209131, and is funded by the Departments of Education in the United Kingdom and by the European Union to promote international education through exchange and interchange.

Director: Tony Male

Seymour Mews, London W1H 9PE
✆ 0171-486 5101   fax 0171-935 5741

Offices also in Edinburgh
✆ 0131-447 8024
and Belfast
✆ (01232) 664418

USING THIS GUIDE

This guide, the sixth edition of **VOLUNTEER WORK**, aims to offer information, advice and encouragement to all those thinking about volunteering. It sets out to present a clear view of the wide range of options that are available and to direct potential volunteers to those organisations who can make the best use of their skills, time, enthusiasm and commitment. The term *volunteer work* can cover an enormous variety of activities, from spending a few years working on a development project in an Indian village to devoting just a few hours a week to conservation work in a local urban wildlife area. Perhaps the one thing that such different activities have in common is that they involve an element of service which brings rewards not just to the environment or locality in which the work is being done, but also to the volunteers themselves, in contributing to the enrichment of community life and expanding individual horizons and experience. To some extent the terms *volunteer* and *voluntary* can be misnomers, implying that volunteers give of their time and labour but receive nothing material in return. In actual fact most of the placements listed here are paid in some way, whether by nominal pocket money or a wage equivalent to local workers; and accommodation is usually provided, sometimes on a half or full-board basis.

VOLUNTEER WORK focuses on long-term voluntary placements in the UK and abroad, most of which have a time commitment of at least six months, although there are also suggestions for shorter-term and more informal voluntary work. Most projects listed here are full-time and residential: volunteers live away from home, perhaps with other volunteers, often in surroundings that are radically different from those they are used to. Section VII, however, has information on part-time, non-residential opportunities in the UK.

SECTION I TO BE A VOLUNTEER and **VOICES OF EXPERIENCE** provides an introduction to the volunteering ethic, offers advice and information for those thinking of undertaking voluntary service, personal checklists to evaluate potential, a discussion of the key elements of being a volunteer, and what you need to think about before applying to work on a development project in the Third World. It also discusses the pros, cons and options of a period of voluntary service and includes details on opportunities for volunteers in developed countries. **VOICES OF EXPERIENCE** includes personal insights from past volunteers, who discuss their own experiences of voluntary service and give their impressions on how they felt the projects benefited themselves and the community they were working for.

SECTION II UNDERSTANDING DEVELOPMENT and **INFORMATION RESOURCES** lists organisations who campaign on, and raise awareness about, development and development education issues, and are a valuable source of information, especially for volunteers going to, or returning from, the Third World.

Suggested further reading and other useful sources of information and advice covering voluntary work, development issues, taking a year out and travel are listed here under **INFORMATION RESOURCES**.

SECTION III PREPARATION & TRAINING, RETURNING HOME and **TRAVEL ADVICE** covers preparation, briefing and orientation for potential volunteers, including what to expect of the sending agency and what needs to be researched on an individual basis, and lists organisations arranging specialist courses for those about to be placed overseas.
RETURNING HOME gives details of organisations offering advice on resettlement, reorientation and continuing commitment.
TRAVEL ADVICE covers travel, health and insurance, and forward information on returning, including insights from returned volunteers on preparing for the reverse culture shock.

SECTION IV OVERSEAS SERVICE lists, in alphabetical order, those organisations arranging volunteer placements overseas.

SECTION V PROFESSIONAL RECRUITMENT, lists those organisations working in development who, rather than looking for volunteers, recruit personnel with considerable skills, qualifications and overseas work experience.

SECTION VI SERVICE IN BRITAIN & IRELAND, lists organisations recruiting for full-time, residential projects in Britain and Ireland.

SECTION VII NON-RESIDENTIAL SERVICE and **SHORT-TERM VOLUNTARY WORK**, lists opportunities for more informal, non-residential voluntary work in Britain and Ireland.

SHORT-TERM VOLUNTARY WORK offers advice for those who are unable to commit themselves for medium or long-term voluntary service, or who do not yet have the necessary skill/qualifications. Details are also given of projects suitable for those who may wish to participate in a short-term project in order to gain some experience.

Information on each organisation is provided in a set format to aid selection and provide easy comparison:

Name and address of organisation including the title of any contact person to whom potential volunteers should apply.

Telephone number Where no number is given this is at the specific request of the organisation concerned.

Countries/areas lists the countries (or within some countries, the areas) in which volunteers may be placed. In some cases the destination depends on the projects in operation during a particular year or is at the discretion of the organisation.

Profile A general description of the philosophy, aims and activities of each organisation.

Opportunities Details of the type of opportunities available, with a description of what work volunteers are expected to undertake. Where possible, details of the number of volunteers recruited each year are given.

Requirements Age limits for applicants, plus details of the personal qualities, skills, experience and qualifications that volunteers will require. Any language requirements and nationality restrictions are specified. Where applications from people with a disability are considered, this is indicated as follows:

B	Blind or partially-sighted
D	Deaf or hard of hearing
PH	Physically handicapped
W	Wheelchair users

Duration Length of the placement, including any minimum and maximum periods. In general, in the main sections, residential placements last from six months to three years.

Terms and conditions covers details of any costs to volunteers, hours of work, salary or pocket money provided, board and lodging, holiday entitlement, National Insurance, grants and whether travel and insurance costs are covered.

Briefing Details of any orientation course held prior to departure or any debriefing at the end of the placement, plus information on any in-service training or supervision, and language courses.

When to apply Applications and requests for information should be made to the organisations direct, and not via the Central Bureau. Early application is always advisable, giving time to prepare for departure. When writing to any organisation you should mention that you saw the opportunity listed in **VOLUNTEER WORK**, and enclose a large stamped, self-addressed envelope, or, in the case of an organisation based overseas, an addressed envelope and two International Reply Coupons, available from post offices.

Publications Details of newsletters, annual reports and other publications which may be of interest to volunteers.

SECTION VIII INDEX AND REPORT FORM includes three types of index: as well as referring to the alphabetical index of organisations, you can also find a suitable agency by looking up the countries in which you would like to work or the type of project you are interested in.

At the end of your voluntary placement, we would appreciate it if you could complete and return the **REPORT FORM**, which will enable us to keep up-to-date records of the various organisations listed, as well as giving us some idea of volunteers' personal experiences.

SECTION 1

TO BE A VOLUNTEER

VOICES OF EXPERIENCE

TO BE A VOLUNTEER

For many, the word volunteer conjures up the image of a young enthusiast working on a development project somewhere in Africa, Asia or Latin America. The volunteer could be teaching, training, nursing, distributing food, digging wells, building clinics, advising on agriculture ... the list is a long one, but in some way she or he is assumed to be contributing to the development of the host country.

This section sets out to force self-analysis of just what volunteering can achieve - for the volunteers as well as the community - to challenge any myths and stereotypes that may exist, and to cover most of the pros, cons and options. In doing so, potential volunteers should arrive at their own reasoned decisions for volunteering, aided in their choice of agency, project and country, and crystal clear of their ultimate goals.

This section is to help you, as a potential volunteer, consider your motivation and commitment towards volunteering, to provoke you into thinking carefully about what is meant by *development* and to offer you some insight into exactly what type of person the volunteer-sending agencies are looking for. Projects are essentially mutually rewarding and beneficial; both volunteer and co-worker are expected to be enriched by the experience of working on a common task and to have contributed positively, even if fractionally, to the betterment of humankind.

There is now a greater understanding that without the partnership and willing cooperation of agencies, officials and individuals in the country in which projects are established, volunteers and indeed development aid generally may be distorting and harming the very development it is hoped to foster, and interfering intolerably with the right of the societies in question to determine their own destiny.

However, to argue as some have done, that volunteer aid for development is outdated and that such benefit as accrued from it comes in terms of personal experience for the volunteers, is to ignore the vital importance of personal contacts for the growth of mutual understanding and the transmission of skills. In this greater mutual understanding lies the best hope for a real improvement in the human condition worldwide. The witness of returned volunteers in their own community is or should be an important influence for change, without which mutual understanding will be increasingly replaced by self-interest and protectionism.

Motivation Your reasons for thinking about voluntary service may be many and varied, but they are definitely worthy of careful analysis. It is very important that you get at least some understanding of your motivation before deciding whether or not to volunteer, either at home or abroad. You must be absolutely clear, positive and honest with yourself about your reasons for even thinking about volunteering. All volunteers will share a certain amount of idealism, but a realistic expectation of what can be accomplished through voluntary service, and what you will return with in exchange, needs to be set down from the outset. Although rigid preconceptions are the last things expected of today's volunteers, some idea of what you are expecting, and why you are starting out from that position, needs to be examined. Which of the following, if any, apply to you?

☐ I feel voluntary service will give me valuable experience and improve my career prospects

☐ I want to get away from problems at home, at work or at university

☐ I did consider volunteering in my home country, but going abroad is more exciting

☐ I have a political commitment to the struggle of exploited people

☐ I have felt a call from God

☐ I'm fed up of this country, I'm heading for the sunshine

☐ I honestly haven't really thought about why I want to volunteer

Considering the importance of the answer, the question of why one is volunteering is often passed over by both volunteer and sending agency alike. You may find difficulty in answering; there may not even be a clear-cut answer, but the process of examining the reasons for even thinking about volunteering is a vital one.

If you're considering undertaking a project in the Third World, for example, your understanding of why those countries are *underdeveloped* also needs careful examination:

Why are there people in need who have to rely on other people's voluntary help?

How do the people of such countries come to be so poor, badly housed and underfed, and what are the industrialised nations doing to help?

What about disadvantaged people in your own country - couldn't you volunteer to work with them?

One thing is clear: one or two years spent in voluntary service is a considerable slice of one's life and is far too valuable to squander. For such an investment of time and energy it is essential that there is a clear understanding of what volunteers expect and what is expected of them. Read through the following ten reasons for volunteering - some may strike a chord. You may not be prepared for the responses, but these are aimed at provoking you into really thinking about your commitment.

☑ I want to help the less fortunate

A perhaps well-meaning but rather patronising attitude. Have you given any thought as to how and why these people you want to help actually are *less* fortunate? What sort of help do they need, and how are you in a position to give it? In what way do you consider yourself *more* fortunate? Better off, better educated, more intelligent, in some way superior? Are these people less fortunate in a cultural sense? If you are applying this reason to volunteering overseas, remember that Third World countries are no longer colonies. Perhaps you need to acquire some understanding of international citizenship and development issues. Perhaps a change of attitude is required.

☑ I'm sure they'd benefit from my technical skills/expertise

But are these appropriate to the conditions existing in the country where you will be working? The idea that the developed West can solve all the Third World's problems is a dangerous one. Hi-tech methods are not invariably the best ones, and may disrupt perfectly adequate systems that have been in use for generations. Will you be taking a course in the local language? Do you think you'll be able to communicate well enough to transfer your skills to the people that matter? Is the introduction of technology going to have a material benefit in their day-to-day lives? Has it occurred to you that you will perhaps learn more than you can teach?

☑ I want to show solidarity with the poor and oppressed

And presumably you want to work to put an end to poverty and oppression. Do some research. Is the agency you have in mind really working to change things, or is it just treating the symptoms, rather than the causes of poverty? Will the project you will be working on really benefit those who need it, or just help the elite and perpetuate an oppressive system? What kind of government does the country have, and what sort of Human Rights record? Couldn't you work for change far more effectively from your home country? What about the poor and oppressed in the *developed* world; aren't they also in need of solidarity, or are you really just looking for foreign travel?

☑ My life's going nowhere, I want a change, a break from the pressures of the rat race

Volunteering abroad will certainly be a change, but it won't solve your problems. If the rat race is getting you down now, will it be any easier after being abroad? Running away from problems won't necessarily make them disappear. Nor should you consider volunteering to be an easy way out. And how do you feel you're in a position to help anyone, when you're in no position to sort out your own problems effectively?

☑ I want to do something worthwhile

Define *worthwhile*. What is it that you want to give or gain? If you expect to get immediate good feelings about setting the world to rights you may be disappointed. Volunteers usually take time to settle in and find out what is required of them. It may take several months before they feel they're making any progress at all. Many volunteers return feeling that they actually contributed very little to changing the world or helping others, it is they themselves who have gained most from the experience.

 I've just left university and I'm having difficulty finding suitable work here

Unfortunately, applying for voluntary work abroad is not the answer. The majority of volunteer-sending agencies take on employed people with professional qualifications, and are not likely to be able to offer you a placement unless you have considerable work experience and appropriate skills. Those agencies who do recruit less-experienced people may expect them to raise quite a sum of money to contribute to the cost of their placement. There are, however, many opportunities for voluntary work in Britain, which may help in giving you experience and proving to potential employers that you are a responsible and caring person. But remember, you need commitment to volunteer. It is not some sort of easy alternative to work; indeed it requires all the skills and expertise of permanent employment plus more.

 I want to experience the culture and way of life of a far away country

Very honest! Is a period as a volunteer the way to do this? How much have you experienced the culture and way of life of another area or country whilst on holiday? Getting to know the people and what makes the country tick takes time and effort. Will you be living in the community or in an expatriate compound which will remove you from the daily lives of local people? Even as a volunteer you may be considered to be in a position of power and authority - is this what you want? How will it affect your working and social relationships? How much do you know about the country already? Can you speak the local language fluently? How much chance do you think you'll get to become involved in the way of life and the culture whilst working? You will be working, not on some extended holiday. Do you have to go abroad to experience another culture and way of life? What about getting to know members of other cultures in your home country, including working to improve their lot in life?

 I'd benefit from the challenge and experience of working abroad

You might benefit, but who else will? You may enjoy being thrown in at the deep end, but wouldn't you be of more service if you already had experience of voluntary work and development issues? Perhaps you could consider working as a volunteer in Britain, or campaigning for a development organisation before trying an overseas placement.

 My western lifestyle has been very privileged and I want to do something in return

It might also be considered a privilege to take two years out to travel to a far off country and work in the sunshine every day - not everyone can afford to do this! And watch out: this idea of privilege also has a patronising *west is best* air about it. Just how privileged is the lifestyle of other members of *your* community? Virtually all countries have extremes of wealth and poverty, bad housing, illiteracy, high unemployment and immigrant or minority populations discriminated against on many levels. What do you do on a regular basis to help improve their condition? If you do consider yourself fortunate, there are lots of ways to give a little back, and volunteering abroad may not necessarily be the best one, especially if you lack the skills to contribute. Working for fundraising, campaigning or development networks at home can also bring results.

 The situation out there is so desperate, I've just got to do something

Hold on a minute. First of all, what sort of skills have you got that can help? Sympathy and compassion are all very well but they alone can't change things. In cases of famine and disaster for example, the need may be more for cash than people, so your energies would be better channelled into fundraising and working for change from home. How much do you actually know about this crisis that has arisen? Isn't the help you can offer only very short-term? What can you do on a long-term basis that would be more effective? And in the long-term, shouldn't people be given the chance to solve their own problems instead of being told what to do by well-meaning foreigners? Do we really have all the answers?

Working out your motivation and expectations may prove complicated, but it is nonetheless important to try sorting out what you expect to give and gain from volunteering, and whether these expectations are realistic. The most useful projects may come about as a result of the needs and the initiatives of people at the grassroots, where volunteers help those people develop *themselves*.

Janet Taylor has undertaken two voluntary work placements for Christian Outreach, first as a mother, child and community health nurse on the Thai-Cambodian border, and secondly working as part of an emergency team sent out to run a therapeutic feeding programme for the Kurdish refugee community in northern Iraq and Turkey. She feels strongly not only that volunteers should carefully consider their motivation, but also that the aid agencies themselves should make sure that the projects are really needed:

Whilst it is good and encouraging that people do volunteer to help those in need, anyone who feels that this is what they would like to do should examine first their own attitudes and motives for wanting to do the work, before applying to any organisation. An overwhelming desire to meet the needs of the people of the country is essential and should overlie all other agendas of an organisation and the people employed by them. If the nationals you aim to help don't want a project/programme, or see no need for it, or are not included in the planning of it, then they will not work alongside you or be in support of the programme, which will lead eventually to the programme failing to achieve anything. To carry on regardless in this instance is a total waste of resources. In addition, any volunteer should be seeking to make his/her role redundant, replacing the position with a local who has received adequate training by the expatriate. This situation must always be preferable to having expatriate control of all programmes.

The project Janet worked on in Thailand is now being wound down; as refugees return to their country and as the existing national staff are now better trained, the number of volunteers needed is greatly reduced. The emergency programme amongst the Kurdish refugees was also closed down as, after evaluation, it was felt to be no longer necessary.

Qualifications and experience

The days of agencies sending unskilled school leavers to work in the Third World are long gone. Although there are a number of organisations placing those taking a year out on worthwhile community schemes overseas (further information in *A Year Between*, see **INFORMATION RESOURCES**), agencies now look for useful qualifications and transferable skills, usually backed up by solid experience of putting such skills into practice. Even recent graduates are unlikely to be placed as volunteers if they lack basic work experience. This is understandable: someone who has made the transition from being a student to working within the structured discipline of a work environment will have gained valuable management and organisational skills and will be better placed to organise their work in a new situation overseas. Most agencies look for at least two years' work experience; others, especially those covered in the **PROFESSIONAL RECRUITMENT** section, will expect applicants to have already worked in development overseas. If you lack experience and still want to volunteer you should first consider doing a voluntary placement in your home country. Alternatively, you could postpone volunteering until you have more experience under your belt; this has the advantage of giving you more time to consider the options, find out what specific skills are needed and get yourself properly prepared. The following tips may help you better plan any period of preparation for voluntary service:

Pick up some basic skills: learn to drive - in many areas this is an essential skill, as is a knowledge of vehicle maintenance. If you already hold a driving licence, try to get experience on a range of vehicles, including four wheel drive and minibuses. Take evening classes in administration and office skills such as book-keeping or word processing, or practical subjects such as bricklaying or plumbing. The ability to turn your hand to a variety of tasks will always be worthwhile on a development project.

Go for breadth of experience: at village level there is likely to be a need for generalists rather than specialists, so if your present job moves you around departments, take advantage of this to get as broad a training as you can. The more adaptable you can be, the better. Apply any skills you have to the benefit of your own community, gaining more practical experience and training.

Go for hands-on experience: look out for any chance to get real practical experience, find out how and why jobs are done in a certain way, find out how to do-it-yourself. The more hands-on experience you get in doing tasks, the better able you will be to do them overseas, even if materials are not ideal and tools are missing. A knowledge of simple, practical jobs is likely to be most useful to you in the field.

Get experience of teaching: most agencies expect volunteers to transfer their skills to those around them, so start now by learning to be a communicator. You could perhaps help to run a youth group, volunteer to teach basic English, literacy or maths, or take a Sunday school class. Anything involving the sharing of skills and ideas is bound to stand you in good stead.

Learn about the issues: the organisations listed in the **UNDERSTANDING DEVELOPMENT** section offer a variety of resources concerned with development issues. It is also worth reading up about development work in your own particular field, be it health, agriculture, technology or teaching. Getting involved in campaigning or fundraising will also be an excellent way of learning about the problems facing Third World countries and the means that exist to solve them.

Skills Working overseas on a development project will usually mean that you will have more responsibility than you currently have. The full range of your professional and interpersonal skills will be tested and developed, as you develop new perspectives in your chosen field. New in-service skills will have to be quickly acquired, in areas such as cross-cultural communications, project planning and adaptation on the ground. Time scales will have to be revised, particularly if the project you are placed on has not been in operation for long. It can take many years before the process of development can be measured within the local community, and as an outsider you may have even more difficulty in recognising the changes that have already taken place.

If you are going to transfer your skills to the host community, and share in what they can offer you, effective communication goes way beyond the boundaries of language proficiency. You will need to understand the various aspects of life in the new society, study the cultural background and be sensitive in developing and adapting to new situations.

To many new volunteers the given level of independence and high-level decision making can be as frightening as it is challenging. You may well be looked to for leadership and resourcefulness, and it will be your imagination, determination and flexibility that will get the project completed at the end of the day. You will also be living and working in close proximity with fellow workers, and all your organisational and interpersonal skills will be put to the test. Your ability to adapt and cope with ever-changing situations will be the key to the success of your placement.

As you have an interest in the politics, history and culture of the host community, so they will be interested in yours. This may mean acquiring background knowledge of the political, economic and geographic situation of your own country before your overseas placement, as well as expanding your interest and in-depth knowledge of worldwide current affairs. This international component of your skills, the degree of your international and intercultural understanding, will be as valuable on your placement as your professional qualifications and skills.

Personal qualities Qualifications, skills and experience, however impressive, are no good unless a volunteer has the right personal qualities. To begin with, if you can't communicate your skills to, and learn from, other people, then you are unlikely to be of much use to any development project. The ability to make friends and get on with all kinds of people is vital. Volunteers also need to be able to show sensitivity and tolerance towards cultures different from their own, as well as enough flexibility, patience and humour to enable them to work with people who may be used to doing things in a different way and perhaps have a different sense of priorities. You may well find yourself in a more responsible position than you have been used to, with people coming to you for advice and treating you as an expert, so a considerable amount of initiative, confidence, self-reliance and decision-making ability will be required.

Prospective volunteers should take careful note of the personal qualities required by the agency. How many of the following can *you* check positively:

- [ ] I get on with people
- [ ] I can work independently and show initiative
- [ ] I am prepared to learn from the community I will be working in
- [ ] I can work as part of a team
- [ ] I can bridge the gap between what the project will expect of me and what I am
- [ ] I can work the way others want me to work (I don't *have* to do things *my* way)
- [ ] I could learn the language
- [ ] I am adaptable and flexible
- [ ] I am tolerant and sensitive to other cultures
- [ ] I have got good communication skills
- [ ] I am patient and tactful
- [ ] I am independent and self-disciplined
- [ ] I have a sense of humour
- [ ] I have a desire to seek challenges

Aside from the working environment, you may also have to deal with your own feelings of isolation and homesickness, not to mention strange food, the heat, weird insects, and a lack of basic amenities. Luc Bertrand, UNAIS Field Coordinator in Burkina Faso, has experience of life in a small African village, and says it can be a strange and somewhat disconcerting experience for many project workers. Here he offers some insights:

If you have to live in a small village, you would do well to prepare yourself psychologically. There will be no cinema, nowhere to go out, and you may find it difficult to make local friends. Moreover, there will be little or no cultural activity and any intellectual exchanges will be at the most basic level. Loneliness is one of the greatest problems faced by a project worker in a village. Unless you make friends with local officials or teachers you will find it an intellectual desert. You must therefore be able to adapt yourself to your surroundings, and cultural adaptability is a most important characteristic for a successful project worker.

When you first arrive you will attract a great deal of attention. The people living around you will be very curious and may appear somewhat intrusive. The way of life of a white person is very different from what they are used to; his or her possessions and how they are used will also be novelties. You need to accept and even expect visitors who will come to your home merely to 'be there' and not necessarily to talk or chat to you. From their point of view, the fact that they are there is enough. For a westerner, this can seem most strange, as receiving a visitor usually implies extending a welcome and therefore some kind of personal exchange, at least a conversation.

At the same time, the person at the receiving end of this strange experience has a need for a degree of solitude, or privacy. He or she has to integrate into the village and therefore requires time to take in all these new and disconcerting experiences.

For project workers living in this kind of environment, two or three days in a lively town once a month becomes an absolute necessity ... to eat different foods, to enjoy the choice of a thousand different leisure activities, to go to the cinemas, bars and restaurants - to experience the variety of urban life.

Coming to terms with cultural differences constitutes a major aspect of living and working in a new environment. If you've grown up with a certain set of beliefs, viewpoints and ways of working you may take it for granted that these are *right*, especially if they have never seriously been challenged before. Everyone has their own preconceptions or prejudices, usually determined by their upbringing and the social attitudes of the culture to which they are accustomed. In order to break down barriers it is therefore important for you to be able to see where your own assumptions come from and to try and understand and live with the way other people see things. It would be inappropriate for you to impose what may be a western, urbanised outlook on a completely different, rural community. Be open to differences, even if you think they are *wrong*. They have been developed over generations, are probably well-adapted to the surrounding environment and may teach you a lot about your own beliefs and attitudes. The following comments from a volunteer who worked in Zimbabwe are a good illustration of this:

Coming to Zimbabwe has shown me many things about my own cultural assumptions and habits of thinking and behaving. Things I used to regard as generally valid I now see, in the light of a quite different rural and communal way of life, as specialised and even odd social traits ...

I came out with typical criticism of my project like there's no system to working, everyone spends too much time talking together in the office, or they come to decisions in such a roundabout way. It was just that I often didn't understand what was being said, or the significance of it, the relationships between people and the importance of showing hospitality. People joked about me always being busy, unable to spend time with them.

In agricultural work one day we were shifting earth from one place to another where trees were to be planted. All project members were working. The bucket chain broke down after a little while and everyone began to carry the buckets of earth from A to B in pairs or groups. I started to argue about inefficiency - the first time I'd expressed frustration I'd experienced in other situations, but of course I spoke up in work I thought any fool could organise (more fool me). Some workers just smiled, others were hurt and humiliated by my condemnation. One woman spoke up: *We are not machines,* she said, *we are people.* And the work continued.

The best way to gain an understanding of another society's customs and values is through personal contact. If you know which country you will be going to, try to get the chance to talk to a native of the country before you leave. There may, for example, be an immigrant community near where you live, or a refugee group. The cultural section of the relevant embassy may organise social events or put you in touch with a society for promoting understanding between Britain and that particular country. People are usually happy to talk about the way things are back home and you may learn a lot more from them than from reading books.

Which agency? The volunteer-sending agencies ask volunteers about their background, competence, views and intentions; volunteers have an equal right to ask similar questions of the agencies, and they owe it to themselves, the organisation and most importantly the people they will be working with to ensure that they are well-informed. You may be anxious to be selected, but remember that it is a two-way process; as much caution should be shown to the agency as they will show the potential volunteer. Talk to representatives, ask to see field reports and contact returned volunteers who can provide information based on personal experience. Make sure that your own motivation for volunteering does not conflict with the general aims of the agency you have selected. Ask for further information about its background and philosophy, details of aims and objectives, its scale of operation, the type of enterprise, how it is run, and its support system both at headquarters and overseas. The agency should be honest enough to provide you with details of the problems to be encountered, the projects that failed and the basic dilemmas still unresolved after years of activity, as well as their successes. They should offer their views on development and underdevelopment, and explain what role they feel volunteers have to play in this.

Which country? Many agencies take the view that volunteers should be prepared to serve where they are needed, their own choice of country being of secondary importance. How do you feel about this? If you have a specific preference then you should state this when applying, giving your reasons. Questions you should ask yourself about the proposed host country include its location, climate, history and current political situation:

- [ ] Where in the world *is* the country?

- [ ] Could I cope with the heat, the dust, the mosquitoes, the lack of basic facilities?

- [ ] Could I come to terms with the practices and customs of the local host community?

- [ ] Are the priorities of the government of the country the same as those of the majority of the people?

- [ ] If not, why not, and what as a volunteer can I or will I, do?

Terms and conditions As far as terms and conditions of work are concerned, many agencies provide accommodation, board, travel, remuneration and insurance; further details about this are given in each entry or are available from the agencies on application. Some agencies also provide allowances covering equipment, settlement/ resettlement, dependants and holidays. You should ascertain how you are to be paid, and by whom, how social security and pension rights are affected and what sort of insurance provision is available. Find out about job security - you may find yourself doing a completely different job from the one you expected, or no work at all, and you will need to know to whom you can turn in such an event. The political and social climate in some countries is not always stable, so find out what security provisions and support you can count on in case of political or social conflict. And what will be your position if, in exceptional circumstances, you return before the end of the contract?

Projects You should do your best to find out as much as you can about the project to which you will be assigned, bearing in mind the points made under **Motivation** about the need for projects to be actually required by the people for whom they are set up. Some agencies recruit on behalf of organisations overseas and so will not themselves be in control of the project, but you should still endeavour to find out the answers to key questions such as:

- [ ] Why was the project chosen?
- [ ] How does it relate to local needs?
- [ ] Who set it up?
- [ ] Who finances it?
- [ ] What do the duties entail?
- [ ] Who would you report to?
- [ ] How are the decisions reached?
- [ ] Why does the project need the skills of a volunteer?
- [ ] Whose interests will your presence promote?
- [ ] How interested is the agency in the work you will be doing?

If the project is well-established you should be able to see the field reports, evaluations and debriefing records of previous volunteers. If the project is successful, you could ask why the agency has not by now trained a local person to fill the post, and in any case, you should check carefully that by going there you are not putting a local out of a job.

Volunteering nearer home If you have no special qualifications, skills or experience, then opportunities to work on a development project overseas are now extremely limited. As well as the fact that developing countries may themselves already have large numbers of unskilled, unemployed people, it is also the case that most volunteer-sending agencies need to recruit people who can put specialist skills and experience into practice. Those agencies who do organise volunteer placements abroad for those without particular skills will generally expect them to raise quite a large sum of money to cover the placement fee, travel and living costs, viewing the placement not simply as a period of service, but also as an educational and cultural experience.

However, you don't *have* to travel far afield to find out about other cultures. Britain's population, for example, is made up of many cultures and many faiths, and there are plenty of opportunities to work with them. You could also volunteer in another European country or in North America. Working to overcome the problems caused by disability, poverty, bad housing, illiteracy, unemployment or discrimination against an immigrant population presents a worthwhile challenge. Or if you are motivated by a desire to work for world development you can do this from home - see the **UNDERSTANDING DEVELOPMENT** section for a list of organisations, many of which need volunteers to help with fundraising, campaigning or administration. Voluntary work experience in your own country may make it easier to be accepted as a volunteer overseas, quite apart from the contribution you can make to the welfare of the community with which you will be working. Jonathan Allat, a former volunteer with The Missions to Seamen, found that he could work for the improvement in education, welfare and conditions of people from all over the world without leaving the UK:

I had hoped to spend a year abroad, so I was disappointed when I was posted to Southampton, but the multinational, multi-cultural clientele at the Mission meant the world came to me. I spoke to British seafarers in transit to and from the Gulf War, Indians at the time of Gandhi's assassination, and Yugoslavians when their civil war started.

Many of the options for long-term voluntary work in western countries are in the field of social and community service. This can be a particularly valuable experience for everyone, especially those contemplating a career in health care or social work. Although the work is classed as voluntary, this does not necessarily imply that you work for nothing. Most placements covered in this guide are residential: board and lodging are provided, plus, in some cases, a certain amount of pocket money to cover personal expenses. Often, volunteers live and work together with the people they are there to help, and in order to promote a family atmosphere, emphasis is placed more on common humanity rather than on any distinction between volunteer and resident. Volunteers tend to learn and gain a lot from the people with whom they are working, whether these be people with a physical disability, an illness, learning difficulties, a need for food and shelter, or simply difficulty in coping with the pressures of society.

Despite the many rewards, this type of voluntary service can, at least to begin with, be both mentally and emotionally draining. You will be in a very new situation, probably away from your home and family, living amongst people who may be demanding in a way you have not had to deal with before.

It is therefore important that you consider your own strengths and weaknesses before formally applying and discuss any doubts or questions with the people running the project. In all likelihood they will be able to offer a lot of training and support, but you will also need to be fairly self-reliant. The ability to take initiatives within the framework of the project team, to cope with crises, to exert discipline without being authoritarian, and to maintain a sense of humour and perspective, is usually essential. You may not be aware of possessing all these capabilities, but the training and experience provided by a period of community service may well bring them to the fore. This can only stand you in good stead and prepare you for any future challenges you may have to face.

Jane Manning worked for Cambridge Cyrenians as part of a team living at a direct access hostel for nine homeless people:

I see my time as a volunteer worker as one where I used my abilities to assist people to improve aspects of their lives or to accept them. As a live-in volunteer the project had an aspect of family community that many residents had not experienced for many years. This made the residents feel more at ease talking to me and I was viewed less as an outsider.

In the six months I was at the project I found myself in an environment that was often challenging, frequently confronted with new situations. However I feel that what I put into the work was a fraction of what I received back from it. I forged and maintain many friendships with the residents and in the local homeless population. I would recommend voluntary work as a way of discovering parts of your own expectations in life and realising the hidden problems that exist in our society.

Volunteering from home If you've never done any voluntary work before and feel a little daunted by the prospect of committing yourself on a long-term residential basis there are still countless opportunities to volunteer in your home area on a part-time basis. **SECTION VII** (pages 196-230) has detailed information on no-residential service and short-term voluntary work.

In its recent Survey of Voluntary Activity in the UK the Volunteer Centre UK defined voluntary work as *any activity which involves spending time, unpaid, doing something which aims to benefit someone (individuals or groups) other than or in addition to close relatives, or to benefit the environment.* A very broad definition, which can encompass an enormous variety of opportunities. It has been estimated that in the UK between one third and one half of the population devotes some spare time to organised voluntary work. So you don't have to be an extra special person with proven skills - *anyone* can volunteer!

Faced with such a wide variety of opportunities, the first thing you need to do is decide what sort of voluntary work is right for you. Your motivation might be political, environmental, humanitarian or religious; perhaps you have a desire to help other people, look after children, campaign for change, stop pollution, reduce poverty and need, care for animals or offer help in emergencies. Discover what it is that you really care about, and look for an organisation that has this issue at its heart.

You should also be aware of what it is you are good at and what sort of work you enjoy doing. There's no point volunteering to do practical work if you don't know one end of a screwdriver from the other. If you like talking to people then you might not be very happy stuck in an office doing the filing. On the other hand, if you're neat and methodical you may quite enjoy the administrative side of things. Everybody has their strong and weak points, and all types of people are needed to keep a voluntary organisation going: campaigners and lobbyers; people to offer support and friendship; practical people who like to be where the action is; counsellors, advisors and problem-solvers; clerical workers, administrators, secretaries, organisers and managers.

In addition to checking out the opportunities is **SECTION VII**, ask around your local area to find out about voluntary organisations; check in your local library; consult the phone directories; or contact your local volunteer bureau. The organisations listed in the **INFORMATION RESOURCES** section should also be able to help you. Once you've found a voluntary organisation you would like to work for, ask to speak to the volunteer organiser, who will be able to tell you what sort of work is available. You will probably have to fill in an application form and attend an interview - this will help them to place you in work to which you are most suited. You may be asked to provide references, either from a past employer or someone who knows you well, just to confirm that you are who you say you are and that you'll be able to do the work. If you are going to be working with children, you may also be asked to disclose any police record. The interview is also an opportunity for you to find out all you can about the organisation and where volunteers fit into the structure, so don't be afraid to ask lots of questions.

As a volunteer, even though you may feel you are working fairly informally for no financial reward you still have rights and should not just be treated as an extra pair of hands or someone to do the dirty work. Volunteering is a matter of free choice, and your willingness should not be exploited, so don't feel pressurised into doing something you really don't want to do. Your hours of work should be agreed and put in writing - you have other demands on your time, and therefore should not commit yourself to giving more time than you can afford. You should have some kind of verbal or written description of the job you will be doing, and if the job is likely to change it is only fair that you should be consulted. Make sure you know who is supervising your work and whom you can approach to talk through any problems. If your work is likely to incur any expenses, find out how to claim these back; if any special clothing or equipment are needed then these should be supplied by the organisation, not by you.

You should be adequately insured by the organisation whilst at work, and as with all employees, you should not be expected to work in unsafe or unhealthy conditions. Above all, make sure that the work you are doing is genuinely voluntary - you should not be putting someone out of a job by doing work which was previously paid.

Volunteering should give you a chance to enhance the skills you already have and learn new ones, either on-the-job or in some cases through a training course. As your skills develop, so should your work, and like any job it should be reviewed at regular intervals. If you find the work tedious and unsatisfying, then make your voice heard and ask if you can do something that is more demanding or entails more responsibility. Remember, it's in everyone's interest for you to feel fulfilled and happy in your work, because then you're much more likely to carry on with it!

If you are claiming benefits such as Unemployment Benefit or Income Support you must inform your local payment office if you are doing any voluntary work. Payment of benefits will not usually be affected as long as you are still available for and actively seeking work. This means that you must be willing to give up your voluntary work at 24 hours' notice to attend an interview or take up a job, and that you must be able to show for each week you claim benefit that you have taken reasonable steps to find a job. Your local social security office, unemployment benefit office or Jobcentre should be able to give you further advice. If you incur any out-of-pocket expenses whilst undertaking voluntary work, such as travel costs, for example, the reimbursement of such costs should not affect the payment of benefits.

Obviously, residential voluntary projects will require more of a full-time commitment from volunteers than more informal voluntary work, and because of this you may not qualify for benefits as you will not be able to say you are actively seeking work. However, you will not be entirely without resources as most residential projects provide board and lodging and will supply volunteers with pocket money to cover basic personal expenses.

Pauline Manning does voluntary work for ACET, a Christian charity which recruits volunteers to provide practical home care for people ill with HIV/AIDS:

Working as a volunteer for ACET has been one of the most challenging and fulfilling experiences of my life. I have met people from a wide variety of social backgrounds, ages, lifestyles and cultures, and have been continually surprised and delighted at the hope and courage of so many people who are suffering so much.

It has helped me to put my own life and my full-time work into perspective, and made me more aware of what HIV and AIDS actually are, and how the disease affects those who have contracted it.

ACET have continually encouraged and supported me as a volunteer, so that I do not feel on my own when I make a visit. I see myself as a small part of a larger organisation, of which I am incredibly proud to be a part.

VOICES OF EXPERIENCE

In the sections of practical information and advice there are accounts from volunteers and sending agencies alike, to give some idea of the realities of voluntary service. Here we have included some personal insights into what it actually means to give and receive.

Many project placements are unique and every volunteer different, and each will have their own idea of what it is they have personally gained from volunteering. Nonetheless it is always worth getting some first-hand information before you start any project. A friend who has been a volunteer may be able to give you some advice and information, and the organisation you will be working for should be happy to provide you with a list of returned volunteers whom you can contact.

Sarah Lane answered a UNAIS (United Nations Association International Service) advert for a speech/language therapist to work in Sucre, Bolivia. Over a year later, after completing a six month course in Cochabamba learning Spanish and about life in Bolivia, she finally arrived in Sucre. Here she shares her first impressions of the place where she will be working and living for the next two years:

Sucre was as beautiful as everyone had told me, full of colonial buildings, freshly painted and dazzling white. It's a small city, surrounded by mountains, so that when you look along a street you can see where the city ends and the hills start. I have a wonderful view from my window at work, no comparison at all to the brick wall I used to see from my office in Camberwell!

I've been here three weeks now, and the city is small enough so that when you walk around town you are very likely to bump into someone you know, which gives a nice feeling of belonging here - though of course I don't know anyone well yet.

My first encounter with Hermano Maximiliano, who runs the Centro Psicopedagogica, a centre for children with learning difficulties and physical handicaps, was interesting.
He was of course, nothing like my stereotyped idea of a monk, added to which he speaks Spanish very quickly with a strong accent, so I had great difficulty understanding him. How can I possibly be a Spanish language

therapist when I don't speak the language well? How will anyone have any confidence in my ability to do this job? However, my first impressions of the Centre were very positive - everyone seemed very welcoming and demonstrated a warm and caring attitude towards the children.

It's a time of change here, and therefore a good time for me to be starting. However it has been two years since the centre requested a speech/language therapist, and I have a feeling they are expecting miracles!

I am trying to lower expectations a little, and am also talking about different aspects of language and communication, not just speech, but the understanding of language too.

I'm the only speech/language therapist in Sucre; there are a few elsewhere in Bolivia; but all have been trained abroad as there is no training available here yet. There is obviously a great need for such training, however; I keep meeting people who know someone who has some kind of difficulty. My job will involve working with out-patients as well as children at the Centre. My first couple of weeks at work have been spent getting to know people, and thinking about the best way of using my time here over the next two years.

Training will be an important part of my work, so that when I leave the teachers will be able to continue working with the children to facilitate their language development. Regular training sessions have already been arranged for 8 am every Monday morning! I have ambitious plans for producing a manual which teachers can use to assess the children's language abilities, together with some ideas for suitable activities to stimulate language development and communicative ability.

I'm still working out the best way to approach things, though - where to start, what to do first and who does what. Roles are slightly different here; for example the physiotherapists work very much under the direction of one of the doctors, and make few decisions themselves. Also, the scarcity of resources is a major factor, even more so than in the NHS.

For example, there are no small wheelchairs; the few wheelchairs there are are too big for the small children who need them, so consequently a few children spend most of their time lying on the mattress looking at the ceiling - which is hardly stimulating!

Although at times I feel fairly daunted by the task ahead, I feel excited about the opportunity to work at the Centre, and potentially to make a difference to the lives of some of the children there, both now and in the future (at least that's the theory).

And I also feel lucky to be living in such a beautiful place, and in such an interesting country.

I'm still getting used to speaking Spanish all the time - on the whole it's not too difficult with the children, but problems arise when I want to explain something to teachers and parents. I often find myself saying something that only approximates to what I want to say.

The last three weeks here have rushed by. I haven't had time to do any of the touristy things like visiting the cathedral ... well, I've got two years here, I'm sure I'll manage it sometime!

Maintenance officer Andrew Dutton is on placement with VSO, restoring neglected school facilities in Papua New Guinea:

The water's off again, mister has got to be the phrase I've heard more than any other since arriving at my new posting in Papua New Guinea. I'm a maintenance officer at Kupiano Provincial High School, situated in Central Province, three hours southeast of the capital, Port Moresby.

Little maintenance has been done since the school opened in the mid-70s, and the conditions are far from satisfactory. This problem extends throughout PNG - Central Province alone has eight high schools which need upgrading, but Kupiano is one of the more run-down schools. I'm working within the Province's new maintenance programme, along with a manager and a fellow volunteer at a neighbouring school.

When I arrived the students' toilets and washrooms were in such poor condition that the majority couldn't be used. This was due to a combination of neglect, vandalism (on the boys' part) and mainly an erratic water supply. The 150 boy boarders were reduced to washing under a single standpipe and using two badly constructed pit latrines (a student told me that the smaller boys used the floor because they were frightened they might fall down the hole). The girls, who tend to take more care of their facilities, were still using their toilets and washrooms, though they were far from perfect.

Over the last two months, Wilson, a young man from the local village, and I have repaired six 9,000-litre water tanks that have been leaking for years, and connected the tanks to provide round-the-clock water. Upgrading the dormitories will be the next project.

Kupiano is my second posting in PNG - I did a similar job at a school in Milne Bay Province for two years. My time here has been one of the most enjoyable and satisfying periods of my life. It's not always easy, and at times it can be very frustrating, but that all adds to the challenge.

I have found the people here very understanding and accepting of my disability (I lost my right arm in an accident some years ago). My fellow workman have an uncanny ability to offer help when it's really needed and have no prejudices, which cannot always be said in the UK.

Marek worked as a full time volunteer for Independent Living Schemes in Lewisham. The job consisted of working alongside a team of two volunteers, helping a severely disabled man to live an independent life in his own home in the local community.

I found the experience both challenging and rewarding. It proved interesting getting to know the user and other volunteers, plus the other people that were involved more indirectly on the project, all of whom were from a varied background.

Most volunteers stay on the scheme between four and eight months, and after I completed my term I felt a sense of achievement. Before coming to Lewisham I had been unemployed, so I felt I had served a useful purpose on the project and regained much self-confidence.

Of course working there was not all a bed of roses. One had to learn to live on a small amount of money, budget oneself, and live alongside and get on with the other volunteers who stayed in the workers' flat. But I felt that all this was a very good learning experience particularly for younger volunteers who were away from home for the first time.

Working on an Independent Living Scheme can teach independence and gives an opportunity to get to know a different area away from one's home background. Whatever one's reasons are for becoming a volunteer I am sure everyone gains something from the experience, like I did, through learning a bit about oneself and others. If one has time on hand the Scheme is definitely worth a gamble.

Sharon is a disabled woman whose life has been changed through Independent Living Schemes:

I am in my early forties with a teenage daughter. In late 1993 I started an Independent Living Scheme which is important to me as an individual and as a mother. In 1994 my daughter made me a grandmother - she and her baby live with me in my adapted bungalow. My mother pops in most days, so we are a big, close family.

Because of multiple sclerosis I cannot walk and have limited use of arms and hands. This means I have to use a wheelchair. I am Registered Blind and have a small amount of vision. Being on an Independent Living Scheme, I can do what I want, when I want. I am getting better at managing my three volunteer helpers so they understand it is my home and that I want to live my life without anyone telling me what to do. However, I do listen to my volunteers as they can have problems of their own. Sometimes I can help them as well - must be the wisdom that comes from being a grandmother!

I am lucky because I have never been in a residential home where, even with the best will in the world, I would lose my freedom and individuality. To paraphrase the old adage, I would say Civil Rights start in the home!

Clare Hall-Matthews has worked as a volunteer in Kent's L'Arche Community for four years. Here she writes about what she has gained from her experience:

I came to L'Arche from an academic background, having completed my degree. I was looking for something different - I wanted to work on relationships, on the heart, after years of educating the head. I certainly found it. Living closely with others, in a caring and open atmosphere, I learned a lot about myself.

I didn't like all of it - I discovered my anger, tension and frustration; I realised there were people I didn't get on with. Sometimes I felt I was pushed to my limits. But still I was accepted and supported. L'Arche has been a place of enormous growth for me.

The way of life seems very normal. We get up and have breakfast, go to work or work in the houses, come home, have supper together, relax in the evenings, go out or shopping at weekends. But there is a place for everyone, however handicapped - they are included and accepted, enabled to join in.

There is something very simple yet profound in this. Life is very ordinary, full of everyday joys and sorrows. We laugh together, we enjoy each other's company. We go through difficult times together, argue, work through problems, share crises. We learn and grow and pray together.

In L'Arche the assistants are enabling those with learning difficulties, but it also works the other way round; the people with learning disabilities, in sharing with the assistants, enrich the quality of our lives, teach us to care, enable us to grow. The atmosphere of care extends to everyone - the assistants are supported in their difficulties and weaknesses too.

People with learning difficulties have a lot to teach us. Our society values achievement, success, technology, physical beauty and prowess. Where does that leave those who do not succeed? In L'Arche we learn the unique value of every person, however handicapped; we learn to appreciate their gift. When we slow down to their pace, we gain a new perspective on life and learn what really matters. We learn to value relationship and things of the heart. People are important, not status or success.

When the element of competition is removed and a place is made for each person, there is a place for me too. I was able to open up, and to share vulnerability. Living with handicapped people I discovered my own handicap, my own brokenness. I was also accepted and loved. I came to L'Arche with little self confidence, and although I have along way to go, I gained an enormous amount.

Chris Minton spent nearly three years teaching English in Hungary on a placement organised by East European Partnership (EEP):

Like many volunteers, my motives were mixed - I'd been pressed to take early retirement and the selection by EEP was extremely important psychologically. For this reason, I think older people made redundant or pensioned-off make particularly good volunteers for organisations such as EEP. It was an advantage to be able to return home at Christmas and in the summer, and, though it wasn't necessary I could have come back in an emergency. Also, family members and friends could visit me and learn about life in an unfamiliar country.

My salary, paid in local currency, was adequate, because my accommodation was paid for, and it was easy to earn extra through private teaching, to pay for fares home at Christmas. It was also important that National Insurance contributions were paid and my teacher's pension in the UK wasn't affected by my working abroad.

While in post, I was able to arrange for a small number of students to visit the UK, and plans are in train for a group of British singers to visit Hungary and a Hungarian music school choir to come here. The students were particularly pleased to visit an ordinary part of the country, not just London.

Of course, it was a privilege to be welcomed into the homes of my colleagues and students, from whom I learned much about hospitality, cooperation and generosity - they gave me far more than I could give them. For me, now, Hungary is my second home.

Arthur Trees' placement in Poland was also organised by East European Partnership; he worked training teachers of English:

I came to volunteering rather late in my career. I was 66 when I went to Poland. I was, and still am in good health, have no major financial problems and my family has grown up. This enabled me to go with my wife to Poland for a year. Moreover, I have lived and worked abroad for a total of about ten years. On the other hand, volunteers going to Poland for the first time adjusted remarkably well.

This placement was one of the most satisfying and fulfilling professional experiences of 43 years of teaching. I worked with students ranging from 18 to 30 from varied backgrounds, with a tremendous range of skills. Some had already done a lot of teaching; some were at the very beginning of their training.

Not only was the work satisfying, but life outside the classroom was equally fascinating. I lived in a flat that was part of a complex that housed a few hundred Polish students. They behaved in an exemplary manner. Kept their disco-type entertainment away from old Father Time, were always polite and on hand to help with language problems. Assistance from the staff who administered the accommodation was also readily available.

Getting about the country was quite painless. A very efficient train service on the main lines operated in all directions. It was a different story when off the beaten track. But there were buses. A car was extremely useful and enabled us to see quite a lot of the country. We have come back with some heartwarming memories of outstanding generosity from Poles who 'regard the Guest as God'. We felt very much part of the local scene. And I really believe I gained as much as, and possibly more than the students did from the experience.

To get a lot from volunteering I believe you need to have a sense of humour, a sense of proportion and the ability to keep an open mind.

Volunteering is a creative and proven way of tackling today's social needs. For over 30 years Community Service Volunteers (CSV) has created opportunities for people to play an active part in the life of their community through volunteering, training, education and the media. CSV believes that everyone has got something to give and aims to enable every citizen to invest their energy to help others. CSV's Roger Mortlock and Donna Miller here outline the challenges and rewards of community involvement.

Community Service Volunteers challenges all young people to experience the rewards, hard work and fun of working as a volunteer. CSV involves over 3,000 volunteers every year on community projects working face-to-face with people who need their help. CSV was founded in 1962 with the firm belief that everyone has something to offer the community. It gives everyone the chance to volunteer; no one is rejected. Volunteers may be graduates, school leavers, professionals, homeless, under the care of local authorities, young offenders or substance abusers.

The first CSV volunteer may have been an Oxbridge candidate, but 30 years on, a volunteer is just as likely to be unemployed, disadvantaged or a young offender.

All the volunteers provide an effective and innovative response to recent changes in health and social service care; in particular the 1991 Children Act and the 1990 Community Care Act. CSVs provide much-needed respite care and support to hard-pressed carers of elderly relatives or family members with disabilities.

They help other young people get established when leaving local authority care by teaching them basic skills to live on their own, like cooking, budgeting or looking for employment. In Coventry, volunteers organise other young people to educate their peers about the hazards of unprotected sex and issues surrounding HIV/AIDS. After 20 years of working with young offender institutions, CSV now recruits full-time volunteers from adult open prisons. Young people can come to CSV for a meaningful activity while on a community sentence or after release from custody. Being a volunteer may be the first time a young person has experienced real responsibility and shown that they care for other people. Offenders join other young people from different walks of life and have the chance to break the stereotypes and prove it's the person - and not the offence - that counts.

When she received her Probation Order, Anita's Probation Officer suggested CSV. Working in a home for adults with learning disabilities for six months proved a challenge and a turning point for Anita. She was accepted without question by the people she worked with and found that working in new surroundings helped her to break away from a pattern of offending.

In these and many other settings young volunteers complement the work already being done by professional staff and do not attempt to replace it. The contribution made by CSV volunteers can make the difference between living and just being alive for the people they help.

By the year 2000, more than one third of the UK's population, over 17 million people, will be aged over 50. Improvements in health care and working conditions mean that most people remain healthy and active well into their later years. But once the honeymoon period of retirement has ended and the time at home begins to drag, more and more people are deciding to use their skills, time and energy to help others in the community.

CSV's Retired and Senior Volunteer Programme, RSVP, not only helps local communities, it enables older people to stay fit, healthy and active through volunteering. RSVP believes that all volunteers have the knowledge and wisdom to be of immense value to their local community. Jean Anderson, an RSVP volunteer in Glasgow believes it gives her a purpose in life: I feel if I wasn't doing this I'd need to look for something else to do because I'm on my own now. Why retire and just sit there and vegetate when you can be of use to the community and give?

RSVP is targeting the largest untapped source of voluntary help there is, a reserve of people with time and skills to invest which is continually growing as the UK population grows older. At the same time within every local community and in hard-pressed health and social services, there is a need for the enthusiasm and energy of volunteers - in schools, hospitals, day centres, museums, in protecting the environment and visiting the sick and housebound.

RSVP brings together those organisations who are clamouring for volunteers with older people looking to fill their lives actively and positively. RSVP is pioneering a new approach to volunteering that is entirely volunteer-led.

Many older volunteers are reinvesting their skills and experience in schools - sharing memories and living history of the Second World War, organising carpentry or cookery groups and working with pupils on reading and numeracy programmes. Generation gaps close quickly and genuine friendships are made in the classrooms or the playcentre when older volunteers sit reading an afternoon story or helping out with a craft project.

Research undertaken by RSVP and carried out by older volunteers shows that most people are keen to take part and get involved in their community; they just need to be asked. Over 80% of older people who volunteer feel that they are making a real contribution to their communities. Over half have fun in the process.

Increasingly, CSV proves how its policy of community involvement can be applied across the spectrum of social care. Through CSV Education's partnership with over 3,000 schools CSV encourages young people in full-time education to become active citizens and serve their community as part of their studies.

The nationwide programme of student tutoring, CSV Learning Together brings the enthusiasm and experience of undergraduates into the classrooms. The idea is a simple one. Students from over 80 universities volunteer to work alongside teachers for an afternoon a week, helping pupils with their studies, raising their aspirations and encouraging them to go on to higher education.

Across the airwaves, CSV has pioneered social action broadcasting since the mid-seventies, forging innovative and adventurous working partnerships with over 40 BBC and independent radio and television stations across the country and in Europe. CSV Media informs millions of people every year and energises them to take action in their communities.

SECTION II

UNDERSTANDING DEVELOPMENT INFORMATION RESOURCES

UNDERSTANDING DEVELOPMENT

There is a certain amount of controversy about the extent to which the industrialised nations are responsible for the under-development of the Third World and what steps should be taken to effect a change in the relationship. If you are considering volunteering as a development worker overseas you should make every effort to find out more about the issues involved and how they affect the situation in the country in which you will be working. If you have recently returned from a period of voluntary work overseas you may be keen to work in the field of development education and awareness-raising.

The following organisations, based in Britain, campaign on a variety of development and environmental issues and/or produce reading materials and other resources of interest to potential and returned volunteers. None of them actually sends volunteers overseas, but some of them do recruit volunteers to help with administration, fundraising, campaigning or publicity in the UK, or there may be a local group, part of a campaigning network involving volunteers. See **SECTION VII NON-RESIDENTIAL** for further details.

AMNESTY INTERNATIONAL BRITISH SECTION 99-119 Rosebery Avenue, London EC1R 4RE ✆ 0171-814 6200
A worldwide human rights movement which is independent of any government, political faction, ideology, economic interest or religious creed. Its 1.1 million members work within a closely-defined mandate to: seek the release of prisoners of conscience - those imprisoned for their beliefs, colour, sex, ethnic origin, language or religion - who have not used, or advocated the use of violence; work for fair and prompt trials for all political prisoners; oppose the death penalty, torture, and other cruel, inhuman or degrading treatment or punishment of all prisoners; end extrajudicial executions and 'disappearances'. Amnesty International also opposes abuses by opposition groups: hostage-taking; torture and killings of prisoners; and other arbitrary killings. Annual *Amnesty International Report* details its work and main concerns in more than

120 countries and has a factual country-by-country account of Human Rights abuses; also *Country Reports* and *Theme Reports*. Local groups campaigning network.

APPROPRIATE HEALTH RESOURCES & TECHNOLOGIES ACTION GROUP (AHRTAG) Farringdon Point, 29-35 Farringdon Road, London EC1M 3JB ✆ 0171-242 0606
Committed to strengthening primary health care and community-based rehabilitation in the South, by maximising the use and impact of information, providing training and resources and actively supporting the capacity-building of partner organisations. Its objectives are to disseminate practical information on primary health care and disability through a publications programme; to provide an information and enquiry service to health and community workers; to strengthen human resources and institutional capacities of partner organisations by providing technical support and training in publications and the development of resource centres and information systems; to undertake participatory research projects in collaboration with partner organisations; to promote health awareness in education; and to plan and develop new programme initiatives and respond to new opportunities with partner organisations. Library and resource centre available to health workers going to work in developing countries; contains a wide range of relevant books, journals, documents, regularly updated bibliographies and training information. *Publications List* includes newsletters, resource lists, briefing packs and directories covering primary health care.

CAFOD Romero Close, Stockwell Road, London SW9 9TY ✆ 0171-733 7900
The official Catholic Church agency in England and Wales for overseas development, aiming to increase awareness of poverty and injustice in the world and the structures which cause them. Promotes human development and social justice in witness to Christian faith and Gospel values, through authentic and practical partnership between communities in the Third World and people in England and Wales.
Provides emergency relief and supports over 1,000 projects in community development, vocational training, preventive health care, food production, water development and non-formal education in some 75 Third World countries. Also runs fundraising and awareness-raising in England and Wales for which voluntary clerical and administrative support is often needed. *Resources Catalogue* lists general books and materials; simulation games; country profiles; and campaigning, theological, social, teaching and liturgical material.

COMMONWEALTH INSTITUTE Kensington High Street, London W8 6NQ ✆ 0171-603 4535
The centre for Commonwealth education and culture in Britain. It aims to promote knowledge and understanding of the Commonwealth through a programme of permanent and special exhibitions, cultural events and festivals, and educational activities. Its Commonwealth Resource Centre has multi-media resources and a reference collection providing general factual information about the individual countries, peoples and organisations making up the Commonwealth.

COUNCIL FOR EDUCATION IN WORLD CITIZENSHIP Seymour Mews House, Seymour Mews, London W1H 9PE ℗ 0171-935 1752 Fax 0171-935 4741
A non-political and non-sectarian organisation promoting such studies, teachings and activities as may best contribute to mutual understanding, peace and cooperation, and goodwill between all peoples. Regular *Broadsheets* provide background information on countries and issues in the news; each has an accompanying *Digest* for younger students and an associated *Activities Sheet*. Bi-monthly *Newsletters* publicise opportunities for young people and their teachers and include reviews of new resources to support education for international understanding selected from more than 200 organisations. Also supports a range of local, regional and national workshops and conferences for young people and their teachers, and its *World Citizenship in the National Curriculum* identifies, for each subject and cross-curricular theme, where the knowledge, skills and understanding relating to international citizenship occur. Resource centre, information service and speakers service; the information service is for members only and will provide information on international issues, as well as on opportunities for volunteering. For personal visits, please arrange an appointment. CEWC receives grants from the education departments and others and its membership is open to individuals, schools, colleges, organisations and local authorities.

FRIENDS OF THE EARTH 26-28 Underwood Street, London N1 7JQ ℗ 0171-490 1555
A network of independent national groups in over 50 countries, with an international secretariat based in Amsterdam. In the UK, Friends of the Earth represents the environmental concerns of many thousands of people, blowing the whistle on those who destroy the environment, and putting pressure on those who have the power to protect it. It has over 250 local groups across the UK campaigning against the destruction of the environment and providing information about environmental issues and ways in which individuals can help save the natural world.

GREENPEACE Canonbury Villas, London N1 2PN ℗ 0171-354 5100
An international environmental pressure group which actively campaigns for a nuclear-free future, to stop pollution of the natural world and to protect wildlife. Greenpeace campaigns have one common purpose: to preserve or recreate an environment in which living things, including people, can survive without threat to their lives and health. Campaigns involve non-violent direct action and the lobbying of relevant authorities and international conventions, backed up by scientific studies and careful research. Local support groups countrywide organise fundraising initiatives and occasionally help with lobbying and campaigning.

INTERMEDIATE TECHNOLOGY DEVELOPMENT GROUP Myson House, Railway Terrace, Rugby CV21 3HT ℗ Rugby (01788) 560631
Founded by the late Dr E F Schumacher in the 1960s, aims to enable poor people in the South develop and use productive technologies and methods which give them greater control over their own

lives and which contribute to the long-term development of their communities. Runs a UK schools programme, and has local supporters' groups. *Publications Catalogue* covers a wide range of books on appropriate technology and development issues, including titles on agriculture, building and construction, cooperatives, education and training, energy sources, health, manufacturing, handicrafts, industry and business, roads and transport, water and sanitation. *Appropriate Technology* quarterly magazine provides reports from the field for those interested in development practice. All publications and subscriptions enquiries to IT Publications, 103-105 Southampton Row, London WC1B 4HH.

THE LATIN AMERICA BUREAU 1 Amwell Street, London EC1R 1UL ✆ 0171-278 2829
A small, independent, non-profitmaking research organisation established in 1977, concerned with Human Rights and related social, political and economic issues in Central and South America and the Caribbean. Carries out research and publishes books. Library has a collection of periodicals from and about the region. Acts as subscription agent for the magazine *Report on the Americas* published 5 times a year by the North American Congress on Latin America (NACLA). *Books Catalogue* includes publications, resources for education, studies in Latin American culture and country guides.

MINORITY RIGHTS GROUP 379 Brixton Road, London SW9 7DE ✆ 0171-978 9498
An international non-governmental organisation that works to secure rights and justice for non-dominant ethnic, linguistic and religious communities. Informs and warns governments, NGOs, the international community and the wider public about the situation of minorities worldwide. Its international fora advocate measures to avoid escalation of conflict and to encourage positive action to build trust between majority and minority communities. Confronts prejudice and promotes public understanding through information and education projects. Publishes reports, books and papers; 85 titles currently in print.

OVERSEAS DEVELOPMENT INSTITUTE Regent's College, Inner Circle, Regent's Park, London NW1 4NS ✆ 0171-487 7413
Founded in 1960 as an independent non-governmental centre for development research and a forum for discussion of the problems facing developing countries. Produces regular *Briefing Papers* which analyse contemporary development issues, available free. *Publications List* includes books, working papers, reports and journals covering a range of subjects including finance and economics, trade and industry, environmental economics, development policy, agricultural development and disasters. The ODI Library, a specialist collection of approx 20,000 books and 400 periodical titles covering a variety of development issues is open to visitors from 0930-1730, Tuesdays to Thursdays.

OXFAM 274 Banbury Road, Oxford OX2 7DZ ✆ Oxford (01865) 311311
Oxfam works with poor people throughout the world, regardless of

race or religion, in their struggle against hunger, disease, exploitation and poverty, through relief, development, research overseas, and public education at home. Oxfam is first and foremost a development agency and, although it still provides relief in times of crisis, its main concern is long-term sustainable development. Oxfam does not recruit volunteers to work overseas but volunteers work at the headquarters in Oxford, at regional offices and in some 850 shops throughout Britain. Unpaid education workers visit schools, and there are local groups countrywide involved in campaigning. Publications, newsletters and other resource materials are distributed for sale as part of Oxfam's education, campaigning and information programme, and cover a variety of countries and topics including trade, environment, land and food, development practice, training, gender and health, as well as reference guides, maps and activity packs for primary and secondary teachers and youth workers. All publications and subscriptions enquiries to Oxfam Publishing, PO Box 120, Oxford OX2 7FA ✆ Oxford (01865) 311311.

POPULATION CONCERN
178-202 Great Portland Street, London W1N 5TN ✆ 0171-631 1546
Seeks to heighten public awareness of global population issues. Raises funds to support family planning and development programmes worldwide and an education programme in the UK. Sees family planning as a basic human right integral in establishing a balance between world population and natural resources. Publications include: *Annual Report*, published in January; yearly *Newsletter* published in July; and various publications for education and advocacy programmes.

SURVIVAL INTERNATIONAL
11-15 Emerald Street, London WC1N 3QL ✆ 0171-242 1441
A worldwide movement to support tribal peoples, standing for their right to decide their own future and helping them protect their lands, environment and way of life. Stocks a wide selection of books, reports and other documentation on tribal peoples and the issues affecting them, and produces a biannual *Survival Newsletter*. Audio and visual materials, including slide sets, video tapes and photo exhibitions are also available for sale or hire. Volunteers are needed to work on a variety of tasks in the London office.

THIRD WORLD FIRST
217 Cowley Road, Oxford OX4 1XG ✆ Oxford (01865) 245678/ 723832 Fax (01865) 200179
A national movement in colleges and universities, explaining and campaigning against the causes of poverty, hunger and exploitation in the Third World, and supporting the growing efforts of the poor as they organise together to determine their own development. *Publications List* covers books, magazines and fact sheets on world development issues including health, women, aid, disarmament, racism, trade, environment and debt.

TOOLS FOR SELF RELIANCE
Netley Marsh Workshops, Netley Marsh, Southampton SO4 2GY ✆ Southampton (01703) 869697
Founded to increase the self reliance of villages in the Third World by providing handtools. A network of local groups collect unwanted

handtools, which are refurbished and sent to Third World communities. Volunteers are always needed. Also promotes an awareness of bonds with the Third World to establish a more fair and just society.

UK COMMITTEE FOR UNICEF 55 Lincoln's Inn Fields, London WC2A 3NB ℡ 0171-405 5592
UNICEF is an agency of the United Nations, focusing on children in 137 countries in the developing world. UNICEF's work includes nutrition, water/sanitation, primary health care, formal/non-formal education and emergency relief. The annual *State of the World's Children* reports on the progress of strategies for child survival, and the simple and low-cost methods that could bring about a dramatic improvement in the wellbeing of the world's children. Produces books, information packs and study materials.

WAR ON WANT Fenner Brockway House, 37-39 Great Guildford Street, London SE1 0ES ℡ 0171-620 1111
International aid agency actively campaigning against injustice and oppression in developing countries and for increasing awareness in the UK of the causes of world poverty. Funds long-term and emergency relief in famine areas torn by military struggle, where little international aid is sent. Network of local groups in Britain where those interested can find out more about the issues and help with fundraising.
Also recruits volunteers for administrative work in London office. *Resources* list covers leaflets, information packs and publications concerned with health, childcare, women, famine, development issues, politics, exploitation and oppression.

WORLD DEVELOPMENT MOVEMENT 25 Beehive Place, London SW9 7QR ℡ 0171-737 6215
Britain's leading campaigning organisation on Third World issues. Unshackled by charity law, WDM's campaigns create political changes that directly benefit the world's poorest people. Has a nationwide network linking individual members, local action groups, lobby teams and staff. Volunteers play a vital role in WDM both in activities in their local area and working in the London office.

WORLDAWARE Centre for World Development Education, 1 Catton Street, London WC1R 4AB ℡ 0171-831 3844
An independent agency whose main aim is to promote education in Britain about world development issues and Britain's interdependence with the Third World; funded partly by the Overseas Development Administration. Annual *Catalogue* includes a wide range of handbooks, guides, booklets, information sheets and other materials on world development and interdependence; employment, technology, industry and energy; EU and the Third World; aid; disasters and refugees; immigrants and migration; population and education; and health, food and agriculture.

INFORMATION RESOURCES

The information provided in the main sections on the volunteer-sending agencies includes details of relevant briefing and other information resources. This list recommends further reading material, including additional volunteer placement opportunities and background material on volunteering and development issues. It also covers organisations offering advice on volunteering at home and abroad.

VOLUNTARY WORK
Returned Volunteer Action produce a range of publications on development work overseas including introductory booklets on volunteering and the main sending agencies in the UK through to more in-depth, critical analyses of the work and roles of the agencies and of the practice of development work overseas. Popular titles include *Questioning Development, Handbook for Development Workers Overseas, Thinking About Volunteering Overseas* and *Volunteering And Overseas Development: A Guide to Opportunities.*
A full resource list with current prices can be obtained from RVA, 1 Amwell Street, London EC1R 1UL
✆ 0171-278 0804.

The HPA Guide to Voluntary Nursing Overseas £3.50 including postage, provides information on the many organisations which send nurses abroad, as well as general information on working overseas. Available from Health Projects Abroad, PO Box 24, Bakewell, Derbyshire DE45 1ZW.

Working Holidays £8.99 is an annual guide to thousands of seasonal work opportunities in Britain and 70 countries worldwide. Gives details of a wide variety of short-term voluntary placements, including workcamps, community work, archaeological digs, conservation and restoration projects, as well as paid work opportunities. There is also helpful practical advice on travel, insurance, accommodation and further sources of information. Published by the Central Bureau for Educational Visits and Exchanges, Seymour Mews, London W1H 9PE.

The Third World Directory £9.95 covers 200 organisations working for overseas development, with information on possibilities for volunteering in the UK and overseas. Edited by Lucy Stubbs; published by the Directory of Social Change, Radius Works, Back Lane, London NW3 1HL.

Directory of Volunteering & Employment Opportunities £7.95 is a comprehensive guide to the opportunities for both voluntary and paid work in over 500 of the UK's major charities and voluntary organisations. Edited by Jan Brownfoot and Frances Wilks; published by the Directory of Social Change, see above.

The Voluntary Agencies Directory £15.95 is a comprehensive listing of voluntary agencies in England, compiled by the National Council for Voluntary Organisations. It lists 2,000 agencies ranging from small, specialist self-help groups to established national charities. An invaluable source of reference for anyone thinking about doing volunteer work in the UK. Published by NCVO Publications, Regent's Wharf, 8 All Saints Street, London N1 9RL ✆ 0171-713 6161.

STS Directory is a yearly manual of short-term Christian service opportunities in the UK and abroad, ranging from 1 weekend to 2 or 3 years. Price £1.75 plus 75p postage. *Who Needs You?* gives information on opportunities for voluntary Christian service for those working from home, price 30p plus an A5 SAE. Both available from the Christian Service Centre, Holloway Street West, Lower Gornal, Dudley, West Midlands DY3 2DZ ✆ Dudley (01902) 882836.

World Service Enquiry's free *Guide* gives information on agencies producing resources and contacts for people wishing to volunteer. *Opportunities Abroad* is a monthly list of vacancies through 40 agencies working in development or mission, price £10 for one year's subscription. *A Place For You Overseas* leaflets cover specialist subjects and include relevant agency contacts.
All available from Christians Abroad, 1 Stockwell Green, London SW9 9HP (add 30p to cover postage).

International Directory of Voluntary Work £8.95 is a guide to short and long-term volunteer opportunities in Britain and abroad.
The Directory of Work and Study in Developing Countries £7.95 is a guide to employment, voluntary work and study in the Third World.
Both published by Vacation Work, 9 Park End Street, Oxford OX1 1HJ ✆ Oxford (01865) 241978.

Volunteer! The Comprehensive Guide to Voluntary Service in the US and Abroad $11.95 plus $7 airmail postage, lists over 200 voluntary service organisations offering voluntary opportunities ranging in length from a few days to a few years. Published by the Council on International Educational Exchange and available from CIEE, Publications Department, 205 East 42nd Street, New York, NY 10017, United States.

Volunteering in the 90s are two booklets listing organisations running workcamps. Book 1 covers Africa & Asia; book 2 covers Europe & North America. Published with the support of UNESCO by the Coordinating Committee for International Voluntary Service, UNESCO, 1 rue Miollis,

75732 Paris Cedex 15, France. Cost £1 or 5 IRCs per volume.

DEVELOPMENT ISSUES
Earthscan Publications Ltd, 120 Pentonville Road, London N1 9JN ✆ 0171-278 0433 is an editorially independent subsidiary of Kogan Page Ltd, publishing in association with the International Institute for Environment and Development and the World Wide Fund for Nature (UK). Its *Catalogue* covers a wide range of books on environmental and development issues.

IT Publications, 103-105 Southampton Row, London WC1B 4HH is the publications wing of the Intermediate Technology Development Group and is an excellent development/ environment bookshop. Its *Publications Catalogue* includes books on appropriate technology and development issues, including titles on agriculture, building and construction, cooperatives, education and training, energy sources, health, manufacturing, handicrafts, industry and business, roads and transport, water and sanitation. *Appropriate Technology* quarterly magazine provides reports from the field for those interested in development practice.

New Internationalist, 55 Rectory Road, Oxford OX4 1BW ✆ Oxford (01865) 728181 is a monthly magazine covering major world issues. Produced by a cooperative based in Oxford and with offices in Aotearoa/ New Zealand, Australia and Canada. Originally started in 1973 with the backing of major aid agencies such as Oxfam, but now independent with over 70,000 subscribers worldwide. Each month the magazine covers a different Third World/environmental theme, such as global warming, Southern Africa or animal rights, with plenty of analysis, facts, opinions, photographs and charts.

Oxfam Publishing, PO Box 120, Oxford OX2 7FA ✆ Oxford (01865) 311311 cover a variety of countries and topics including trade, environment, land and food, development practice, training, gender and health, as well as reference guides, maps and activity packs for primary and secondary schools and for youth workers. *Development in Practice* journal published four times a year provides a forum for the exchange of ideas and information among policy makers and staff both North and South, and carries articles and assessments of the experiences of Oxfam and other NGOs. *Gender and Development* journal published three times a year links theory and practice from both North and South and carries articles, evaluations, reviews and interviews in the field of gender.

Zed Books, 7 Cynthia Street, London N1 9JF ✆ 0171-837 8466 publishes titles covering a wide range of issues and areas including Development and the Environment, Women and World Development, Third World Women, Health, the Middle East, Africa and Asia.

Economic and Social Development in the United Nations System: A Guide for NGOs (8th Edition) contains brief entries for all of the major UN agencies, programmes and funds working for economic and social development, and contact points for NGOs involved in development education, information and policy advocacy work. *The NGLS Handbook* provides information on 23 agencies of the UN system working in the field of economic and social development. In addition to information on the historical background, structure and policies of each agency, the handbook outlines programme activities of interest to NGOs. The final section of each entry discusses cooperation with NGOs. Both publications available from UN Non-Governmental Liaison Service (NGLS), Palais des Nations, 1211 Geneva 10, Switzerland or Room 6015, 866 UN Plaza, New York NY 10017, United States.

Further details on publications and other resources covering development and related issues are given in the previous section.

TAKING A YEAR OUT

A Year Between £8.99 is a complete guide for those taking a year out between school and higher education or work, or higher education and a career. Carefully researched with the aspirations of school leavers and graduates in mind, it offers authoritative advice and guidance, as well as relating the experiences of people who have themselves taken a year out. Published by the Central Bureau for Educational Visits & Exchanges, Seymour Mews, London W1H 9PE.

Opportunities in the Gap Year £3.50 looks at what is available to sixth-formers wishing to take a break between school and university or college. It weighs up the pros and cons of a year out and gives hints on how to make the best of a once-in-a-lifetime opportunity. Published by the Independent Schools Careers Organisation, 12a-18a Princess Way, Camberley, Surrey GU15 3SP ✆ Camberley (01276) 21188.

Taking a Year Off £7.95 takes a new look at the option of taking time out before, during or after higher education or during employment, encouraging the reader to identify his or her own needs by placing emphasis on case studies, group discussions and interviews, letters, a quiz, checklists, and the experiences of young people who have taken time out. Published by Trotman and Company Limited, 12-14 Hill Rise, Richmond, Surrey TW10 6UA.

TRAVEL

Sources of Information for Independent and Overland Travellers £5 is a reference guide giving details on where to get the best information about health, equipment, visas, insurance, maps and so on. Published by the Expedition Advisory Centre of the Royal Geographical Society, 1 Kensington Gore, London SW7 2AR ✆ 0171-581 2057.

The Travellers' Handbook £14.95 (£9.95 to members) is a 900-page reference and source book for independent travellers, with chapters on travel, health, clothing, luggage and survival kits, where to stay, photography, choosing maps, passports, visas, permits, insurance, currency and Customs. Also includes special chapters for students, single women and people with a disability. Published by WEXAS International, 45-49 Brompton Road, London SW3 1DE ✆ 0171-589 0500.

Travellers' Health - How to Stay Healthy Abroad £7.99 is considered the definitive guide to all aspects of health abroad, and offers comprehensive advice for those planning journeys anywhere in the world. Author Dr Richard Dawood; published by Oxford

University Press, price £7.99, available from most good bookshops and specialist travel shops.

The Tropical Traveller £7.99 is an invaluable handbook for those travelling to, in and through tropical countries. Contains a wealth of practical information on planning your journey, what to take with you, health precautions and how to make the most of your time in the tropics. The author, John Hatt, has based the book on years of personal experience, as well as tips from readers of previous editions. Published by Penguin, and available in most good bookshops and long-haul travel chains.

Lonely Planet's *Travel Survival Kits* and *Shoestring* guides are detailed travel handbooks to countries in Africa, Asia, Australasia, Europe and the Americas, giving background information on the country, advice on places to visit, information on where to stay, what to eat, how to get there and ways to travel around. Also produce a range of useful *Phrasebooks* containing essential words and phrases for effective communication with local people. Available in most good bookshops and long-haul travel chains. Prices range from £1.95 for some of the smaller phrasebooks through to £16.95 for the bigger travel guides.

Rough Guides are a series of practical handbooks to most countries in Europe and some areas of Asia, Africa, South America and the United States, giving full details on cities, towns and places of interest, plus a wealth of practical information on places to stay and how to get around. The range also includes *Women Travel*, a guide for women travellers; also *Nothing Ventured: Disabled People Travel the World* containing first-hand accounts of disabled people's travel experiences and practical advice on planning a trip. Published by Penguin and available in most good bookshops; prices range from £6.99-£11.99.

Culture Shock! is a series of guides written for international travellers of any background, introducing the people, customs, ceremonies, food and culture of a country, with checklists of dos and don'ts. Countries currently in the series include Australia, Canada, China, France, India, Indonesia, Israel, Italy, Japan, Korea, Malaysia, Nepal, Pakistan, the Philippines, Singapore, Sri Lanka, Thailand and the US. All guides cost £6.95 and are available from bookshops or through Kuperard (London) Ltd, No 9 Hampstead West, 224 Iverson Road, West Hampstead, London NW6 2HL ✆ 0171-372 4722.

ADVISORY BODIES
The Christian Service Centre, Holloway Street West, Lower Gornal, Dudley, West Midlands DY3 2DZ is a member organisation of the Evangelical Missionary Alliance and the Evangelical Alliance, offering information and advice to those interesting in doing long-term or short-term Christian service. It links the personnel needs of missions and Christian organisations in Britain and abroad with those offering themselves for service, and also provides a counselling and advisory service for those considering Christian work. Advice is offered through a national network of voluntary advisers with experience of Christian work at home or overseas. *Jobs Abroad* directory lists hundreds of opportunities of interest to Christians, published twice a year; *STS Directory* is a yearly manual

of short-term Christian service opportunities in the UK and abroad; *Who Needs You?* offers information on opportunities for voluntary Christian service for those working from home.

Christians Abroad, World Service Enquiry, 1 Stockwell Green, London SW9 9HP ✆ 0171-737 7811 is an ecumenical body founded in 1972 and supported by aid and mission agencies. Provides an information and advisory service on working overseas to people of any faith or none. World Service Enquiry encourages people to be involved in development and its issues either in the UK or overseas. An experienced advisor is available for personal discussion - face to face or through a telephone interview. A written advisory service is also available. A database is maintained of over 3,000 skilled professional personnel which is searched at the request of aid and development agencies. Information and advice about openings through a variety of organisations working within the UK and overseas is offered to those with or without professional skills. Information is held on many opportunities from two week summer projects and gap year activities to long term contract employment. Assistance is offered to those returning from abroad who face the challenge of sharing their experiences and of using what they have learnt, and surmounting the problems of readjustment. *World Service Enquiry* produces a free *Guide* (available on receipt of a large SAE) outlining development issues and containing useful resource information as well as schemes and agencies of interest to a volunteer. Also includes information on finding paid work in development. *Opportunities Abroad*, produced 10 times a year, lists current vacancies through over 40 partner agencies; bumper editions printed twice a year.

The Coordinating Committee for International Voluntary Service (CCIVS), 1 rue Miollis, 75015 Paris, France ✆ (33 1) 45 68 27 31/32 is a non-governmental international organisation founded in 1948 on the initiative of UNESCO, with a membership of over 100 organisations engaged in volunteer work, including those from eastern and western Europe, Latin America, Africa and Asia. Through the promotion and development of the voluntary movement on regional, national and international levels it works towards peace, international understanding, development and the furtherance of the efforts of developing countries in strengthening their national independence, and in solidarity with people in observance of the Universal Declaration of Human Rights. Works for the benefit of people affected by all forms of social and economic exploitation, unemployment, bad working and living conditions and promotes awareness and action against these forms of degradation. Organises seminars and conferences, sponsors training courses for volunteer workers, participates in solidarity action and raises funds for concrete projects carried out by voluntary organisations in order to attain genuine development. CCIVS replies to requests for information received from individuals and organisations. Publications include: *Volunteering in the 90s*, two booklets listing youth volunteer organisations in Europe & North America and Africa & Asia; *Running a Workcamp*; *How to present a project*; *CCIVS News*, bulletin issued 3 times a year.

The National Association of Volunteer Bureaux (NAVB), St Peter's College, College Road, Saltley, Birmingham B8 3TE ✆ 0121-327 0265 was set up in 1986 to increase public awareness of volunteer bureaux and to assist in their establishment and development. Volunteer bureaux aim to help people overcome the obstacles which might prevent them volunteering, whether through a lack of information or a stereotyped view of what volunteering entails. The central concern is the welfare of volunteers themselves and the development of volunteering locally. Enquirers can be put in touch with their local bureau, who will be able to advise them of a range of volunteer work locally. Publish *Volunteer Bureaux Directory*, revised annually and available in December.

National Social Service Board, 71 Lower Leeson Street, Dublin 2, Ireland ✆ (3531) 661 6422 Fax (3531) 676 6908 advises on the development of social services and promotes, encourages and resources services which disseminate information and advice to the public. The Board's main activities include the development and support of its network of 81 Citizen's Information Centres and assisting the training of those involved in disseminating information. It also administers a group insurance scheme for voluntary organisations. Publishes an annual report, *Relate* monthly bulletin, the *Directory of National Voluntary Organisations* and a range of literature on aspects of the social services.

The Northern Ireland Volunteer Development Agency, Annsgate House, 70-74 Ann Street, Belfast BT1 4EH aims to promote volunteering throughout Northern Ireland and provides a central resource of support, information and training for all those involving volunteers. The Agency provides a forum for all those involved with volunteering; practical support for projects involving volunteers; information and advice on issues relating to volunteering; training courses and materials for those who work with volunteers; and a focus for research and evaluation of current trends, policy and practice.
It provides advice and information on where to apply in Northern Ireland for volunteer opportunities, and publishes *Residential Volunteer Opportunities in Northern Ireland*, a volunteer information kit.

Returned Volunteer Action, 1 Amwell Street, London EC1R 1UL ✆ 0171-278 0804 is the only British organisation of and for prospective, serving and ex-volunteers and others who have worked overseas, existing independently from the sending agencies. It believes that voluntary service abroad fails to achieve its full value unless it becomes part of an educative process for the volunteer, and much of its work involves face to face contacts between more recently returned volunteers and those who have been back for up to two years. Helps returned volunteers make use of their overseas experience in Britain by providing support and advice, training courses in communication skills and a channel through which volunteers can comment on and influence the policies of the sending agencies. Also gives advice on action to take on returning from a period of service. Publications include *Volunteering and Overseas Development: A Guide to Opportunities*, an advisory pack containing information on the sending agencies and general advice for the prospective overseas worker; *Questioning Development, Handbook for Development Workers Overseas, Thinking About Volunteering?* and *The EVI Charter; Comeback* quarterly magazine; *Development Action* monthly bulletin; pamphlets and information sheets. Price list on request.

The Scottish Council For Voluntary Organisations, 18-19 Claremont Crescent, Edinburgh EH7 4QD ✆ 0131-556 3882 is an independent national council with the prime objective of promoting and supporting voluntary service and action throughout Scotland, enabling other voluntary organisations to be effective. It extends the range of voluntary endeavour, advocates particular issues, promotes and safeguards the values of voluntary endeavour and provides services to these ends. It has information and referral services and produces various publications, including two directories: *Scottish Grant Making Trusts* and *National Voluntary Organisations for Scotland*; also *Inform*, a fortnightly current awareness bulletin; and *Third Force News*, a fortnightly newsletter.

The Volunteer Centre UK, Carriage Row, 183 Eversholt Street, London NW1 1BU ✆ 0171-388 9888 Fax 0171-383 0448 can provide information for those who want to volunteer for the first time, or for those who are already involved and want to know more. It runs events and training courses for those responsible for organising volunteers and coordinates UK Volunteers Week which takes place annually in June. It has an extensive library and a free information service, as well as a *Signposts* database on volunteering opportunities. Publications include *Volunteering* magazine published 10 times a year.

The Wales Council For Voluntary Action, Llys Ifor, Crescent Road, Caerphilly, Mid Glamorgan CF8 1XL ✆ Caerphilly (01222) 869224 is an independent national organisation established to promote, support and facilitate voluntary action and community development in Wales. It provides thorough the work of its staff and committees a service of information advice and consultancy to all voluntary organisations which seek assistance, including funding advice; an intelligence service by monitoring developments in the voluntary sector in Wales and throughout the UK, as well as in government policies and current trends in society; an educational programme through the provision of a range of educational events from conferences to workshops; a representational role by responding to government consolations, taking the initiative to bring into the forum of public debate issues of importance for the development of voluntary action in Wales; a Volunteering in Wales fund; and assists in the development of new projects which will link voluntary, statutory and commercial resources towards work creation and new forms of community benefit. Its information service directly responds to enquiries from all those with an interest in the voluntary sector in Wales.
Publications include: *Network Wales* monthly newsletter; *WIN Directory of voluntary organisations in Wales 1995*; *A Short Guide to Voluntary Work Opportunities in Wales* information sheet; *Wales Funding Handbook*; *Annual Report*; and general and funding information sheets.

A year out, between school and university or work, is a rare chance to stand back, assess where life has brought you so far, and seize the freedom offered to take on a completely different challenge. All the vital advice and information you need to arrange a successful and enjoyable year out is in the Central Bureau guide **A YEAR BETWEEN**.

A YEAR BETWEEN lists over 100 organisations and employers offering year between placements in Britain and 80 other countries. Whatever the opportunity, in whatever country, the guide gives very full details. Any age restrictions are noted, the period of work on offer, salary and terms, including whether accommodation, insurance or travel are included is listed, and application deadlines are given together with details of where the work is overseas, and any address in the home country to which application can be made. But we don't stop there.

A YEAR BETWEEN carries information on a wide range of other useful details: a personal checklist covering the pros, cons and options of taking a year out, offering a programmed series of questions to enable participants to evaluate their potential; authoritative advice on planning & preparation, useful books and other resources; accounts from students and placing organisations alike, providing first hand reports vital to those considering taking a year out; and for potential volunteers, some challenging words on commitment.

A YEAR BETWEEN has opportunities detailed under seven headings: Training/work experience; Discovery/leadership; Conservation/land use; Teaching/instructing; Community & social service; Youth work/childcare; and Christian service. The guide also provides advice on further study options, on travel, insurance and health requirements. In fact, just about everything you'll need to know in order not only to get a successful placement but to make the whole experience worthwhile, fulfilling and as trouble-free as possible.

A YEAR BETWEEN has opportunities for those aged 17+; from 4 weeks up to a whole year; from accountancy placements to zoology expeditions; from Australia to Zimbabwe. For further information on the Bureau's publications and programmes contact the Information Desk on ✆ 0171-725 9448.

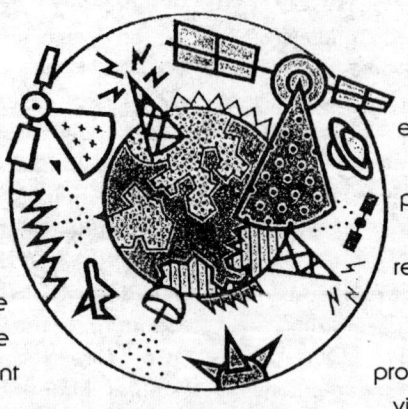

From industrial placements in research in the UK to working on a cattle ranch in Australia; from trekking through Bali, Lombok and Java to tracking Arctic foxes in Norway; from teaching in Spain to working with kids on community projects in Scotland, **A YEAR BETWEEN** *has hundreds of opportunities and a wealth of information for a great gap year.*

A YEAR BETWEEN is published biannually.   Second edition   ISBN 0 900087 98 6   £8.99

SECTION III

PREPARATION & TRAINING

RETURNING HOME

TRAVEL ADVICE

PREPARATION & TRAINING

Some preparation is obviously needed, and it is in the volunteer's interest to be well informed about the country in which they will be living and working, as well as to request adequate training before setting out. Any agency with a sense of responsibility will make available time and find funds for proper training, and such an orientation period should last long enough for you to both take in and digest the information.

You may be about to live and work in a society where much will be strange and different, and the training is basically to help you understand and cope. There should be a chance to discuss development and other issues of concern to the host country, as well as arrangements for you to meet other volunteers, both those who are about to leave and those who have recently returned. A knowledge of the relevant language is also vital in enabling you to make contact with ordinary people. Even in countries where English is an official language only a small proportion of the population may speak it (often a privileged minority) so the agency should provide at least basic language instruction. You should also receive up-to-date and relevant technical advice relating to your sphere of work, and any special technologies that fit within the context of development.

In some cases more emphasis is placed on training within the host country, and, depending on the agency, you may on arrival spend anything from a few days to a few months on an orientation programme, acclimatising yourself, learning the language, finding out about the culture and people and the type of work you will be doing. Training should also be a continuing process carried on at intervals throughout the period of service, allowing volunteers to update their skills and make regular reports about their project, and including some preparation for the return home.

There is usually more than enough time before placement and actual departure to allow personal preparation and information gathering to be undertaken. In addition to acquiring a knowledge of the future host country/area through analysis of its socio-economic background, politics, history, culture and living conditions, try to assimilate some popular aspects through food, crafts, arts and music. It is often possible to meet with some nationals of that country, for example higher education students studying in your own country.

Involve your family and friends as much as possible. This will help when the trauma of the departure day itself actually arrives, and will help in maintaining contact throughout your placement. Training should be seen as an opportunity not only to be briefed for the work you will be undertaking, but also to prepare for many of the events and eventualities you will face.

In this way, the inevitable stress brought on by months of anticipation, the change in home, in cultural environment, in the work environment if not the job itself, and in friends, will to some extent be cushioned. If the shock of a new culture, to be experienced on many levels, is seen as a positive element of the whole process of a placement, then the rewards will be gained earlier and less painfully. Being immersed in an environment and community radically different from one's own can have a variety of effects, and at different stages of the project.

The initial feeling on arrival at the placement, often after a lengthy period of preparation, may be simply one of euphoria, where cultural and other differences may be brushed aside as you come to terms with the reality of months of anticipation. Much may be viewed in a too positive light, the *mañana* attitudes of co-workers seen as relaxing, not inefficient, the overwhelming friendliness as a natural welcome, not overfamiliarity. You are not isolated in your new surroundings, as you may have imagined, but are overwhelmed.

Before long however, you will need to build yourself a new social structure. Without some established order, minor difficulties may take on the form of major disasters. Remember that your personal state will very much affect the success, or otherwise, of the project. This stage of adjustment will be similar to that gone through with any new job, where tension and anxiety can quickly build up as you strive to prove yourself while at the same time coming to terms with great changes on many fronts. On a voluntary placement in another country, these tensions may be compounded by language, indifferent health in foreign surroundings, utter loneliness, and an inability to adapt quickly enough.

How long this culture fatigue lasts will depend on you, the thoroughness of your preparation, the support from the placing agency, the length of the project itself, and above all your tolerance. It is no accident that many volunteer-sending agencies put a sense of humour fairly high on the agenda of required qualities. The ability to laugh, particularly at yourself, will see you through many a dip as goals seem ever unachievable, as success seems distant, and as homesickness or boredom threatens to overwhelm.

One particular problem will be to separate your private life and your work life. Your personal skills may be as much in demand on the placement as your professional skills. The size and form of your host community may make any sort of privacy almost impossible. Much however, will depend on the nature of the task in hand, how you view the challenges ahead, and above all, how prepared you really are for a new work and life style.

Further information about specific countries and development issues can be obtained from the organisations listed in the **UNDERSTANDING DEVELOPMENT** section. The following agencies also arrange specialist briefing courses for those about to go overseas:

**ACTION HEALTH
The Gate House, 25 Gwydir Street, Cambridge CB1 2LG
✆/Fax Cambridge (01223) 460853**
An international voluntary health association working for better health

care in parts of Asia and East Africa by creating greater awareness of the issues involved and giving practical support to appropriate health programmes.

Organises a 3 day orientation course for health personnel and development workers planning to work overseas, covering health and development, country briefings, personal health care and survival, travel, insurance, fundraising and communication skills. Opportunity to meet and talk with those who have worked in developing countries. A series of follow-up detailed project briefing sessions are provided, together with language training, when appropriate.

THE CENTRE FOR INTERNATIONAL BRIEFING
Farnham Castle, Farnham, Surrey GU9 0AG
✆ Farnham (01252) 721194

A non-profit educational organisation providing residential briefing courses lasting 1-4 days for those, including volunteers, who have been appointed to work in the developing countries of Africa, Latin America and the Caribbean, Asia and the Pacific, and the Middle East. The courses provide an understanding of the working environment and cover the culture, values and attitudes, history, the political, social and economic structure, current affairs, future trends and living conditions of the destination country. Intensive language tuition is available throughout the year for most languages. The Centre also arrange courses on Britain for those from overseas who have recently arrived to take up residence, especially on professional development assignments.

THE CHRISTIAN SERVICE CENTRE
Holloway Street West, Lower Gornal, Dudley, West Midlands DY3 2DZ

Member of the Evangelical Missionary Alliance and the Evangelical Alliance, offering information and advice to those interesting in doing long-term Christian Service.

Organises regular Which Way? weekends and days for those seriously considering where God wants them. Subjects include world mission, guidance, training for service, opportunities available and personal evaluation. For further details and a booking form write enclosing SAE. Also publish directories listing opportunities for short and long-term Christian service in Britain and overseas.

CHRISTIANS ABROAD
1 Stockwell Green, London SW9 9HP ✆ 0171-737 7811

An ecumenical body, supported by aid and mission agencies, with over 20 years' experience of vocational guidance for those seeking overseas opportunities. Also provides preparation conferences for those participating in overseas service. Arranges New Eyes half-day workshops for groups interested in exploring the possibility of working overseas. Staff work with groups of 10 or more to enable group members to look objectively at their skills, experience and circumstances; present a range of opportunities for overseas work; provide tools for decision-making and explore ways of preparing to apply to work overseas. Sessions include a skills audit; how an individual's circumstances may affect openings; a discussion of available options; decisions; and developing a portfolio.

RETURNED VOLUNTEER ACTION 1 Amwell Street, London EC1R 1UL
✆ 0171-278 0804

An organisation of, and for, serving and returned volunteers, those interested in or active in development work, and others who have worked overseas.

Organises a programme of training events in various cities throughout the year. These enable prospective volunteers to find out more about what it means to be an overseas development worker, and to meet returned workers. In addition, RVA publishes a number of booklets, ranging from general information on volunteering, to critical perspectives on volunteering and development issues.

THE VOLUNTEER MISSIONARY MOVEMENT
Comboni House, London Road, Sunningdale, Ascot, Berkshire SL5 0JY ✆ Ascot (01344) 875380

An ecumenical movement within the Catholic Church which recruits, prepares and sends Christian volunteers with a skill or profession to work as lay missionaries in projects linked with local churches. Organises and runs a 5 week residential preparation course to help those who are going overseas to reflect upon and examine their motivation, and to provide them with relevant up-to-date in formation. The course covers all aspects of life and work overseas and participants learn about the people with whom they will be working and the countries and projects in which they will work. Underlying the course is the missionary element, with special emphasis placed on prayer, spiritual formation and guidance, with returned volunteers sharing their experiences.

RETURNING HOME

Some six months before the end of the assignment you should begin to prepare yourself for the return home. The sending agency should be ready to help and advise on resettlement, and you should request information about job openings and other practical matters whilst still overseas. Many volunteers find the culture shock of returning home equal to that of going; those who come back not expecting to meet practical problems concerning health, housing, employment and state benefits can find themselves under considerable stress.

As indicated in the entries throughout this guide, many agencies arrange debriefings. In some cases these can be fairly perfunctory, but those agencies who are genuinely concerned for the welfare of their development workers will give you the opportunity to report back and evaluate the project in which you have taken part. In this way you can begin to effectively utilise the experience gained overseas: by pointing out successful methods, drawing attention to failures and describing the working conditions your reports and comments will be able to aid the agency in its work in the future. Another way in which you can apply what you have learnt abroad is to take part in briefing courses for prospective volunteers, speaking to trainees about your experience, offering advice and practical information.

Two years or so of working overseas, especially as a development worker in the Third World, is bound to change you in many ways. You will have seen things from a different perspective and your views on development and underdevelopment, and the role played by industrialised countries may have sharpened somewhat, to say nothing of the fresh eye with which you will view your home surroundings. If your experience urges you to carry on working for development from home, then check the **UNDERSTANDING DEVELOPMENT** and **NON-RESIDENTIAL** sections for organisations who would appreciate your help in their work towards raising people's awareness about development issues. The agency that sent you abroad in the first place may also put you in touch with development organisations, or they may even help you set up a development education project.

Learning to learn from the South is the theme of the Manchester-based project where Celia Marshall works:

You'll often hear returned volunteers saying that they gained more than they gave when they went overseas. After three years as a volunteer in Ghana, I definitely fall into that category. I went to share my skills, as the VSO motto says, but I returned to Britain a good deal wiser about the meaning of sharing. When I came home I felt very strongly about the need for development education, but not so much on a political level - looking at why famine occurs and how much money the South 'owes' Northern banks - as on a personal level. I felt it should be about people in the UK learning from people from the South; and people from the South living in Britain being valued for the contribution they can make here, and welcomed as brothers and sisters, as I was when I lived in Ghana.

The Southern Voices Project, where I now work full-time, is a start. Set up in 1990 through a VSO Development Education Award, it seeks to involve people from the South who are living and studying in the Manchester area with schools, community groups, workshops and conferences, and to create opportunities where people can learn from each other.

I work as part of a team of overseas students and community workers, talking to people, making links and offering support. In all the contact we arrange, the emphasis is on the human dimension.

For example, Kwame, a Ghanaian student in Manchester, has spoken to a group of students on how the debt crisis is affecting ordinary people in Ghana. Martha, from Ecuador, has made several visits to a primary school to talk to children about her country and culture - they learned games, listened to stories and cooked an Ecuadorian meal together.

I hope that the Southern Voices Project will continue to make a contribution - even if only a small one - to helping people here in the North learn how to receive from the South with an eagerness equal to their desire to give. Until we are open to receiving, we will be unable to share.

The first part of effectively utilising the experiences gained overseas is to engage in constructive evaluation of the project. Returned volunteers should also take up any opportunity to participate in briefing courses for prospective volunteers, being able to provide a range of alternative reference points. All too often returned volunteers find that the opportunities to apply what has been learnt abroad to life and work in the home country are limited.

Alex Lipinski of Returned Volunteer Action, an organisation of, and for, returned volunteers, outlines some of the problems to be faced by the returning volunteer:

Coming back home after being abroad can be as much a jolt to the system as going out in the first place, and can cause as many problems for the unprepared. The experience of living in a totally different country and culture often changes the way returnees view their own country, and the issue of fitting in again is a concern common to returned volunteers.

Sometimes there is the problem of a lack of money, or having to look for work or somewhere to live again. Or the problem may be a difficulty in adjusting to the pace of life, perhaps even trying to avoid becoming a volunteer bore to friends.

Eleanor Kercher spent two years teaching in Africa:

People expect you to fit straight back in. They ask you how was Africa and expect a two minute answer. After that they aren't interested. Also the culture shock - things like going into a fully stocked supermarket and seeing the waste. Those kinds of things are important as they build up quickly when you return. It made me feel alienated. I wasn't interested in what people had to say about their houses, I wanted to talk about the amazing experience I had. Basically for most people it is so out of their way that they don't know how to react to it.

Volunteers are given extensive training before they leave home, but Eleanor wishes her sending agency had been more supportive on her return:

It's a very solitary thing coming back. You've been through this massive experience, then you come home and have to pick up the pieces again. It's different to when you go out, lots of orientation and training; coming back you get off the plane and - nothing.

Aled Williams was more fortunate and also feels the time spent abroad is in itself a preparation for coping with resettlement:

My social network was quite strong when I returned and I got the support I wanted. Maybe I would have felt different if I was single with no close family. People who go out to a developing country are resourceful and self-reliant; they develop these abilities out there so when they come back they should adopt a similar kind of approach to problems.

Alex Lipinski says that these days the support services available to returnees are much better:

VSO for instance has a returned volunteer office which provides information and advice for its returning volunteers, who may be considering a career change or wish to become more involved in development work, and a new project was launched in 1994 to regain contact with as many former volunteers as possible. Returned Volunteer Action, too, gives advice to returned development workers from any sending agency in the UK and can put them in touch with local support groups.

Despite problems, Eleanor is enthusiastic about the benefits of volunteering:

The most useful thing about it is the experience that you bring back. The effect of your two years work abroad is tiny compared to the effect it has on you. Just living in a totally different culture makes you able to look at your own culture and question its values. I feel that I can now be more effective in working for development in this country.

Aled also sees positive benefits:

The experience has given me the confidence to work anywhere abroad, even under my own steam, without the support of an organisation.

It can take some time before returnees start to settle down and consider their future. Says Eleanor:

A lot of people wish to do something completely different when they come back. In the present economic climate that's often very difficult. It's also difficult to get back into your own professional field because things have moved on. Often employers think you've taken a two year holiday and your experience isn't relevant.

Rather than changing career, Eleanor worked her experience into teaching:

My first idea was to go back abroad immediately but then I realised it would jeopardise any education work I wanted to do. I also wanted to get into development work, but it's a very small field with many people wanting to do it, so I went back to teaching. But things have changed in that I do a lot of development education in school, and because I trained teachers abroad I now run more training courses than I would otherwise.

Aled incorporated his volunteering experience into his career plans. He saw it as an essential part of his professional development:

It's important that the post you go out to contributes to your professional development, otherwise you gain only the social development skills which, though necessary, employers don't always value.

Further help on advice, resettlement, reorientation and continuing commitment can be obtained from the following organisations:

CHRISTIANS ABROAD
1 Stockwell Green, London SW9 9HP ✆ **0171-737 7811**
An ecumenical body, founded in 1972 and supported by aid and mission agencies.
Organises one day *Back to Britain* workshops for groups of people who have recently returned from working overseas. Sessions include pictures of an experience; the coming back occasion; and the next step. Staff work with groups of 4+ people to acknowledge the joys, frustrations, hopes and fears that were part of the overseas experience; affirm what has been learned from that experience; consider the process of returning to Britain; affirm experience as a resource for paid and unpaid work in Britain; and consider the stumbling blocks and supports for sharing what has been learned overseas with others in Britain.

COMHLÁMH 10 Upper Camden Street, Dublin 2, Ireland
✆ **(353 1) 478 3490 Fax (353 1) 478 3738 and 55 Grand Parade, Cork, Ireland ✆/Fax (353 21) 275881**
The Returned Development Workers' Association of Ireland is a membership organisation open to returnees and others interested in promoting international development and awareness of development issues. Has offices in Dublin and Cork and members throughout the country.

Volunteers are encouraged to join groups working in the association's main areas: services to returned development workers, including reorientation weekends, advice on rights and help with adapting to life in Ireland and finding work; development education, including courses on world development, development and the environment and in-service courses for teachers; action and campaigns on human rights and/or development issues; and support and training for other groups involved in these areas.

RETURNED VOLUNTEER ACTION 1 Amwell Street, London EC1R 1UL
✆ 0171-278 0804

The British membership organisation for current and returned overseas development workers and those active or interested in development work. Facilitates returning volunteers to use their experiences to lobby for improvements to overseas programmes and work for change in the UK. Puts returning volunteers in touch with each other through contacts network. Also keeps members up-to-date with development worker issues through training days, monthly newsletter and biannual magazine. Provides a critical perspective on overseas development work - through publications and through training days - to guide people who are considering 'volunteering' overseas. Members are encouraged to contribute their experience to this work.

TRAVEL ADVICE

Some volunteer-sending agencies organise all the travel arrangements for their volunteers, but if you are travelling independently one travel agency which complements the theme of this book is North-South Travel Ltd, Moulsham Mill, Parkway, Chelmsford, Essex CM2 7PX ✆ Chelmsford (01245) 492882, which arranges competitively priced, reliably planned flights. Its profits contribute to the funds of charities working in the developing world.

Key Travel, 92-96 Eversholt Street, London NW1 1BP ✆ 0171-387 4933 Fax 0171-387 1090 specialise in providing low-cost airfares and other travel services for organisations and individuals working in the fields of development or conservation. Also at Etosha House, 46 Ullswater Road, Handforth, Cheshire SK9 3NQ.

Other agencies which specialise in cheaper student/youth airfares include Campus Travel, 52 Grosvenor Gardens, London SW1W 0AG ✆ 0171-730 3402 (Europe), ✆ 0171-730 2101 (North America), ✆ 0171-730 8111 (worldwide) and STA Travel, 86 Old Brompton Road, London SW7 3LQ/117 Euston Road, London NW1 2SX ✆ 0171-937 9921 (Europe), ✆ 0171-937 9962 (intercontinental), ✆ 0171-937 9971 (North America). Both have branches throughout the UK, often on student campuses. Campus Travel's sister company across the Irish Sea is USIT, with main offices at Fountain Centre, Belfast BT1 6ET ✆ Belfast (01232) 324073, and at Aston Quay, O'Connell Bridge, Dublin 2 ✆ (353 1) 778117.

Trailfinders also operate low-cost flights between London and destinations worldwide, and will offer advice to travellers in planning their trip. They have a travel centre in London at 42-50 Earls Court Road, London W8 6EJ ✆ 0171-938 3366 and another branch at 194 Kensington High Street, London W8 7RG ✆ 0171-938 3939 which has a travellers' library, bookshop and information centre, a visa service and an immunisation centre for overseas travel vaccinations. Branches also in Manchester and Glasgow.

If you are really shopping around for a cheap flight it pays to do careful research, checking with travel agencies such as those listed above and also with major airlines to find out what sort of deals are available. Bucket shops usually supply tickets direct from the airline or from consolidators (agencies responsible for filling seats on scheduled flights). They are mostly based in London and advertise their bargain fares in the national press, often in the travel pages of Sunday papers. They can offer discounts on airline tickets, but as they tend not to be covered by travel associations such as ABTA, they are viewed as slightly risky. If you want to be sure that the shop you are dealing with is reliable, check that they are licensed by the International Air Transport Association (IATA) or hold an Air Travel Organisers' Licence (ATOL), and see if they will accept payment by credit card, as credit card companies are usually pretty careful about whom they deal with. The Air Travel Advisory Bureau (✆ 0171-636 5000) should be able to refer you to a reputable agency, or an airline may be able to refer you to their own preferred agent or consolidator.

Always double check your travel details such as flight number, time of departure, check-in time and any Customs regulations that apply. It is easy to forget small but important things: for example you may have to pay airport or departure taxes, so find out whether these are included in the ticket price, and if not, in which currency they are payable. If you've booked a flight some time in advance, don't forget to confirm the booking 24-48 hours before departure.

Visas For entry to some countries a visa or visitor's pass is required. The recruiting agency should inform you about entry and exit visa procedures, but it is always wise to check for yourself whether a visa is required and that you obtain one that is valid for the length of time you expect to be in the country. If you plan to do any extensive travelling, investigate the possibility of getting a multiple entry visa. You can get information on visas from the consular section of the relevant embassy, but make sure you allow yourself plenty of time, as the visa application process can be a lengthy one.

Passports It is essential to check that your passport is valid at least for the time you intend to stay overseas and, as your circumstances may change, it is wise to allow an extra six months. Immigration and other government officials usually turn to a new page when stamping passports, so check that there are enough clear pages for visas and stamps; the British Passport Office issues a 94-page passport which is useful for those doing a lot of travelling through several countries. Always apply at least three months in advance for a passport, especially in the holiday season; a standard UK passport costs £15 (£22.50 if particulars of family are included), the larger size costs £30. Both are valid for 10 years and are obtainable from the following regional offices:

Passport Office, Clive House, 70-78 Petty France, London SW1H 9HD
℡ 0171-279 3434 (personal callers only).

Passport Office, 5th Floor, India Buildings, Water Street, Liverpool L2 0QZ
℡ 0151-237 3010

Passport Office, Olympia House, Upper Dock Street, Newport, Gwent NP9 1XA
℡ Newport (01633) 244500

Passport Office, Aragon Court, Northminster Road, Peterborough, Cambridgeshire PE1 1QG
℡ Peterborough (01733) 895555

Passport Office, 3 Northgate, 96 Milton Street, Cowcaddens, Glasgow G4 0BT
℡ 0141-332 0271

Passport Office, Hampton House, 47-53 High Street, Belfast BT1 2QS
℡ Belfast (01232) 232371

Nationals of other countries will need to consult their own passport-issuing authorities as to the issuing and validity of passports. If a passport is lost or stolen while abroad the local police should be notified immediately; if necessary your nearest embassy or consulate will issue a substitute. It is therefore wise to keep a separate note of your passport number.
The *Essential Information* booklet contains notes on illness or injury

while abroad, insurance, vaccinations, NHS medical cards, consular assistance overseas, British Customs and other useful advice, and is available from all passport offices.

Health Some volunteer-sending agencies will provide in-country medical treatment, but it is still a sensible precaution to have thorough medical and dental check-ups well before you leave. If you need to take prescribed drugs then you must find out beforehand whether these are subject to any regulations in the country or countries to which you will be travelling - some medicines freely available in Britain may be strictly controlled in other countries. A letter from your doctor giving details of any prescribed drugs can help in preventing misunderstandings. Brand names for drugs vary from country to country, so find out the generic name for any prescribed drugs in case you need to get more whilst overseas. If you wear spectacles take a spare pair and make a note of the prescription in case you lose them. Contact lenses can prove to be painful and hard to keep clean in dusty regions, in which case you may consider changing to spectacles.

Changes in food and climate may cause minor illnesses and, especially when visiting the hotter countries of southern Europe, North Africa, Latin America and the Far East, it is wise to take extra care in your hygiene, eating and drinking habits. Native bacteria, to which local inhabitants are immune, may cause the visitor stomach upsets, so it is worth avoiding tap water and doing without ice in your drinks. In a hot climate never underestimate the strength of the sun, or overestimate your own strength. Drink plenty of fluids, make sure there is enough salt in your diet, wear loose-fitting cotton clothes, even a hat, and guard against heat exhaustion, heat stroke and sunburn, especially when working outdoors.

Whilst abroad it is unwise to have your skin pierced by acupuncture, tattooing or ear piercing, for example, unless you can be sure that the equipment is sterile. A major cause of the spread of viruses, including AIDS, is the use of infected needles and equipment. In some countries blood for transfusions is not screened for the presence of the AIDS virus, but there may be arrangements for obtaining screened blood. The doctor treating you, or the nearest consulate may be able to offer advice. If you are concerned about the availability of sterile equipment whilst abroad, emergency medical travel kits are available through MASTA (see under the **Immunisation** heading, below) and other suppliers, and can be ordered through retail pharmacists. They contain a variety of sterilised and sealed items such as syringes and needles for use in emergencies. MASTA also has a range of health care items such as mosquito nets and water purifiers.

In the UK the Department of Health issues a booklet, *Health Advice for Travellers*, available from post offices, travel agents, libraries and doctors' surgeries, or by phoning 0800 555777. This includes details of compulsory and recommended vaccinations, other measures that can be taken to protect one's health, information on rabies, AIDS, malaria and other diseases. There is also advice on types of food and on water supplies which may be a source of infection.

A person is only covered by the NHS while in the UK, and will usually have to pay the full costs of any treatment abroad. However, there are health care arrangements between all countries in the European Economic Area (EEA) - Austria, Belgium, Britain, Denmark, Finland, France, Germany, Greece, Iceland, Ireland, Italy, Luxembourg, the Netherlands, Norway, Portugal, Spain and Sweden. British citizens resident in the UK will receive free or reduced cost emergency treatment in other EEA countries on production of form E111. An application form for E111 is included in the *Health Advice for Travellers* booklet mentioned above, which also explains who is covered by the arrangements, what treatment is free or at reduced cost, and gives the procedures which must be followed to get treatment in countries where form E111 is not needed (usually Austria, Denmark, Finland, Gibraltar, Ireland and Portugal). Form E111 must be taken abroad and, if emergency treatment is needed, the correct procedures must be followed.

There are also reciprocal health care arrangements between Britain and Australia, Barbados, Bulgaria, Channel Islands, the Czech Republic, Hong Kong, Hungary, Isle of Man, Malta, New Zealand, Poland, Romania, Russia and the former Soviet Union (not Baltic States), the Slovak Republic, the former Yugoslavia and the British Dependent Territories of Anguilla, British Virgin Islands, Falkland Islands, Montserrat, St Helena, and Turks and Caicos Islands. However, private health insurance may still be needed in these countries; *Health Advice for Travellers* gives full details. Despite reciprocal health arrangements it is still *essential* to ensure you have full medical insurance cover whenever travelling overseas. The health treatment available in other countries may not be as comprehensive as in the UK, and *none* of the arrangements listed above covers the cost of repatriation in the event of illness.

Immunisation should be started well in advance, as some courses necessitate an interval between the first and second inoculation, or between one immunisation and another. As immunity may take several days to develop, validity may not be immediate - immigration officials will not accept a yellow fever immunisation certificate until 10 days after the vaccination. And, as you may suffer after-effects from a vaccination it is sensible to allow yourself time to recover before you leave, rather than suffering during the journey and the first few days abroad. A certificate of vaccination against certain diseases (usually cholera and yellow fever) is an entry requirement for some countries, and it is best to consult embassies on this point, since requirements are continually subject to review. Other immunisations are merely recommended, but may well be even more vital to your health. These include tetanus - especially if you will be doing manual work outdoors; typhoid - particularly important in the tropics; polio - have a booster if it's 10 years since you were last vaccinated; hepatitis - many volunteer agencies will insist on this; rabies - for those at special risk such as vets and zoologists; and malaria - currently one of the worst health hazards for British travellers to Africa, Asia and Latin America. As a general rule it is wise to make sure that your protection against typhoid, polio and tetanus is up-to-date if you are travelling outside Europe, North America or Australasia.

The volunteer-sending agency may be able to advise you on appropriate vaccinations. Within the UK, up-to-date printouts indicating the immunisations and malaria tablets appropriate for any specific journey are also available from the Medical Advisory Service to Travellers Abroad (MASTA). Call ✆ 0891 224100 to leave a recorded message listing the countries you will be visiting, the month of arrival in each and the living conditions. The required information will be sent by return; calls are charged at 39p a minute (cheap rate) or 49p a minute (all other times). MASTA printouts are also available without charge for those attending British Airways Travel Clinics for their immunisations; for details of the clinic nearest to you call ✆ 0171-831 5333.

Insurance It is in your own interests to have adequate insurance, not only for medical treatment, but also life and personal accident cover and to cover cash and possessions. Many volunteer-sending agencies do provide insurance, but this may only be against third party risks and accidents, in which case you will need to supplement the provision. You may already have an insurance policy covering you both at home and overseas, but this may need extending to cover the nature of the situation in which you will find yourself as a volunteer. It is common to include cover in the policy for ambulance transport and in certain circumstances repatriation, including medical attention on the journey and the conveyance of a relative or friend. Cover for personal effects should include baggage in transit and at destination, and expensive individual items such as photographic equipment. Check carefully the limit for the total package as well as for each claim, make sure that the policy does cover you for the type work that you will be doing, and find out whether there is a representative of the insurance company in the destination country to whom claims can be made. Whatever insurance cover you take out, do make sure that you read the small print very thoroughly before you travel, and take a copy of the policy with you, keeping a separate note of the policy number. If a claim needs to be made then the insurance company should be informed of all the details without delay, and where a crime is involved the local police must also be notified.

National Insurance The regulations covering National Insurance contributions and social security are complex and become more complicated for those paying contributions while overseas. Your entitlement to sickness, invalidity and unemployment benefit, maternity allowance, and state pension is governed by your National Insurance record, but this does not affect entitlement to other social security benefits such as income support. Some agencies, especially those funded by the British government, will automatically pay National Insurance contributions for their volunteers (see information below about VDW contributions), but whichever organisation you are working with it is essential to clarify the position regarding National Insurance contributions well in advance of taking up a post; neglecting to make proper arrangements may well prejudice any future claims for benefits. If you are going to one of the EU countries, leaflet *SA29, Your Social Security, Health Care and Pension Rights in the European Community*, available from the Contributions Agency, see *below*, gives details of National Insurance contributions, plus the social security rights and where to claim them.

If you are going outside the EU there are separate leaflets detailing social security procedures in countries with which the UK has a reciprocal arrangement: Australia, Austria, Barbados, Bermuda, Canada, Croatia, Cyprus, Finland, Iceland, Israel, Jamaica, Jersey and Guernsey, Malta, Mauritius, New Zealand, Norway, Philippines, Slovenia, Sweden, Switzerland, Turkey, United States and the Federal Republic of Yugoslavia. For other countries, leaflet *NI38, Social Security abroad* applies.

A special Volunteer Development Worker (VDW) contribution can be paid by volunteers going abroad where the following conditions apply: the volunteer normally lives in the UK, is recruited by an approved organisation, and has gone overseas to work in a recognised developing country. The VDW contribution in most cases is paid direct to the Overseas Contributions Agency by the recruiting organisation; however it is possible in some cases for volunteers to make their own payment arrangements. The payment of VDW contributions will normally provide cover for sickness and unemployment benefit following a person's return to the UK provided the contribution years on which the claim is assessed are covered by the absence abroad. For copies of leaflets mentioned above and any further information, contact the Contributions Agency, Overseas Contributions, Department of Social Security, Newcastle-upon-Tyne NE98 1YX.

Emergencies Find out before you leave what support is available in times of emergency or trouble. Many organisations have country representatives or field officers who will at least act as a point of contact between volunteers and the sending agency. The British Consulate or the Consular Section of British Embassies or High Commissions will be able to offer advice and help, especially if there is no-one else to turn to, but do consider other options such as the local police or a local representative of your bank or insurance company. If you do need help from the Consulate, try to phone or telegraph in advance; the telegraphic address of all British Embassies is *Prodrome* and of all British Consulates *Britain*, followed in each case by the name of the town. Consuls will advise or help in cases of serious difficulty or distress; they cannot give advice on, or pay for, legal proceedings, but will do what they can to help in such cases. As a last resort they can, providing strict conditions are met, make a repayable loan for repatriation to the UK. Before you go overseas, make sure that you have the following, kept separate from your other belongings: passport number, date and place of issue; travel ticket numbers, dates and places of issue; insurance details and 24 hour emergency number; local agency or representative details; embassy or consulate contact address and phone number; serial numbers of travellers' cheques; any medical prescriptions or doctor's instructions.

SECTION IV

OVERSEAS SERVICE

ACTION HEALTH

Information Officer, Action Health, The Gate House, 25 Gwydir Street, Cambridge CB1 2LG

Cambridge (01223) 460853   Fax Cambridge (01223) 460853

India; Tanzania, Zambia, Zimbabwe

Founded in 1984, an international voluntary health association with no political or religious affiliations, working for better health care in Asia and Africa. Aims to work towards the World Health Organisation's target of making basic health care accessible to the world's poorest peoples; provides and encourages links between health professionals worldwide, and is concerned with health care research and education.

Study training programme allows doctors, paediatric nurses, midwives, health visitors, physio, occupational and speech therapists and other health personnel to work as volunteers in rural, semi-rural or deprived urban areas. Recruits 30 health professionals annually.

Ages 23+. Appropriate professional health qualifications necessary. No experience necessary on application, though selected individuals may be asked to acquire specific experience before being sent overseas. Applicants should be resourceful, resilient, sensitive to local cultures and difficulties, compassionate and understanding, and have non-verbal communication skills. A multi-disciplinary approach and the ability to work as part of a team required. Volunteers only accepted after satisfactory medical report. All nationalities considered. **PH**

Six months-two years

Simple housing, adequate local food, insurance, National Insurance, travel costs and monthly allowance of £115-£380, depending on length of service, provided. Participants contribute or fundraise £1,000 towards their programme. Advice given on sponsorship and fundraising.

Short-listed applicants can meet former volunteers at selection weekends. Compulsory, comprehensive three-day orientation course arranged, together with a series of one-day project briefing sessions. Language training is given. Returned volunteers are debriefed and provided with help and advice on resettlement and finding a job, and are encouraged to participate in the society's UK activities.

Recruitment all year; usually a 6-12 month gap between application and departure to allow time for preparation

Newsletter; project reports; information leaflets

AFRICA INLAND MISSION

Assistant Personnel Secretary, Africa Inland Mission, 2 Vorley Road, Archway, London N19 5HE

0171-281 1184

Mainly Kenya, but other African countries as needs arise

AIM is a Protestant missionary society whose aims are evangelism and church planting

There are opportunities for teaching in rural schools and working with young people; some 30 volunteers are recruited each year

Ages 18-70. Applicants must have A levels or a degree for teaching. Knowledge of French helpful for some countries. All applicants must be committed Christians with a desire to serve God in Africa.

One year, departing end of August

Housing is provided but volunteers are required to raise all their travel expenses, insurance, living allowances and administration costs through their churches and Christian friends. Advice is given on obtaining sponsorship.

Compulsory orientation course provided. One-day debriefing seminar on return.

Apply September-May

AIM International quarterly magazine

APSO

Recruitment Section, APSO, 29-30 Fitzwilliam Square, Dublin 2, Ireland

Dublin (353 1) 614411   Fax (353 1) 614202

Over 50 developing countries, mainly, but not exclusively, in Africa

A state-sponsored body established in 1974 to promote and sponsor temporary personal service in the developing countries of the world for their economic and social development, in the interests of justice and peace among nations. It recruits on behalf of governments and non-governmental agencies in developing countries, co-funds volunteers with other sending agencies and seeks to protect the interest of development workers on their return.

Volunteers are needed in the areas of education, health, engineering/ construction, agriculture, administration and social sciences.
There are vacancies for doctors, nurses, pharmacists, physiotherapists, nutritionists and medical laboratory technicians; teachers of English, science, maths, primary education, home economics, secretarial/ commercial skills and technical subjects; university lecturers; mechanical, civil and electrical engineers; carpenters and mechanics; horticulturists and agriculturists; administrators and project managers; social workers and community development specialists. Recruits and funds approx 1,000 volunteers annually.

Ages 21+. Applicants must qualify for an Irish passport.
Basic qualifications required. Experience preferred but not essential.
Applicants must have a genuine interest in helping a developing country.
B D PH W subject to placement opportunities.

Normally 2 years

Return airfares, insurance, accommodation and living allowance provided

Orientation, professional skills training and language courses provided

Recruitment all year

Annual Report, training brochure, newsletter

ASSOCIATE MISSIONARIES OF THE ASSUMPTION

The Director, Assumption Convent, 227 N Bowman Avenue, Merion, Pennsylvania 19066, United States

(1 215) 664 1284

East Africa, Japan, United States and Europe: France, Spain, Germany, Italy and Britain

Founded in 1960, provides lay men and women with the opportunity to share their skills with others in teaching, medical work or towards the development of peoples in another country

Volunteers are needed to teach at elementary and secondary level; or to live and work in communities for people with mental handicaps, retirement homes or nursing centres

Ages 22-45. College graduates or equivalent preferred. Previous volunteer experience essential. Applicants should have a deep faith, generosity, forgetfulness of self, the ability to adapt to new cultures and the willingness to tackle any job they are given. Knowledge of relevant languages helpful.

One year minimum

Board and lodging provided, plus health insurance and stipend of approx $100 per month. One-way fare provided for a one year commitment, return fare for a two year commitment.

Compulsory orientation course arranged prior to departure; plus re-entry weekend on return

Apply by 15 March

ASSOCIATES OF MILL HILL MISSIONARIES

Associate Secretary, Associates of Mill Hill Missionaries, St Joseph's Missionary Society, St Joseph's College, Lawrence Street, Mill Hill, London NW7 4JX

0181-959 8254

Cameroon, Kenya, Sudan, Uganda, Zaire; Pakistan; Chile, Falkland Islands

The work of the Mill Hill Missionaries goes back to the late 19th century and since 1970 associate lay members have joined the service to work with the priests and brothers. The organisation enables lay missionaries to use their talents and skills to build up God's people in mission lands, and to channel and employ the gifts of many for the service of the missionary ideal.

Vacancies exist in the areas of teaching, nursing, social and pastoral work, catechetics, engineering and building work in a missionary context

Ages 21+. Applicants must have Christian and missionary motivation, relevant professional or technical qualifications and skills, and at least 2 years' work experience. Some form of experience doing voluntary or parish work is recommended. The ability to work as part of an international team and the maturity to adapt oneself to different cultures and work in isolated conditions are also important.
All nationalities considered; working knowledge of English essential.

Three years

Board and lodging, insurance, travel costs and local missionary allowance provided

Introductory weekends held regularly for those interested in applying. Compulsory three month preparatory course organised in England and the Netherlands before Associates take up their placements. Oral debriefing arranged on return, plus financial assistance until a job has been found.

Recruitment all year

Two booklets: *A Century of Charity - The Story of the Mill Hill Missionaries*; *The Changing Face of Mission*

ATD FOURTH WORLD

General Secretary, ATD Fourth World, 48 Addington Square, London SE5 7LB

Burkina Faso, Central African Republic, Côte d'Ivoire, Madagascar, Mauritius, Senegal; Philippines, Thailand, Taiwan; Belgium, Britain, France, Germany, Luxembourg, Netherlands, Spain, Switzerland; Guatemala, Haiti, Honduras; Canada, United States

Supports the efforts of the poorest in overcoming poverty and taking an active role in their communities. Involved in grass roots projects, the approach is tailored to the particular requirements in each community. Works to three core objectives: to breakdown ostracism endured by the poor; enable the poorest to participate in and contribute to society as a whole; and develop a constructive public awareness of poverty. It is not aligned with any political or religious group.

Potential volunteers participate in a working weekend and then a 3 month induction programme in London or Surrey, where they live and work alongside full-time workers and undertake manual and office work, assist in projects with poor families and learn about ATD through discussions, books and videos. They also join in planning and evaluation meetings and are expected to write about their experiences. Accommodation provided and, after the second month, a small allowance. Can go on to become core workers abroad, stay on as workers in Britain, or become friends of ATD, encouraging the public to view the very poor as useful members of society.

Ages 18+. No professional/academic requirements; everyone welcome. Applicants should have a genuine interest in learning from the experiences and hopes of very disadvantaged communities as a vital first step to building a future with them, and a willingness to work hard with others in a team.

Three months minimum; at least two years for placements outside Europe

Accommodation provided; volunteers pay food expenses for first month; subsequent increments up to the minimum salary all workers receive after one year. Travel/insurance costs provided for volunteers working overseas.

Working weekend acts as selection period; 3 month induction programme in Britain followed by several weeks in France before joining a team. Intensive in-service training for new volunteers during the first two years.

Recruitment all year; applicants should enclose an A3 SAE

Emergence from Extreme Poverty, a book describing the nature of the work of the permanent volunteers on behalf of the poorest families in Europe

BAPTIST MISSIONARY SOCIETY

Andrew North, Baptist Missionary Society, PO Box 49, Baptist House, Didcot, Oxon OX11 8XA

Didcot (01235) 512077

Angola, Zaire; Bangladesh, India, Nepal, Sri Lanka, Thailand; Jamaica, Trinidad; Albania, Belgium, France, Italy; Brazil, El Salvador, Nicaragua

An organisation of Baptist churches in the UK, aimed at making known the gospel of Jesus Christ throughout the world. Works in partnership with churches overseas.

BMS gets involved in the evangelistic work of the local church. Projects may include church-planting; social projects such as running a day-care nursery; agricultural and development schemes; education and vocational teaching; medical assistance; training and pastoral work; and supporting national Christians in their work and ministry. There are two types of placement: long-term for students furthering their studies, for example in medical work, engineering or teaching; also BMS Action Teams involving young people in short-term missionary work.

Ages 18+ for long-term volunteers who must have qualifications relevant to the task they wish to undertake. Ages 18-30 for Action Teams; no experience or qualifications necessary. All applicants must have a clear call from God, be involved in their local Baptist church and committed to the expansion of God's kingdom on earth.

Volunteers: typically 6-12 months. Action Teams: 1-3 month summer programme or 9 month placement departing October, which includes training, 6 months abroad and 3 months touring Baptist churches in Britain presenting what was done overseas.

Board and lodging provided. Small amount of pocket money for Action Teams. All participants are encouraged to pay as much as possible towards travel expenses.

Training and debriefing provided

Volunteer recruitment all year; apply well in advance for Action Teams

Missionary Herald monthly; *Look!* monthly (for children); information leaflets

BRETHREN VOLUNTEER SE[RVICE]

Coordinator of Recruitment, Brethren Volunteer Service, 1451 Dundee Avenue, Elgin, Illinois 60120, United States

(1 708) 742 5100

United States. Limited opportunities for US citizens only in Haiti, Puerto Rico, Virgin Islands; France, Germany, Ireland, Netherlands, Northern Ireland, Poland, Switzerland; Bolivia, Chile, Ecuador, El Salvador, Honduras, Mexico, Nicaragua, Uruguay; China; Egypt; Israel.

A Christian service programme founded in 1948, dedicated to justice, peacemaking and serving basic human needs. BVS is characterised by the spirit of sharing God's love through acts of service and reflects the heritage of reconciliation and service of the Church of the Brethren.

Over 200 projects, some dealing with immediate needs, others working towards changing unjust systems; the range of personnel is wide and constantly updated. Recent projects have needed agricultural workers, environmentalists, maintenance experts, craft workers, medical personnel, childcare aides, social/youth workers, community organisers, instructors to the disabled, peace/prison reform organisers, refugee resettlement coordinators, teachers and administrators.

Ages 20+. Applicants should be willing to act on their commitments and values; they will be challenged to offer themselves, their time and talents to work that is difficult and demanding. They are expected to study and examine the Christian faith, to be open to personal growth and willing to share in the lives of others. High school education or equivalent required. Programme especially needs those with relevant skills and experience; the less experienced if they bring a willingness to grow and a desire to learn. All nationalities considered. **B D PH**

One year minimum for US; two years service elsewhere

Participants meet their own costs to orientation in the US; thereafter BVS provides travel, insurance and $45 per month allowance, which may be increased in the second year. Board and lodging provided in apartments/houses or occasionally with a family.

Compulsory 3 week orientation course when the project assignments are made. Debriefing provided during in-service retreat.

Apply at least 6 months in advance

BRISTOL LINK WITH NICARAGUA

The Secretary, Bristol Link with Nicaragua (BLINC), 6 West Street, Old Market, Bristol BS2 0BH

Bristol (01272) 411442

Puerto Morazán, Nicaragua

Set up in 1985 to manage and develop a link with Puerto Morazán, a fishing community of approx 2,000 people living on a tidal estuary on the Pacific coast of Nicaragua. BLINC supports a range of small development and educational projects there, and also organises cultural, social and commercial events in Bristol focusing on Nicaragua.

There are opportunities for self-funded volunteers to work on a number of projects in Nicaragua, including working on a shrimp farm or iguana farm, helping in teaching and organising excursions at a Montessori-style nursery school, teaching craft and literacy skills and organising cultural and sports events at a community centre, teaching English at a secondary school, and health education work at a health centre. In both Bristol and Nicaragua volunteers can also do general administrative work to support the twinning process.

Ages 18+. Experience of campaigning and/or development issues preferable but not essential. Volunteers should be independent, confident and enthusiastic, with an interest in development and in the Latin America region and good interpersonal and motivational skills. Knowledge of Spanish essential.

Three months minimum

Volunteers must be self-financing and cover their own travel, insurance, board and accommodation costs

All volunteers must attend orientation before beginning of placement

Recruitment all year

Information leaflets

THE BRITAIN-NEPAL MEDICAL TRUST

Ms D Jacques, The Britain-Nepal Medical Trust, 16 East Street, Tonbridge, Kent TN9 1HG

Tonbridge (01732) 360284

Eastern Nepal

Set up to assist the people of Nepal improve their health. Runs a TB and leprosy management programme; a community health development programme which includes non-formal education and adult literacy projects, school/community health development and street theatre projects; drugs scheme programme and various training programmes.

Very limited opportunities for expatriate workers to act as programme coordinators in Nepal. One or two expatriate staff are recruited every 2-3 years; all other staff are recruited locally.

Ages 25-50+. Applicants must have a community/public health or medical qualification, and preferably a postgraduate qualification. Previous experience in international development work, preferably health care, essential. Good communications and interpersonal skills, and a commitment to a participatory approach to community development also required. Computer skills desirable. Fluent written and spoken English essential; Nepali language skills useful, but a willingness to learn is more important. **D**

Two years minimum

Workers receive £10,000 per annum, a terminal leave grant and £250 equipment allowance. Accommodation and medical/accident insurance cover provided and travel costs paid.

Orientation course, including language training, provided prior to placement. This is compulsory, unless worker already has adequate development work/cultural/language experience.

Posts advertised as required; apply in response to advertisements

Annual Report

BRITAIN - VIETNAM FRIENDSHIP SOCIETY

Britain-Vietnam Friendship Society, Flat 2, Tomlins Grove, London E3 4NX

Vietnam

The Britain-Vietnam Friendship Society was founded in 1992 to develop friendship and understanding between the two cultures.

Through a Teachers for Vietnam programme there are opportunities for volunteers to teach English as a foreign language in the provinces of Vietnam. Approx 10 volunteers placed each year.

Ages 20-40. Volunteers must be UK nationals with a TEFL qualification and overseas teaching experience. They should be understanding of other cultures and interested in helping people in another country.

One year minimum

40 hour week. Board and accommodation provided plus approx $30 per month paid in local currency. Volunteers cover cost of travel to and from Vietnam and arrange own insurance.

Meetings held to discuss results and work of volunteers.

Recruitment all year

BRITISH EXECUTIVE SERVICE OVERSEAS

Public Relations Manager, British Executive Service Overseas, 164 Vauxhall Bridge Road, London SW1V 2RB

0171-630 0644

Over 80 countries in the developing world, Eastern and Central Europe and the former Soviet Union

An independent organisation, initiated by the Institute of Directors and established with the backing of the British government and the CBI. Its aims are the advancement of industrial and commercial training and education in developing countries; the improvement of managerial skills leading to greater efficiency in industry and commerce; the promotion of the science of supervisory management and organisation of systems and methods in the fields of industry, trade and commerce. Recruits executives by enlisting the help of employers, federations, professional institutes and trade associations, and maintains a register of executives.

Professionals with industrial and commercial backgrounds are sent to advise small and medium-sized businesses on specific problems, sharing knowledge and expertise in a practical way with indigenous businesses and helping countries achieve economic independence, self-sustaining growth and a higher standard of living. An increasing amount of work is being done in the social welfare sector.

Volunteers should be retired professionals or executives on secondment from their employers, with a successful record in industrial/commercial fields. Applicants should have a commitment to passing on their skills; level of expertise required depends on individual assignments.

Average period 6 weeks; maximum 6 months

Travel, insurance and incidental expenses of the volunteer and spouse are met by BESO. Accommodation, subsistence and local transportation costs borne by the requesting organisation.

Briefing provided on local conditions

Recruitment all year

Information leaflets; *BESO News* newsletter; *Annual Report*; *Becoming a BESO Volunteer*

CALCUTTA RESCUE

Lyndsay Hurn, Calcutta Rescue, c/o Calcutta Rescue Fund, PO Box 52, Brentford, Middlesex TW8 8PS

Calcutta, India

Runs two street clinics and a school for destitute people in Calcutta. The clinics see over 500 patients and over 200 children attend the school daily. There is also a small sewing programme and plans for further income-generating projects. The Calcutta Rescue Fund exists to create awareness about the situation of destitute people in Calcutta, and about the work being done by Calcutta Rescue.

Opportunities for self-funding volunteers to help out at the clinics and other projects. The main need is for nurses, midwives, pharmacists and administrators. Approx 4 volunteer placements each year.

Ages 22-65. British passport-holders only, resident in Britain; other nationals can apply through offices in mainland Europe. Applicants must have appropriate qualifications such as RGN and at least a year's post-registration experience. They should also have flexibility, adaptability, diplomacy, enthusiasm and commonsense, and the ability to work well in a multi-cultural team. Previous experience of working in India preferred.

Six months minimum

Volunteers work approx 40 hour week. They must be entirely self-financing; estimated costs for six months are £400 to cover return flight, £150 to cover insurance and £660 to cover living expenses.

All volunteers must attend orientation course prior to placement. Returned volunteers are contacted and invited to local Calcutta Rescue meetings.

Applications accepted year-round

Information leaflet

CAMPHILL AM BODENSEE

Sekretariat, Camphill am Bodensee, Heimsonderschule Brachenreuthe, 88662 Überlingen-Bodensee, Germany

(07551) 80070   Fax (07551) 8007 50

Near Überlingen, Germany

A residential school for mentally handicapped children, based near Lake Constance. The school cares for 90 children aged 4-17, and consists of 10 house communities, a therapy building, a community hall, a garden and a farm. Emphasis is placed on catering for the needs and problems of autistic children. The work is based on the teachings of Rudolf Steiner, and aims to help the children achieve individual independence within the Camphill Trust communities.

Volunteers are required to live and work with the children, helping out in classes and with bathing, dressing and other personal tasks. Volunteers are also encouraged to participate in the cultural, recreational and social aspects of community life.

Ages 19+. No previous experience or qualifications necessary. Volunteers should be caring, enthusiastic and willing to help wherever they are needed. A fairly good command of German is essential.

6-12+ months, usually starting mid August

Volunteers work a 6 day week, and have 5 weeks holiday in a year. Full board single/double room accommodation, insurance and DM350 per month pocket money provided. Volunteers pay their own travel expenses.

Those staying for a year have the opportunity to take part in a training course in curative education

Recruitment all year

Information leaflets

CAMPHILL SPECIAL SCHOOLS
(BEAVER RUN)

- Applications Group, Camphill Special Schools, RD1, Beaver Run, Glenmoore, Pennsylvania 19343, United States

- Pennsylvania, United States

- A children's village community of approx 150 people, of which nearly half are mentally handicapped children and adolescents

- Volunteers are required to live and work in the community, caring for small groups of children in family homes and in the school, assisting in land work and craft activities such as weaving, woodwork and pottery

- Ages 19-35. Some previous experience of work with children with or without mental handicaps is desirable. Volunteers should be enthusiastic and keen to learn.

- One year placements from September-July preferred

- Volunteers work approx 50 hours per week and are provided with board and lodging in a village home, plus approx $130 per month pocket money. Group medical and dental insurance provided. Student visa arranged but participants must pay their own travel costs.

- Ongoing orientation for those new to the work

- Apply 4-6 months in advance

CAMPHILL VILLAGE KIMBERTON HILLS

The Admissions Group, Camphill Village Kimberton Hills, PO Box 155, Kimberton, Pennsylvania 19442, United States

(1 215) 935 0300

Pennsylvania, United States

An agricultural community based on a 430 acre estate in the rolling hills of southeast Pennsylvania. There is a total population of 130, including some 50 adults with mental handicaps. The community raises vegetables, grains, fruits and meat, and produces milk and cheese from a small dairy herd. Their own baked goods are sold in a health food store nearby.

Volunteers are required to live and work as co-workers within the community, working shoulder-to-shoulder with mentally handicapped adults. Work takes place on the farm, in the bakery, co-op, coffee shop and orchards, in the administrative office and in expanded-family homes. Some 10-15 volunteers are recruited each year.

Ages 19+. No previous experience or qualifications necessary. Volunteers should have idealism, enthusiasm and an interest in personal growth.

Three months minimum

Board and lodging provided in a village home. In the first 3 months volunteers receive $75 per month pocket money, after which they may choose to join the community's system of spending flexibly according to one's own perceived needs and those of others in the community. Health insurance provided after 6 months, but not travel costs. Advice given on obtaining sponsorship.

Orientation course available during placement

Recruitment all year; apply at least six weeks in advance

Information leaflets and brochures; *Village Life* publication

CAMPHILL VILLAGE USA INC

Associate Director, Camphill Village USA Inc, Copake, New York 12516, United States

(1 518) 329 4851

New York State, United States

An international community of 220 people, about half of whom are adults with mental disabilities. Situated in 650 acres of wooded hills and farmland 110 miles north of New York City, the Village includes a farm, a large garden, 7 craft workshops, a store and 20 extended-family houses shared by 4-8 adults with disabilities and 2-4 co-workers.

Volunteers are required to live and work as co-workers within the community, taking part in work on the land, household chores, crafts, worship, full social and cultural activities. 25 volunteers join each year.

Ages 18+. No previous experience or qualifications necessary. Volunteers should have an open mind and a willingness to join in and experience community life. **PH** depending on ability.

Six months minimum, one year preferred. Some three month placements during June, July and August.

Co-workers are provided with board and lodging in a village house, plus $50 per month pocket money. Those staying 12 months receive $400 towards a 3 week vacation. Health insurance provided, but not travel costs.

5-8 hours per week orientation course provided. Three year training in social therapeutic work offered to volunteers staying at least one year.

Recruitment all year, although to participate in training programme volunteers should plan to join in mid September

Information leaflets and booklets; *Village View* newsletter

CENTRO STUDI TERZO MONDO

The Director, Centro Studi Terzo Mondo, via G B Morgagni 29, 20129 Milan, Italy

(39 2) 2940 9041

Angola, Chad, Ethiopia, Mozambique, Somalia; India, Indonesia; Brazil, Ecuador, Peru

Founded in 1962, the centre has a wide-ranging involvement with the Third World, which includes arranging development projects, organising courses, initiating studies and research, and issuing documentation, books and journals. Also recruits volunteers for other Italian organisations employing volunteers overseas.

Volunteers are needed to work as teachers, in the medical and social services, in community work, and to organise integrated projects. Recruits 25 volunteers annually.

Ages 18+. Applicants should be reliable and have a serious commitment to voluntary work. Qualifications not always necessary but often desirable, depending on the post. All nationalities considered.

Open-ended commitment

Board and accommodation depends on the country, but usually provided in private house. $100 per week pocket money and insurance provided. 36 hour week. Travel costs are met for periods of at least 6 months service. Advice given to participants on obtaining sponsorship.

Compulsory orientation course organised for those without qualifications and experience. On return, advice/debriefing meetings organised every two months.

Recruitment all year

Terzo Mondo quarterly journal; *Quaderni di Terzo Mondo* occasional publication

CHRISTIAN APPALACHIAN PROJECT

Carla Durand/Kathy Kluesener, Christian Appalachian Project, 235 Lexington Street, Lancaster, KY 40444, United States

(1 606) 792 2219   Fax (1 606) 792 6625

Eastern Kentucky, United States

Founded in 1964, the Christian Appalachian Project (CAP) is a non-profit, interdenominational Christian service organisation that operates in the Appalachian region of eastern Kentucky. Offers over 60 programmes that help the people of Appalachia help themselves. Works with people at different levels of poverty, and seek to involve all the people of Appalachia without discrimination.

Opportunities for volunteers to work in child development centres, teen programmes, adult education, emergency outreach services, elderly programmes, family life services, infant and toddler programmes, respite care, programmes for people with disabilities, home repair and used clothing stores. 77 one-year volunteer placements and 65 summer camp placements each year.

Ages 20+, one-year volunteers; 18+, short-term volunteers. Volunteers must be open and tolerant of living in a community housing situation, sharing evening meals, chores and daily prayer. Skills and experience according to placement. Volunteers must speak English. **PH W**

One year commitment preferred; limited temporary voluntary opportunities with a three week minimum commitment. Summer camp volunteers 3-7 weeks.

40 hour week. Room, board, health insurance and transportation to and from work site provided. Volunteers cover cost of travel to and from Kentucky. Long-term volunteers receive $100 per month pocket money. Overseas volunteers must make own visa arrangements.

One-day general orientation, 1-3 week programme orientation and ongoing training provided

Apply at least one month in advance

CHRISTIAN FOUNDATION FOR CHILDREN AND AGING

The Director of Voluntary Service, Christian Foundation for Children and Aging, One Elmwood Avenue, Kansas City, Kansas 66103

(1 913) 384 6500

Kenya, Madagascar, Uganda; India, Philippines; Bolivia, Brazil, Chile, Colombia, Costa Rica, Dominican Republic, El Salvador, Guatemala, Honduras, Mexico, Nicaragua, Peru, Venezuela; Haiti, St Kitts; United States

Founded in 1981, a non-profitmaking, interdenominational organisation dedicated to help overcome hunger, disease, loneliness and suffering by caring for homeless, orphaned, crippled and abandoned children, refugees and the aged. Provides food, shelter, clothing, medicine, education, vocational and nutritional training, and pastoral and social service to people in need regardless of age, race or creed.

Volunteers needed include childcare centre workers, health care instructors, nurses, nutritionists, social/community workers, agriculturists, craft workers, teachers, recreation organisers, house parents and group home staff. Recruits approx 100 volunteers annually.

Ages 21+. Applicants should be motivated by gospel values and a Christian love which calls them to serve the poor, recognising their dignity and working with them towards self-sufficiency. Some professional skills preferred, although direct experience not necessary. Spanish/Portuguese required for Latin American placements. As part of the screening process, candidates are invited to Kansas City for a discernment period; this is an opportunity for CFCA and the volunteer to find out more about each other before a commitment is made.

One year or more. Summer programme varies each year.

Board and lodging provided on site by the host missionary or volunteer. Travel, insurance and pocket money provided by volunteer.

Orientation provided on the mission site. CFCA stays in contact with volunteers through the laity and the religious who coordinate the CFCA child/aging sponsorship programme overseas.

Recruitment all year

Information leaflets; newsletters

CHRISTIAN MEDICAL FELLOWSHIP

Dr Peter F Green, Acting Overseas Support Secretary, Christian Medical Fellowship, 157 Waterloo Road, London SE1 8XN

0171-928 4694   Fax 0171-620 2453

Throughout the Third World

Founded in 1949, Christian Medical Fellowship provides advice for Christian doctors and medical students wishing to work abroad

Does not actually recruit volunteers, but has a list of short, medium and long-term openings for doctors to work in mission/church hospitals. Also openings for medical students wishing to do their elective period in a Third World country.

Applicants must be committed Christians. Placements are for fully qualified doctors with at least two years work experience, or for medical students in their fourth year.

Length of placement varies depending on requirements of each hospital. Generally 6+ months for doctors; 2-3 months for medical students.

As a rule, doctors are paid a subsistence allowance, while medical students are expected to cover all their costs. Accommodation is usually provided, but volunteers cover their own food and living costs. No insurance or travel costs paid.

Organises a refresher course each year at the end of June for doctors who have been working in Third World countries, or those who are likely to proceed overseas shortly

No specific deadline for applications as this depends on individual agencies

Newsletter, journal, members handbook

CHRISTIAN OUTREACH

The Personnel Officer, Christian Outreach, 1 New Street, Leamington Spa, Warwickshire CV31 1HP

Leamington Spa (01926) 315301

Mozambique, Sudan, Tanzania, Zaire; Cambodia, Thailand

Founded in 1966, Christian Outreach is a voluntary agency providing relief and development opportunities to disadvantaged children and refugees through the provision of primary health care and other facilities

Skilled volunteers are required to provide health care in children's homes, refugee camps and rural health projects; or to assist with administration, construction projects or community development. Nurses, midwives, nutritionists, engineers, sanitation experts, builders, mechanics and community development workers are needed. Recruits 20-25 volunteers annually.

Ages 23+. Applicants should have Christian commitment, adaptability and a desire to help others. Relevant qualifications required, plus work experience in a related field. Some positions also require previous overseas experience. All nationalities considered, but recruitment is done in the UK and a good command of English is necessary.

One year contract, renewable

Volunteers are housed in local accommodation, with meals prepared by staff and approx £50 pocket money per month paid in local currency. Medical insurance, holiday allowance and travel costs provided.

Compulsory orientation course arranged; verbal debriefing and courses for returned volunteers

Recruitment all year

Prayer Letter quarterly newsletter

CHRISTIAN WELFARE AND SOCIAL RELIEF ORGANISATION

Volunteer Recruitment Officer, Christian Welfare and Social Relief Organisation, 39 Soldier Street, PO Box 981, Freetown, Sierra Leone

(232 22) 224096

Sierra Leone, West Africa

Established in 1980 as a non-profitable body, CWASRO is engaged in education and training, exchange programmes, farming, construction and emergency relief work. Also involved in caring for displaced children and refugees.

Variety of projects requiring volunteers in both urban and rural areas. Work may involve agriculture, tree planting, gardening, construction, caring for handicapped or displaced children, teaching, health care and social work.

Age limits vary depending on project; usually 18-45. Previous voluntary work experience preferred. Applicants should have a real commitment to the project and be open to new cultures and lifestyles. Fluent English or French essential.

One month to three years

Board and accommodation provided. Volunteers pay a fee, from £350 for one month, to cover registration, orientation, immigration, residence permit and communication/local transport costs. Volunteers must also arrange and pay for their own international travel and insurance.

Orientation programme held in Freetown during first week of stay. A field supervisor is around at all times to advise, support and guide volunteers.

Apply at least two months in advance

CHRISTIANS ABROAD

Projects Manager, Christians Abroad, 1 Stockwell Green, London SW9 9HP

0171-737 7811

Mainly in Africa, the Caribbean and the Far East

An ecumenical body founded in 1972 and supported by aid and mission agencies. Provides an information and advice service on work abroad to help volunteers discover how their skills can be used and which organisations can be approached; see page 45. The recruitment and project management service is provided for overseas projects seeking personnel.

Volunteers are recruited primarily to work as teachers, both primary and secondary, the greatest demand being in maths, English and sciences. EFL teachers, medical and other development specialists are also occasionally recruited.

Ages usually 21+. Requirements vary according to demands of overseas organisation. Qualifications and experience are more important than age. Applicants, who should have a Christian commitment, must be suitably qualified and experienced, with a wish to learn as well as to give. They should have a willingness to adjust what they know to new situations, an ability to cope with loneliness and frustration and to respect the expectations of people overseas.

Mainly 2 years; varies according to employer

Terms of service vary; accommodation and travel usually provided, local salary paid. Some posts are paid on local terms, some carry inducement allowances paid in the UK.

Candidates participate in a preparation conference prior to departure, any other appropriate training and undergo a medical examination.
A Back to Britain day is available to those returning from overseas.

Recruitment all year

See page 41 for details of publications

CHURCH MISSIONARY SOCIETY

Vocations Advisor, Church Missionary Society, 157 Waterloo Road, London SE1 8UU

0171-928 8681

Africa, Asia, Middle East, Britain and mainland Europe

Founded in 1799 in response to Christ's command to proclaim the Good News, a voluntary society set within the worldwide Anglican Communion, which sees its role as a source of interchange, not only of people with varied skills, experiences and spiritual gifts, but also of material resources, ideas, news and mutual prayer support

Opportunities are available for volunteers to gain a cross-cultural experience of mission. Up to 30 people recruited for placements each year.

Ages 21-30; 18-30 for British placements. Emphasis is on gaining cross-cultural experience and relating to the overseas church. Professional skills and training can be matched with specific openings in the host country. Applicants should have a positive, growing, Christian faith and a desire to share this with others while working in partnership with an overseas church. They should be flexible, willing to work with others and able to live with frustrations and disappointments.

6-18 months, usually commencing in September or January

Overseas accommodation provided by host or CMS; this often includes an allowance equivalent to that of a similarly qualified national or missionary. In certain locations the volunteer receives board and lodging plus pocket money. Return airfare, medical insurance and National Insurance contributions provided. Participant pays cost of interview travel expenses before the placements, medical costs, airfare and living expenses while overseas. CMS pays training and re-orientation course costs and the cost of post-placement travel.

Compulsory 10 day training course at a missionary training college provided. Individual debriefing and corporate reorientation weekend arranged on return.

Recruitment all year

Information leaflets

COMMUNITY FOR CREATIVE NON-VIOLENCE

Intern Coordinator, Community for Creative Non-Violence, 425 2nd Street NW, Washington, DC 20001, United States

(1 202) 393 1909

Washington DC, United States

Has worked with Washington's homeless since 1971 and provides food, clothing, shelter, medical care and other services to some 2,000 people each day. It aims to provide a service to the poor whilst strongly advocating an end to policies that create poverty. CCNV has a spiritual foundation expressed in many ways: whilst predominantly Christian, its religious make-up is very varied, with volunteers drawn from an assortment of backgrounds.

Volunteers are required to assist in the running of a 1,400 bed shelter that includes a medical clinic, infirmary, drugs and alcohol programme, social services, outreach, central kitchen, jobs programme, library, arts and education centre. Volunteers spend four weeks working in each area of the shelter for three days; they are then placed where they are needed, with emphasis on where they prefer to work.

Ages 19+. No special skills or experience required, but volunteers must have a sincere desire to address the issues of poverty and homelessness in a concrete, hands-on way and in an extremely diverse environment. All nationalities welcome; good knowledge of English essential.

Six months minimum

Full board dormitory accommodation provided, but no fares or wages paid. Volunteers are responsible for arranging their own US visa.

Write for further information

CONCERN

CONCERN WORLDWIDE

Concern Worldwide, First Floor, 248-250 Lavender Hill, Clapham Junction, London SW11 1LJ

0171-738 1033

Concern Worldwide, Level 2, 80 Buchanan Street, Glasgow G1 3HA

0141-221 3610

Concern Worldwide, 47 Frederick Street, Belfast BT1 2LW

Belfast (01232) 231056

Concern Worldwide, Camden Street, Dublin 2, Ireland

(353 1) 475 4162

Concern Worldwide, 104 East 40th Street, Room 903, New York, United States

(1 212) 557 8000

Angola, Burundi, Ethiopia, Kenya, Mozambique, Rwanda, Somalia, Tanzania, Uganda, Zaire; Bangladesh, Cambodia, Laos

A non-denominational voluntary organisation devoted to the relief, assistance and advancement of peoples in need in less developed countries of the world. Established in 1968 as a response by ordinary people to the tragedy of the Biafran famine, Concern Worldwide has since responded to both emergency and non-emergency situations in various African and Asian countries. Priority countries came to be chosen on the basis of their need for Concern Worldwide's services. This is often in the context of responding initially to an emergency situation, after which Concern Worldwide may stay on to run welfare and basic development programmes in partnership with local organisations. Concern Worldwide's income is derived from public donations in the UK, Ireland and the US, and from co-funding agencies such as the UN, the British and Irish governments, the European Union, official aid agencies and voluntary agencies. *continued opposite*

Concern requires the skills of qualified nurses, teachers, engineers, agriculturists, foresters, community development and social workers, accountants, and experienced administrators to implement and support programmes in the areas of health care and nutrition, women's development, education and training, water supply and sanitation, slum upgradance, construction, natural resources and emergency relief. Other skills are also occasionally needed that do not fit in to the above categories. Concern currently employs approximately 5,000 worldwide, with over 200 expatriate volunteers and staff working overseas on both long-term development and emergency relief programmes. Volunteers are recruited to provide management skills and technical advice for overseas programmes, working hand in hand with local staff, assisting in the sharing of knowledge and skills throughout the community.

Ages 21+. Volunteers must be in good health and, in the majority of cases hold a relevant third level qualification. In most cases a minimum of 18 months relevant post-qualification experience is required.

Two years minimum; 3-6 month contracts for people with previous experience to assist with emergency and relief programmes. Given the demand for experienced personnel in situations such as Somalia and Rwanda, the need to recruit personnel without previous experience, but who have skills and experience that are relevant to the needs of Concern Worldwide's emergency operations, is increased. Salaried positions are available for people with previous experience on both short and long-term assignments.

Concern Worldwide provide return air fares, food, accommodation, pre-departure and post-assignment medicals including vaccinations, life, accident and medical insurance, holiday, monthly and resettlement allowances.

Pre-departure training, in-country induction and language training available

Apply 4-6 months in advance

CROSSLINKS

International Secretary, Crosslinks, 251 Lewisham Way, London SE4 1XF

0181-691 6111   Fax 0181-694 8023

Kenya, South Africa, Tanzania, Uganda, Zimbabwe; France, Portugal, Russia, Spain; Bolivia, Peru. Also opportunities in Asia.

Founded in 1922 as the Bible Churchmen's Missionary Society, Crosslinks is an evangelical missionary society of the Church of England, working in partnership with all branches of the Anglican Communion overseas. Their motto is God's Word to God's World, reflecting their commitment to the Bible and to the international nature of mission. There is an increasing awareness of mission being a crosslinking of men and women, old and young, rich and poor in every continent.

Requests from overseas churches are for accountants, administrators, agriculturists, Bible teachers, evangelists, primary and secondary teachers, doctors, student workers, and people skilled in broadcasting, bookselling and literature production

Ages 21-65. Volunteers should have a commitment to Jesus Christ as Saviour and Lord, a sense of God's call and a willingness to work in partnership with the overseas church as a dedicated servant of God. Qualifications and experience in an appropriate field required. Professional, and often postgraduate qualifications needed for medical and teaching personnel. Knowledge/study of languages required as appropriate. All nationalities considered.

Two years minimum

Most overseas institutions and dioceses provide basic accommodation but not food. Monthly allowance is designed to provide a reasonable standard of living. National Insurance contributions and travel provided.

Training at All Nations Christian College or similar institution desirable but not essential. Orientation provided before departure. Consultation with one of the regional coordinators provided as debriefing.

Recruitment all year

Mission quarterly magazine; *Crosslinks* newsletter

DIENST OVER GRENZEN

The Secretariat, Dienst Over Grenzen, PO Box 177, 3700 AD Zeist, Netherlands

(31 3404) 24884

Mainly in Africa, with limited opportunities in Asia and Latin America

Founded in 1962, a personnel recruiting agency serving as a mediator rather than employer, working on behalf of churches, church-related organisations and governments in the Third World. When a request for personnel is received, an insight into whether the project concerned contributes to the improvement of the socio-economic situation of underprivileged groups in the developing countries and as to the precise task of the development workers within these projects is involved. Keeps a register of volunteers qualified in different professions and the agencies abroad can submit requests for personnel.

Vacancies in the medical, technical, educational, administration, financial and community development fields. Personnel required include doctors, nurses, physiotherapists and analysts; construction, mechanical and agricultural engineers; teachers in science, agriculture, mechanics, technical and vocational subjects; and social workers.

Ages 25+. Dutch nationals only. Volunteers should be qualified to MSc/BSc degree level or equivalent. Previous experience an advantage.

Three years minimum

Appointment is in principal based on local contract with the host country organisation, including local salary. Through Dutch government sponsored co-financement scheme supplementary arrangements can be made regarding costs of preparation, travel, salary, allowance, costs of housing, insurances, social benefits and other related costs.

Compulsory orientation course arranged by a joint institute of the Protestant Missions in the Netherlands. Additional training such as language or professional courses can also be arranged. Advice and debriefing provided on return if necessary.

Recruitment all year

Doggersbank quarterly communication bulletin, published in Dutch; information leaflet

EAST EUROPEAN PARTNERSHIP

Recruitment Coordinator, East European Partnership, Carlton House, 27a Carlton Drive, London SW15 2BS

0181-780 2841   Fax 0181-780 9592

Albania, Bulgaria, Czech Republic, Estonia, Hungary, Latvia, Lithuania, Macedonia, Poland, Russia and Slovakia

An initiative set up in 1990 by VSO. It posts men and women abroad in response to requests from ministries, non-governmental organisations and other institutions to help in the process of reconstruction which is taking place in the face of enormous political, social and economic difficulties. Volunteers share their skills with local colleagues to help re-establish the self-sufficiency of the host country. It is hoped that after several years the skills which EEP has been asked to supply will be available locally, and a volunteer programme will no longer be required.

Opportunities are focused in three main areas:

Education: teachers of English and British studies for secondary schools, universities and teacher training colleges; teachers of business studies, economics and commerce to set up new programmes in schools and colleges; occasional requests for teachers of other subjects such as maths.

Health and social welfare: social workers with experience in learning disabilities are needed to set up new training courses and community initiatives and to establish health education campaigns to address key health issues including HIV/AIDS, hepatitis, smoking and alcohol related diseases and environmental pollution; paediatric and mental handicapped nurses to work as in-service trainers in intensive care and oncology; haematologists for blood transfusion services; teachers of the deaf; and cleft lip/palate specialists.

Business advice: advisers/trainers to work with chambers of commerce and business advice centres, to help in the preparation of business plans, budgets and evaluation and running a programme of business seminars for the local entrepreneur community.

continued opposite

Ages 22-70. Volunteers must have English to mother tongue standard, appropriate qualifications and a minimum of 2 years, significant full-time work experience. English language teaching posts require graduates with a TEFL qualification; social workers should hold the CQSW; other health specialists need appropriate qualifications. Applicants should have a genuine desire to assist in long-term development. They should be in good health, adaptable, tolerant, resilient in the face of frustrations and able to cope with difficult working and living conditions. **B D PH W**

Two years for teaching posts; 1 year for social work and business advice

The overseas employer provides a salary based on local equivalent (typically £100 per month), accommodation, free medical services and concessions on internal travel and accommodation. EEP provides return travel expenses, training, medical/dental treatment not covered by employer, equipment grant, mid-tour grant and resettlement grant, National Insurance contributions, visa fees and accident insurance.

Compulsory 10-14 day pre-departure training provided. Debriefing and advice on resettlement provided on return.

Most postings are in September or January; apply at least 3 months in advance

Link newsletter

EDUCATION FOR DEVELOPMENT

Education for Development, Woodmans, Westwood Row, Tilehurst, Reading RG3 6LT

Reading (01734) 426772   Fax (01734) 433733

Developing countries worldwide

An independent training, research and consultancy organisation established in 1985 and specialising in the education and training of adults in development. It comprises a group of adult educators who work alongside those engaged in development programmes both overseas and in the UK, to help them become more effective in their work. Has conducted training the trainer programmes in a wide variety of settings using different formats.

One or two self-funded attachments are available each year to work in adult education or development agencies in developing countries

Ages approx 22+. Applicants must have experience of adult education, including management and/or teaching skills. **B D PH W** willing to consider each application on its merits.

No specific time limits; dependent on individual projects

All volunteers are entirely self-funded, and must therefore be prepared to pay all the travel, insurance, accommodation and other costs involved

Orientation can be provided if required. Personal discussion with returned volunteers.

Apply at any time; no set recruitment period

Publishes training materials and reports relating to adult learning and development, including *Teaching Adults in Extension; Teaching Methods in Extension; Literacy in Development: language, people and power;* and *Adults Learning for Development*. Full list available on request.

FOOD FOR THE HUNGRY

Food for the Hungry, 7729 East Greenway Road, Scottsdale, AZ 85260, United States

(1 602) 998 3100

Food for the Hungry UK, 6 Galtres Avenue, Stockton Kane, York YO3 OJT

York (01904) 424136

Ethiopia, Kenya, Mozambique, Rwanda, Somalia, Sudan, Uganda, Zaire, Zimbabwe; China, Japan, Laos, Philippines, Thailand, Vietnam; Bolivia, Dominican Republic, Honduras, Nicaragua, Peru; Romania

An international Christian relief and development organisation founded in 1971, Food for the Hungry is dedicated to meeting the physical and spiritual needs of hungry people in the poorest areas of the world

Opportunities for relief and development work in agriculture, community health, TEFL, engineering, teaching and small business management. All positions involve Christian outreach and Bible studies. Approx 40 volunteers recruited each year.

Ages 21+. Volunteers must be Christians who are willing to invest themselves and their skills to help the very poor. Experience according to placement. Volunteers range from skilled professionals to those with no experience. **PH**

Minimum 3 years; projects are ongoing

Volunteers must raise funds through friends, family and church to cover all costs incurred

Compulsory orientation course provided. One week debriefing at Scottsdale office.

Apply one year in advance

FÖRENINGEN STAFFANSGÅRDEN

The Director, Föreningen Staffansgården, Box 66, Furugatan 1, 82060 Delsbo, Sweden

(46 653) 16850

Delsbo, Sweden

A Camphill village consisting of a training school for adolescents with mental handicaps and a nearby farm for handicapped adults. The community also has a garden, a bakery, eight family houses, and workshops for weaving, woodwork and candlemaking.

Co-workers are required to live and work with mentally handicapped people, playing a full part in village life including domestic tasks, crafts and farmwork

Ages 19+. No previous experience or qualifications necessary, but applicants must have a strong desire to share a period of their life with handicapped people. Applicants should speak Swedish or another Scandinavian language. **B D PH**

One year minimum preferred

Co-workers receive board and lodging in a village home shared with 10-15 other people, plus pocket money to cover their immediate needs. Accident and health insurance provided. Volunteers pay own travel costs.

Training seminars and courses organised in arts, therapy and the philosophy of anthroposophy

Recruitment all year

FRONTIERS FOUNDATION / OPERATION BEAVER

The Program Coordinator, Frontiers Foundation/Operation Beaver, 2615 Danforth Avenue, Suite 203, Toronto, Ontario, M4C 1L6, Canada

(1416) 690 3930

Alberta, Ontario and Northwest Territories, Canada

Works in cooperation with requesting communities to fulfil basic housing needs. Volunteers from all over the world make practical efforts in reducing poverty, do volunteer work, and meet people from culturally diverse backgrounds. Also run recreation programmes, providing stimulating and creative alternatives to the boredom and social problems endemic in many Native American communities.

About 80% of volunteers work on practical projects in cooperation with Native and non-Native peoples in rural communities in Ontario, Alberta and Northwest Territories. Construction projects involve building or renovating wood frame or log houses. Volunteers also work in Alberta with local youth workers organising games, camp-outs and other activities for the youth of the community during the summer months.

Ages 18+. Older applicants must feel competent to perform manual labour. Applicants should be hardworking, open-minded, flexible and culturally sensitive. They must also be able to live without television, flush toilets, and in some cases without running water or electricity. Volunteers with construction skills are given first priority, and previous voluntary experience is also an asset. For recreation projects applicants should have experience of working on camps or with children.

12+ weeks (16+ weeks Northwest), beginning April-October; most volunteers arrive for the summer session, June-August. Service can be extended for up to 18 months, depending on initial performance.

Salary not provided, although a modest living allowance is paid after 12 week minimum period. Accommodation, food, local travel expenses and insurance provided. Travel to Canada and to the orientation site (Toronto or Edmonton) is the volunteer's responsibility.

Volunteers receive detailed information in the application kit. Intensive 2 day orientation for summer session volunteers; others participate in a less formal 1 day orientation.

Apply at least 3 months in advance enclosing 3 IRCs; recruitment all year

FUTURE IN OUR HANDS MOVEMENT

Future in Our Hands Movement, FIOH (UK), 120 York Road, Swindon, Wiltshire SN1 2JP

Swindon (01793) 532353

Kenya, Sierra Leone, South Africa, Uganda; Orissa and Tamil Nadu (India)

Set up in 1974 with the aims of encouraging a simpler and more ethical lifestyle, particularly in the rich countries; and promoting an emphasis on values such as sharing, cooperation and fellowship rather than dogmatic approaches to world problems

Offers approx 4 self-funded placements each year. These include a learning and exposure opportunity on a project in Tamil Nadu, and other volunteering opportunities with contacts in India and Africa.

Ages 18+. No specific experience or qualifications necessary, but volunteers should be able to show initiative and a commitment to the aims of the organisation and the project in which they are placed.

No set time limits; this is to be agreed between project and volunteer

Volunteers must be entirely self-funded. Accommodation and food provided at a small charge; volunteers arrange and pay for own travel and insurance.

No official briefing arranged, but volunteers may visit FIOH office to get advice. Get-together of returned volunteers arranged for those who wish it.

Best to apply at least 2 months in advance

GERMAN LEPROSY RELIEF ASSOCIATION

The Personnel Manager, Germany Leprosy Relief Association, Deutsches Aussätzigen-Hilfswerk eV, Dominikanerplatz 4, Postfach 11 04 62, 97067 Wurzburg, Germany

(49 931) 3521-0

Ethiopia, Sierra Leone, Tanzania, Togo, Uganda; Bolivia, Brazil, Colombia, Paraguay

Founded in 1957 with the tasks of sponsoring and establishing institutions to combat leprosy and TB; training, education and other means of rehabilitation for leprosy patients; public health education and publicity. The declared aim of the association is to integrate leprosy control services into general health care programmes wherever possible, as well as supporting public health care work and the training of local personnel for the medical and social welfare sector.

There are vacancies for skilled long-term volunteers, helping at treatment and training centres, on national health care and control programmes, and in the general care of leprosy patients

Ages 25+. Applicants must have a commitment to the care of leprosy patients. Academic qualifications required, plus several years of skilled, professional experience. All nationalities considered. Knowledge of English, Spanish and French required, depending on the host country.

Three years

Accommodation in house or apartment, monthly allowance depending on marital status, insurance and travel costs provided. 40-50 hour week.

Compulsory orientation course arranged

Recruitment all year

Information leaflets; several publications in the German language

THE GUIDE ASSOCIATION (UK)

The International Secretary, The Guide Association (UK), 17-19 Buckingham Palace Road, London SW1W 0PT

0171-834 6242

India, Mexico, Switzerland, London

The Guide Association of the United Kingdom, founded in 1920 by Robert Baden Powell, is a voluntary organisation for girls and young women. It gives them the opportunity to follow any number of interests and at the same time learn self-reliance and self-respect. Guides share a commitment to a common standard set out in the Promise and Law.

Volunteer work is available in London and overseas at centres owned by the World Association of Girl Guides and Girl Scouts. Projects may include assisting the development of Guide Associations, training adult leaders or administration duties in connection with Guide House. The work is sometimes strenuous and the hours long.

Ages 18+. Qualifications and experience required vary according to the position. Volunteers must be members of the Association. **B D PH** considered.

Duration variable

Board, accommodation and pocket money provision vary according to the position. Insurance provided in some cases. Travel costs usually paid by the volunteer. Advice is given to participants on obtaining sponsorship. Members are encouraged to write articles for the magazines on their return.

Recruitment all year

The Brownie; Guiding magazines; *The Guiding Manual*

HEALTH PROJECTS ABROAD

Volunteer Coordinator, Health Projects Abroad, PO Box 24, Bakewell, Derbyshire DE45 1ZW

Tanzania

The charity supports the development of access to health care facilities for people living in developing countries and gives young people from the UK the opportunity to participate in projects and learn first hand about the realities of life in a developing country

Volunteers work alongside Tanzanian villagers, helping to complete locally initiated projects. They are usually involved in simple tasks such as assisting with the construction of dispensaries and renovation work at health centres and hospitals. Volunteers work with local people under the guidance of volunteer engineers.

Ages 18-28. Applicants must have enthusiasm and energy, be open minded and receptive to change, sensitive to the needs of the host community and able to work as part of a team. No specific skills, qualifications or experience required. **B D PH** all applicants considered on an individual basis.

Three months, beginning May, July and September. Includes two weeks travel time at the end of each project.

Each volunteer is required to raise £2,650 towards the cost of their own participation. This covers flights, accommodation, food, medical insurance, language training and support for the project. Advice is given on raising funds.

Applicants are selected at an assessment and briefing weekend. Two compulsory training weekends are held before departure; language training is provided on arrival in Tanzania and a follow-up weekend is held about 6-8 weeks after volunteers return.

Apply by end June for May departure; end August for July departure, end October for September departure. Send a large SAE for details and an application form.

HEALTH VOLUNTEERS OVERSEAS

Health Volunteers Overseas, c/o Washington Station, PO Box 65157, Washington, DC 20035-5157, United States

(1 202) 296 0928

Africa, Asia, Latin America/Caribbean

A private, non-profit, voluntary organisation established in 1986 to foster long-term improvements in the quality and availability of health care in less-developed nations through education and training, using appropriate technology

Over 180 qualified volunteers sent each year to train local health care providers in anaesthesia, dentistry, general surgery, internal medicine, oral and maxillofacial surgery, orthopaedics and paediatrics, focusing on local pathologies and medical problems. Locally available equipment and supplies used to teach relevant and realistic interventions.

Only fully qualified and trained physicians, nurses, dentist and physical therapists recruited. Volunteers should have a desire to share their knowledge and skills with colleagues in less developed nations. Cultural sensitivity, flexibility, a sense of humour and commitment to helping others are important qualities for successful volunteer experiences.

One month minimum

Volunteers are responsible for their own travel expenses, insurance and minimal living costs. Depending on the project, accommodation and food will be provided at little or no cost. Those wishing to volunteer must first become members of HVO; cost from US$15-US$100 depending on status. Members receive a quarterly newsletter which includes updates on openings at all programme sites.

Orientation course held each year in Tucson, Arizona, for participants interested in upgrading their knowledge of conditions in the developing world. Teleconferencing debriefing for returned volunteers with programme directors, HVO staff and new volunteers.

Application process generally takes one year

A Guide for Short-Term Medical Workers in Developing Countries manual, price US$6; quarterly newsletter for members

HELP INTERNATIONAL

Help International, International House, Asfare Business Park, Hinckley Road, Wolvey, Leicestershire LE10 3HQ

Wolvey (01455) 221119

Third World and Eastern Europe

Founded in 1985 as a Christian relief and development agency, Help International provides primary relief aid in crisis situations as well as more long-term development aid

Various opportunities for a limited number of volunteers to work overseas. Work is variable and ranges from care work, medical/health care through to different types of practical aid.

Ages 18+. The precise requirements vary according to project, but as a rule placements are for those already professionally skilled and experienced in their chosen field. In terms of motivation, volunteers should show altruism and a pioneering spirit.

Variable

Terms and conditions depend on the specific project and on what funds are available. Volunteers may have to be self-funding, or raise the money for the return trip through sponsorship. Provision is made for full insurance cover.

Orientation usually held prior to placement. Full counselling by professionals for returned volunteers.

Positions are advertised; speculative applicants are interviewed if a suitable project arises

THE INDIA DEVELOPMENT GROUP

Mr Surur Hoda, India Development Group (UK) Ltd, 68 Downlands Road, Purley, Surrey CR8 4JF

0181-668 3161

Uttar Pradesh, India

A registered charity devoting its energy towards bringing new hope to the future generations of India, and giving employment and self-respect to hundreds of millions of Indians. The Group is trying to create a new vision of development by keeping people instead of products at the centre of attention. Works in cooperation with the Appropriate Technology Development Association and the Schumacher Institute of Appropriate Technology in India to run training programmes, set up small-scale cottage industries in rural areas and promote and develop appropriate technology for the purpose of rural development.

Some 5-10 placements each year are available to work in the areas of rural development, primary health care, social forestry, primary education and community development, all using appropriate technologies

Ages 18-60. Volunteers must be highly motivated with a good basic education and/or vocational training. They should also have experience and skills in workshop technology, nursing, paramedics, primary education, community development or environmental work. **B D** if disability is not severe.

Six months minimum

Volunteers must be entirely self-funding in order to cover their own travel, insurance, food, accommodation and personal expenses

Orientation course available. On return, volunteers are expected to submit a report of their work.

Apply at least three months in advance

Information leaflet

INNISFREE VILLAGE

The Volunteer Coordinator, Innisfree Village, Route 2, Box 506, Crozet, Virginia 22932, United States

(1 804) 823 5400   Fax (1 804) 823 5027

United States

Innisfree's goal is to provide a lifetime residential facility for adults with mental disabilities. The staff consists of volunteers who live and work together with mentally disabled co-workers in a natural and humanistic environment.

Acting as houseparents and co-workers, volunteers are needed to work on the 600 acre farm in the foothills of the Blue Ridge Mountains with the choice of working in the bakery, weavery, woodshop, garden or free school. Recruits 18-20 volunteers annually.

Ages 21+. Volunteers need energy, enthusiasm, patience, and a willingness to work with the differently abled. They must be in excellent health, and interested in the community process in a very rural setting. Volunteers must be college graduates or equivalent, preferably with some experience of working with mentally disabled, recently brain injured or emotionally ill people. Craft skills greatly appreciated. All nationalities considered. Fluent English required.

One year minimum

Volunteers work a 5 day week, with 2 consecutive days free and have their own room and board in a house of 6-10 people. $160 per month spending money, $100 Christmas bonus, medical insurance and up to $250 for dental expenses provided. Travel costs paid by volunteers. Annual holiday entitlement 21 days, with an additional holiday allowance of $30 per day. In addition, severance pay is accrued at $45 per month.

First month is a mandatory trial period with four orientation sessions covering a brief history of the village and its guidelines. Volunteers are encouraged to get to know the village as well as possible before settling down in one house. At the end of this period, the community evaluates and decides the best placement for the volunteer. Can provide applicants with the names and addresses of former volunteers whom they may wish to contact for further information.

Recruitment all year

INTERNATIONAL COOPERATION FOR DEVELOPMENT

The Recruitment Officer, International Cooperation for Development, Unit 3, Canonbury Yard, 190a New North Road, London N1 7BJ

0171-354 0883

Namibia, Zimbabwe; Haiti, Dominican Republic; Yemen; Ecuador, El Salvador, Honduras, Nicaragua, Peru

A charity receiving funds from the ODA, EU, UK development agencies and private sponsors. Has been recruiting experienced professionals to share skills with communities in the Third World since 1965. Works with locally based partners to improve people's lives and for a just and equal society. Will only work on a project if there is a real need for an ICD worker's skills; it has a strong skills transfer or training element; if the poorer or less advantaged sections of the community are the main beneficiaries; and if the role/needs of women are taken into account.

Areas of work include primary health care and health education; teacher training; food technology and nutrition; environment and public health; literacy education; agricultural training; youth skills training; engineering/mechanics; community-based rehabilitation; cooperative/small business training; popular communication; community education work; information technology. Majority of posts available are for health workers, agriculturalists, popular education and literacy workers.

Ages mid 20s to mid 60s. Applicants must have appropriate professional qualifications with a minimum of 2 years' work experience and preferably a background in formal or informal training. They must be keen to share their skills with communities in the Third World, self-motivated, sensitive and able to adapt their lifestyle to a new culture.

Two years minimum

Pre-departure grant, accommodation, essential household equipment, salary based on local rates, insurance and return travel provided. National Insurance contributions and home savings allowance also paid. Dependants' allowance available in some cases.

Compulsory 2 week course arranged in London, plus orientation on arrival in host country. Debriefing provided on return.

Posts advertised throughout the year; monthly list available. Volunteers may register and will be informed when a suitable post arises.

Information leaflet

INTERNATIONAL HEALTH EXCHANGE

The Director, International Health Exchange, Africa Centre, 38 King Street, London WC2E 8JT

0171-836 5833

Developing countries

A charity founded in 1980 as a coordinating agency for experienced health workers. It is not a recruiting agency, but runs a register for health workers interested in working in developing countries, acting as a clearing house for those planning to work overseas. Also publishes a bi-monthly magazine which, as well as carrying job and course listings, explores practical approaches to primary health care in developing countries.

Runs a register of 1,000 health workers including doctors, nurses, physiotherapists, nutritionists, health administrators and health educators. Bi-monthly magazine which goes to all register members and is available on subscription, lists health posts, agencies and details of training courses.

Nurses must be SRN and have at least two years' post-qualification experience; most useful areas are midwifery and community nursing. Doctors should have at least one year's post-registration experience; most useful areas are paediatrics, general practice, obstetrics and gynaecology. Other requirements depend on the recruiting agencies.

1-2 years, but occasionally there are opportunities for periods of a few months

Contractual details vary according to the recruiting agency and are outside the responsibility of IHE

Recruitment all year round

The Health Exchange bi-monthly magazine; job supplement; *Annual Report*; advice sheets for doctors, nurses and health workers intending to work in developing countries

INTERSERVE

Yvonne Dorey, Personnel Director, Interserve, On Track, 325 Kennington Road, London SE11 4QH

0171-735 8227

India, Pakistan and Nepal; some opportunities in other countries

A member society of the Evangelical Missionary Alliance, Interserve is an international, interdenominational mission fellowship with over 400 partners working in a wide range of ministries in Asia and the Middle East and several serving among Asian ethnic groups in Britain

Volunteers serve local Christian groups and are involved in a large variety of activities including teaching, TEFL, childcare, medical work, engineering, community development and others. Short-term opportunities for school leavers, students, workers and professionals.

Ages 18+. UK residents only. Applicants must be committed Christians who are involved with their local church/Christian Union. They should have a good general education to at least A level standard or equivalent.

2-12 months

Volunteers work an average of 30 hours per week, and stay with Christian families or in a hostel. They are responsible for all travel and insurance costs, as well as board and lodging costs and personal expenses whilst on placement.

Mandatory training and orientation weekend before departure. At each placement there is someone responsible for the support and guidance of short-term volunteers. Personal interviews and follow-up are given on return to UK.

Apply as soon as possible. Closing date is December each year for those wishing to go overseas anytime from the following May.

IRISH MISSIONARY UNION

Recruitment Office, Irish Missionary Union, Orwell Park, Rathgar, Dublin 6, Ireland

Mainly African countries; sometimes South America

Established in 1970, a coordinating body for all mission-sending organisations, both lay and religious. Aims to make a contribution towards the development of a just world by placing qualified Christian development workers overseas.

Laity office is involved in the recruitment, selection and training of laity for mission. IMU holds a register of job openings and refers suitable applicants to sending agencies and mission groups. Opportunities mainly exist in the fields of medicine: nursing, midwifery, laboratory technicians, doctors, hospital administrators, paramedics, pharmacists, physiotherapists; trades: engineers, builders, carpenters, mechanics; education: teachers of English, science, maths, geography, history, economics and commercial subjects; agriculture: practical and teaching; pastoral work: cathechetics, social work, leadership, group work, community development. Some 50 placements available each year.

Ages 21+. Professional skill or qualification required. Applicants must be Irish nationals with a Christian motivation, wishing to share their skills, train counterparts and help people to help themselves.

Two year commitment

Volunteers work in return for accommodation and living allowance. Mid-term grant, resettlement grant, return airfare, accident and sickness insurance provided.

All volunteers must attend orientation course prior to placement. Debriefing and reorientation course arranged for returned volunteers.

Apply 6 months in advance

Information leaflets

JACOB'S WELL APPEAL

Dr B Beynon, Jacob's Well Appeal, Jacob's Well, 2 Ladygate, Beverley HU17 8BH

Hull (01482) 881162

Afghanistan, Pakistan; Bulgaria, Poland, Romania, Ukraine

A registered charity established in 1982 to promote the Christian faith; to supply medical relief to countries in Eastern Europe and Asia; and to help the disabled in the local community

Recruits some 30-40 volunteers a year to provide medical aid. Volunteers are mainly physiotherapists, occupational therapists, doctors, nurses and special needs teachers.

Ages 18-75. Preference given to those with relevant qualifications and experience. Volunteers must be committed, reliable and prepared to work hard. All nationalities accepted. **D PH**

One month minimum

Volunteers must be entirely self-funding, and pay their own travel, insurance, food and accommodation costs. Accommodation is generally with local families.

Apply at least one month in advance

Quarterly newsletter

JESUIT VOLUNTEER CORPS
(UNITED STATES - SOUTHWEST)

JVC: SW, PO Box 23404, Oakland, CA 94623, United States

(1 510) 653 8564

Jesuit European Volunteers, Kaulbachstrasse 31a, 80539 Munich, Germany

Arizona and California, United States

The largest Catholic lay volunteer program in the United States. In the Ignatian tradition, the Jesuit Volunteer Corps seeks to promote justice in the service of faith. Provides direct service to the poor and marginalised, seeking to identify and address the root causes of social injustice. Since its foundation in 1956 around 10,000 lay men and women have worked in a variety of human service agencies.

Various volunteer placements available, including living and working with AIDS sufferers, victims of domestic violence, people recovering from addictions, and the poor and homeless. Some placements also in health care and education. Approx 110 placements available each year.

Ages 21+. Volunteers should have a college degree or equivalent work experience and are usually graduates in their early 20's; all volunteers should be open and willing to learn. Teaching qualifications necessary for some posts and a knowledge of Spanish useful. Volunteers must be committed to the four visions of the Jesuit Volunteer Corps: working for social justice, living in community, living simply, and growing spiritually. Although the JVC is rooted in the Catholic tradition, applicants from other Christian traditions are welcome. **B D PH W**

One year minimum, starting mid-August

Board and lodging, transportation to and from work site, health insurance and $75 pocket money per month provided. Volunteers pay for travel costs to and from orientation program.

Five day orientation program for all volunteers at beginning of placement and final retreat for debriefing at end of year. Active network of former volunteers can be contacted throughout the United States and the rest of the world.

Apply by 1 March, although applications continue to be accepted until all positions are filled

JOINT ASSISTANCE CENTRE

The Convenor, Joint Assistance Centre, G-17/3 Quatab Enclave Phase I, Gurgaon 122002, Haryana, India

Throughout India

A small voluntary group for disaster assistance working in close liaison with other groups throughout India who run various voluntary projects

Operate a scheme whereby volunteers either do administrative work at centres in Delhi or are placed on short-stay workcamps with groups in other areas to help in environmental activities, agriculture, construction, community work, health/sanitation work, preparation work for disasters or teaching first aid. Specific projects also organised including work on playschemes, organising fundraising campaigns and exhibitions to increase awareness, and teaching English in a village school near Delhi. Long-term volunteers may join projects working with children or in orphanages, often involving teaching English and medical social work.

Ages 18+. Experience welcome but not essential. Applicants should have a personal faith in God, an open mind towards new beliefs, be adaptable to difficult situations and have patience, tolerance, understanding and organisational skills. Conditions are very primitive, and the summers (May/June) are very hot. Only vegetarian food is allowed, and applicants must comply with no alcohol/tobacco/drugs rule.

3-6 month commitment preferred

JAC believes that those fortunate enough to have the opportunities of higher education or travel abroad have benefited from the resources available in their society. Therefore each volunteer is required to make a contribution in order to participate in voluntary service; a minimum of £75 for the first month. Self-catering accommodation provided; volunteers share in all housekeeping duties. Registration fee £15. No travel, insurance or pocket money provided. Volunteers must make their own arrangements for obtaining a visa.

No prior briefing arranged, but there are opportunities to take part in disaster management programmes and conferences. Can also put applicants in touch with former volunteers.

Apply at least 3 months in advance to Friends of JAC, c/o 1 Ludgate Barns, Haytor, Newton Abbot, Devon TQ13 9XR; enclose a cheque for £2 made out to *Friends of JAC* to cover postage

LANKA JATHIKA SARVODAYA SANGAMAYA (INC)

The Director, SSI, Lanka Jathika Sarvodaya Sangamaya (Inc), Damsak Mandira, 98 Rawatawatta Road, Moratuwa, Sri Lanka

(94) 1 647159/645255

Sri Lanka

Founded in 1958, the movement is a large, non-governmental people's self-development effort covering nearly 8,000 villages. The people have provided a practical possibility of realising Mahatma Gandhi's concept of a world society where the wellbeing of all shall be ensured. It aims to create awareness among economically and socially deprived communities and to mobilise latent human and material potential for the satisfaction of basic human needs in a manner that ensures sustainable development.

Volunteers needed mainly on village-level development projects in house construction, sanitation, agriculture, animal husbandry, agriculture-based industry, energy conservation, alternative energy source development, appropriate technology and economic activities. Opportunities also for teachers in pre-school and primary education, and for the provision of preventive and curative health care including nursing, nutrition, feeding programmes, health education and rehabilitation of the handicapped.

Ages 21+. A willingness to teach and to learn is the main consideration. Applicants should have an awareness of their responsibility to improve human conditions wherever needed, an ability to work in sometimes difficult circumstances, a commitment to the promotion of peace and international understanding, and to an ideal that leads to the equitable distribution of the world's resources according to need. Recognised skills and experience preferred, but specialised skills not a priority, and academic qualifications are optional. All nationalities considered.

Six months minimum; visas extended at the discretion of the authorities

Board and lodging provided at a cost not exceeding Rs200 per day, but may be less in outstations. Volunteers are expected to meet their own travel, insurance and living expenses.

Compulsory orientation. End of service evaluation; the volunteer's subsequent activities and placement in the home country are discussed.

Recruitment all year, depending on availability of vacancies

Various pamphlets on the work and ideals of the movement

LATIN LINK

Mrs Cathy Travis, Coordinator, Short-Term Experience Projects, Latin Link, Whitefield House, 186 Kennington Park Road, London SE11 4BT

0171-582 4952

Argentina, Bolivia, Brazil, Ecuador, Nicaragua, Peru

A fellowship of personnel in Latin America and elsewhere, who, alongside their supporters and supporting churches, are committed to demonstrating the interdependence of the worldwide church, encouraging cross-cultural mission and channelling resources to and from Latin America for the benefit of the church worldwide

Short-Term Experience Projects provide a means of allowing volunteers to work in partnership with the Latin American church, building and extending orphanages, churches, community centres and schools. Projects involve a wide spectrum of tasks and skills, from evangelism through the graphic arts to bricklaying and carpentry.

Ages 18-35. Older applicants with special skills welcomed. Applicants must have a Christian commitment and outlook and a willingness to work as a team with Latin Americans. No previous experience or qualifications necessary, although skills in music or drama, knowledge of Spanish or Portuguese, medical qualifications and practical skills are useful. **B D PH** depending on extent of handicap.

Spring teams: 4 months, mid March-mid July; summer teams: 7 weeks, mid July-September. Spring team members have the option of staying on to join a summer team project.

Participants responsible for all travel and living expenses during the project. Rough guide to costs would be £1,710 spring projects, £1,380 summer projects, to cover travel, food, accommodation, insurance and pocket money. Advice given on raising funds. Accommodation is self-catering, and the same as that available to local people.

Compulsory orientation course held before departure, and reunion conference held in autumn/early winter

Full project details available 3 months before teams scheduled to depart

LINK AFRICA

Sally Bourne, Link Africa, 11/12 Trumpington Street, Cambridge CB2 1QA

Cambridge (01223) 322983

Limited opportunities in Kenya, Lesotho, South Africa, Uganda. Opportunities in the UK for fundraising.

An education development organisation aiming to develop educational skills and resources in Africa. Works in partnership with local organisations to plan and develop effective educational projects.

Recruits personnel from the UK with appropriate educational skills to provide effective support and training. Project workers have a unique opportunity to gain better understanding of development issues through working overseas in a development capacity. In the UK there are opportunities for volunteers to help with fundraising.

Applicants for overseas positions must be graduates with a background in education and development. Most projects require specialist and experienced workers willing to share their skills. In-service/teacher training experience valuable. For UK positions some financial training is essential.

Projects vary in length

Project workers are paid a local salary and are provided with accommodation. Round-trip travel costs and insurance cover provided.

Compulsory orientation course held before placement begins. Debriefing with project manager.

Speculative enquiries welcome all year; apply in response to specific advertisements

MÉDECINS SANS FRONTIÈRES

Médecins Sans Frontières, 124-132 Clerkenwell Road, London EC1R 5DL

0171-713 5600

Angola, Benin, Burundi, Cameroon, Chad, Congo, Djibouti, Ethiopia, Equatorial Guinea, Ghana, Guinea, Kenya, Liberia, Madagascar, Malawi, Mali, Mauritania, Mozambique, Rwanda, Somalia, South Africa, Sudan, Tanzania, Uganda, Zaire, Zambia, Zimbabwe; Afghanistan, Bangladesh, Burma, Cambodia, China/Tibet, Hong Kong, India, Laos, Papua New Guinea/Bougainville, Philippines, Sri Lanka, Tajikistan, Thailand, Vietnam; Albania, Armenia, Azerbaijan, Belgium, Bosnia Herzegovina, Croatia, former Yugoslavia, France, Romania, Spain; Iraq, Lebanon, Palestinian Authority, Occupied Territories, Yemen; Bolivia, Brazil, Colombia, Cuba, El Salvador, Guatemala, Haiti, Nicaragua, Panama, Peru
Also other countries affected by war, famine or natural disasters.

Founded in 1971, the largest independent humanitarian organisation for emergency medical relief, providing assistance to victims of war, famine or natural disaster, irrespective of race, creed or political affiliation. Run from 6 operational sections in Europe and 12 offices worldwide.

Volunteers are general practitioners, specialist doctors, surgeons, anaesthetists, nurses, midwives and laboratory technicians as well as administrators, engineers and accountants. Over 100 volunteers from the UK are placed each year.

Ages 25-60. Volunteers must be mature, flexible, well-organised individuals, aware of their own strengths and weaknesses, well-informed about the problems of living and working in developing countries, practical with broad-based skills and not too idealistic. Doctors/nurses should have two years post-qualification experience and knowledge of tropical medicine; logisticians must have an engineering background; financial controllers should have experience of accounting and working in developing countries. Knowledge of French and/or Spanish useful.

Six months minimum

Board, lodging, insurance, travel costs and £400 per month provided

Compulsory training courses held in Amsterdam, cost £380 plus airfare; volunteers are reimbursed 75% on placement. Debriefing on return; returned volunteers network provides support; counselling available.

Apply three months in advance; recruitment all year. UK residents apply direct; others should write for details of where to apply.

MEDICAL AID FOR PALESTINIANS

Overseas Postings Officer, Medical Aid for Palestinians, 33A Islington Park Street, London N1 1QB

0171-226 4114

The Occupied Territories, Lebanon, Jordan and Egypt

A non-partisan, non-political registered charity established in 1984 in response to the massacres of Sabra and Shatilla, dedicated to improving the health conditions of Palestinian people by providing material, financial and personnel support to Palestinian health institutions

Specialised medical personnel work on a variety of primary, secondary and tertiary health care projects, including mother and child health care, physiotherapy and occupational therapy, community nursing, intensive care medicine and surgery, Approx 40 volunteers recruited each year.

Applicants must have medical/nursing qualifications and practical hands-on clinical experience, be motivated by a concern for human welfare, culturally and politically aware, and have a desire to learn and develop in a challenging environment. Some familiarity with development work useful. All nationalities considered; knowledge of English essential.
B D PH W considered depending on project and practicalities.

Six months minimum

Accommodation and a living allowance provided, plus full health insurance and return travel. There is also a monthly grant paid in the UK and a resettlement grant on completion of contract.

Compulsory briefing prior to departure. Prospective volunteers are also put into contact with previous volunteers wherever possible. On return, volunteers receive a project debriefing and are encouraged to share their experiences with others through talks and slide shows, as well as help with fundraising and appeals.

Apply 2-3 months in advance of a specific project commencing

Annual Review; Health in Gaza: A Casualty of Occupation; Laboratory Services in the Occupied West Bank and Gaza; regular newsletters.

MENNONITE CENTRAL COMMITTEE

Europe office: Hansulrich Gerber, Mennonite Central Committee, Grande Rue 114, Case Postale 52, 2720 Tramelan, Switzerland

US office: Personnel Department, Mennonite Central Committee, 21 South 12th Street, PO Box 500, Akron, Pennsylvania 17501, United States

Some 50 countries including Angola, Botswana, Burkina Faso, Chad, Egypt, Kenya, Lesotho, Mozambique, Nigeria, South Africa, Sudan, Tanzania, Uganda, Zaire, Zambia, Zimbabwe; Bangladesh, Cambodia, China, India, Indonesia, Laos, Philippines, Vietnam; Croatia, Russia; Bolivia, Brazil, El Salvador, Haiti, Jamaica, Nicaragua; Jordan; Canada, US

Set up in 1920, the relief, service and development agency of the North American Mennonite and Brethren in Christ churches. Seeks to demonstrate God's love through committed people who work among people suffering from poverty, conflict, oppression and natural disaster.

Assignments include agriculture, community development, water conservation, health, education, economic and technical projects, church-related programmes, social services and peacemaking. Also provide emergency services to people caught in drought, warfare and famine. In North America volunteers are involved in education, housing, justice research and advocacy, immigration/Native American concerns, health, social service, administrative support and urban ministry.

Volunteers need not be Mennonite, but must have a personal faith in and commitment to Jesus Christ, and be active members of a Christian church. Work-related qualifications vary according to assignment; for most positions outside North America a relevant degree and work experience required. Applicants should be flexible, eager to learn, with a sense of humour, and hold to the biblical teaching of non-violence.

North America: 3 years; other countries: 2 years. Short-term programmes (2-12 months) are also available to young adults.

Round-trip travel costs plus full maintenance whilst in service provided, including room, board, health insurance and a small monthly allowance

Two week trans-cultural seminar held in June; compulsory 10 day orientation held in US or Canada immediately prior to assignment. In-country orientation on arrival; time set aside for language study.

Apply at least six months in advance

Information leaflets

MISSION AVIATION FELLOWSHIP

The Manager, Personnel Department, Mission Aviation Fellowship, Ingles Manor, Castle Hill Avenue, Folkestone, Kent CT20 2TN

Folkestone (01303) 850950

Chad, Ethiopia, Kenya, Madagascar, Namibia, Tanzania, Uganda

A Christian organisation founded in 1945 and committed to helping the church in isolated areas by providing aircraft, pilots and the back-up that air transport work of this nature demands. The Fellowship aims to spread the Gospel, life and hope in spiritual and physical terms to thousands of people, providing an essential service to national pastors, church leaders, missionaries and medical and relief agency workers, by flying them to places where they are needed most. Also transports food, equipment, medical and agricultural supplies, emergency relief and other essential materials to remote and otherwise inaccessible locations, and is on call as an aerial ambulance service.

Pilots, aircraft engineers, avionics technicians and administrators are needed. Volunteers work in partnership with Christian and other organisations, forming a unifying link between individuals or families working at lonely outposts.

Ages 18+. Volunteers should have a Christian commitment and be active in the life of the church. Staff are selected for their skill, temperament and spiritual maturity. Pilots, aircraft engineers and avionics specialists must hold the appropriate licences and have relevant experience. Advice on the requirements and courses available given to those who would like to take up this opportunity for service to others.

Initially 3 years

Financial support on agreed scales must be raised by sending churches and others interested in the applicants. The level of support covers salary, accommodation, car, travel to and from the UK and the place of work, medical care, and education for children where appropriate.

All personnel are given special training before they become active overseas to help them to adjust to cultural differences. They also receive guidance on their return to the UK.

Applications can be made at any time

Annual Report; *MAF News* quarterly magazine.

THE MISSIONS TO SEAMEN

The Ministry Secretary, The Missions to Seamen, St Michael Paternoster Royal, College Hill, London EC4R 2RL

0171-248 5202

At some 16 seaports in Britain and around the world, including Dunkerque, Immingham, Kobe, Liverpool, Mombasa, New Orleans, Rotterdam, Seaham, Singapore, Southampton and Yokohama

An Anglican missionary society founded in 1856, caring for the spiritual, material and moral welfare of seafarers around the globe. Helps to combat isolation, exploitation and the dangers of the sea, working for improvements in conditions, education and welfare, serving seafarers of every race, colour and creed, offering a ministry of word, sacrament, counselling care and Christian welcome. The most important feature is the visit of the chaplain and staff to each ship on arrival in port.

There are volunteer service schemes for chaplain's assistants, providing an opportunity to be involved in practical Christian service within the shipping industry. Work is varied and involves visiting ships, conducting sightseeing tours, arranging sporting events, visiting hospitals, and helping with worship. Serving in the seafarers' centres can include bar and shop work, arranging video shows, telephone calls, gardening and cleaning. Recruits approx 18 volunteers annually.

Ages 18-24. Applicants should be sympathetic, understanding, good at quickly establishing relationships, prepared to befriend people of all nationalities, with an interest in this particular form of ministry. Specific experience not necessary, but clean driving licence required. Applicants must be members of a Christian denomination, prepared to participate fully in Anglican ministry and worship. Three suitable references needed.

One year, starting September

Board and lodging, travel costs, medical/accident insurance, approx £25 pocket money per week and three weeks holiday per year provided

One day debriefing on return

Completed applications should ideally be sent before the end of March

Information leaflets; *Flying Angel News* newsletter; *The Sea*; Prayer Union

NEVE SHALOM/WAHAT AL-SALAM

Volunteer Applications, Neve Shalom/Wahat al-Salam, Doar Na Shimshon 99761, Israel

(972 2) 912222

Israel

Neve Shalom/Wahat al-Salam, founded in 1972 and situated equidistant from Jerusalem and Tel Aviv-Jaffa, is a cooperative village of Jews and Palestinian Arabs of Israeli citizenship. Members are demonstrating the possibility of coexistence by developing a community based on mutual acceptance, respect and cooperation on a daily basis whilst each individual remains faithful to his/her own cultural, national and religious identity.

Limited number of places (approx 5) for volunteers wishing to live and work in the community. Work may involve general maintenance work around the village, looking after children in the kindergarten and nursery or helping out at the community's guest house.

No set age limits or nationality restrictions. Help given with arranging work permits/visas. At least a basic knowledge of English, Arabic or Hebrew is required. **B D PH W** willing to consider applications from those with a disability.

Minimum six months commitment preferred

Volunteers work approx 40 hours per week in return for food, accommodation and approx £30 per month pocket money. No travel costs paid. Volunteers must arrange own insurance cover.

Can supply addresses of previous volunteers on request

Best to apply 6-12 months in advance as there are only a few positions available

OPTIONS

The Director, Options, Project Concern International, 3550 Afton Road, San Diego, California 92123, United States

(1 619) 279 9690 Fax (1 619) 694 0294

Over 60 countries worldwide including Ghana, Kenya, India, Nepal, Pakistan, Thailand, Guatemala, St Lucia and Romania, as well as in 30 states in the US

Options is the international health recruitment and referral service of Project Concern International, a non-profit organisation working in primary health care training and development. Options provides professional volunteer opportunities linking health and development specialists with programmes, hospitals and clinics worldwide.

Hundreds of volunteers are placed each year, including primary care physicians, surgeons, nurses, physician assistants, dentists, lab technicians, health trainers, public health and hospital administrators, sanitation and water engineers

Relevant health-related qualifications and skills are essential, and previous overseas experience is preferred. For positions in the United States, US credentials are required. Knowledge of languages depends on host country.

Short and long-term assignments, ranging from 2 weeks to 2 years

Options matches the applicant's job preferences to available positions. Terms and conditions are arranged between the volunteer and the facility, but will typically include housing and meals. Membership fee $25.

Follow-up evaluations conducted with each volunteer on completion of assignment

Recruitment all year

Bi-monthly newsletter lists current opportunities

OVERSEAS SERVICE BUREAU

Overseas Service Bureau, PO Box 350, Fitzroy, Victoria 3065, Australia

(61 3) 279 1788

Mainly in southern Africa, south and southeast Asia, Mekong region, Latin America and the Pacific, including Afghanistan, Bangladesh, Bhutan, Cambodia, China, Cook Islands, El Salvador, Eritrea, Fiji, Guatemala, Hong Kong, India, Indonesia, Kiribati, Laos, Malawi, Malaysia, Maldives, Marshall Islands, Mexico, Micronesia, Mongolia, Mozambique, Namibia, Nepal, Nicaragua, Palau, Pakistan, Papua New Guinea, Philippines, South Africa, Solomon Islands, Sri Lanka, Swaziland, Tanzania, Thailand, Tonga, Tuvalu, Vanuatu, Vietnam, Western Samoa, Zambia and Zimbabwe

Established in 1963, provides opportunities for volunteer development workers, living alongside people in developing countries and working in partnership with them in order to foster cross-cultural relationships and international understanding; assist in the development of their own and other communities; and contribute to a peaceful and just world

Many placements in the field of education; also opportunities in the social sciences, health, administration, agriculture, human settlements, trades, engineering, natural sciences, communications and transport

Ages 20+; some countries have upper limit of 60. Applicants must be Australian citizens or hold permanent residency status in Australia, with recognised trade, commercial or professional skills and usually at least 2 years work experience in their field. Some opportunities for young graduates with less than two years' experience. Limited places for experienced people with practical skills but no formal qualifications.

Normally 2 years

Negotiates placements, arranges and covers return airfares and provides insurance. Terms and conditions vary according to overseas employer; some pay a salary based on local rates for similar skill levels, enabling the volunteer to meet basic living costs, others provide a basic allowance plus accommodation and food. Establishment allowance covers incidental travel and arrival expenses; resettlement allowance when the volunteer returns to Australia after assignment completion.

Volunteers attend a residential briefing programme prior to departure; several held each year and OSB covers the cost. Country briefings and language training are also provided where necessary.

Recruitment all year. Successful applicants usually depart 6 months after submitting application; applicants must therefore be based in Australia during the application period.

PEACE BRIGADES INTERNATIONAL

Peace Brigades International, 192 Spadina Avenue, #304, Toronto, Ontario M5T 2C2, Canada

(1 416) 594 0429   Fax (1 416) 594 0430

PBI Europe, Ulli Laubenthal, European Coordinator, Hof Lauer, Kerbesdorf, 6483 Bad Soden-Salmunster, Germany

PBI North America Project, Barb Macquarrie, Project Coordinator, 1-473 Baker Street, London, Ontario N6C 1X9, Canada

PBI Sri Lanka Project, Joy Boustred, 32 Clare Road, Halifax HX1 2HX

PBI USA, 2642 College Avenue, Berkeley, CA 94704, United States

Currently Colombia, Guatemala, North America and Sri Lanka. In the past, teams have worked in El Salvador, the Middle East and Southeast Asia.

Founded in Canada in 1981, PBI seeks to establish international and non-partisan approaches to peacemaking and to the support of basic Human Rights; it challenges the belief that violent institutions and warfare must dominate human affairs; and it seeks to demonstrate that as international volunteers, citizens can act boldly as peacemakers when their governments cannot. PBI is officially recognised by the United Nations, regularly participates in UN fora in New York, and meets with UN representatives in the countries where they work.

When invited, PBI sends unarmed peace teams into areas of violent repression or conflict. These teams are made up of international volunteers and their task is to reduce violence and support local social justice initiatives by: protective accompaniment/escort of those whose lives are threatened; acting as international, non-partisan observers; fostering reconciliation and dialogue; and educating in non-violence and Human Rights.

In Central America, PBI works in Guatemala and in the Bogotá and Middle Magdalena regions of Colombia, offering accompaniment and an international presence for people or organisations that may be the target of armed harassment.

continued opposite

In Sri Lanka, PBI works with lawyers groups and legal witnesses, extends protection to Buddhist and Catholic clergy, trade unionists and grassroots Human Rights and development groups, and provides observers for major demonstrations.

In North America, PBI trainers have provided workshops on Human Rights and non-violence training to First Nations Peoples in Quebec, Winnipeg and Labrador.

Approx 25 volunteers are recruited each year.

Ages 25+. Applicants must have a profound commitment to non-violence and non-partisanship. They must also be able to live with stress and prepared to live in a cross-cultural environment. Skills in peace education helpful. Knowledge of Spanish required for Central American projects; knowledge of French for work in Quebec; English for other projects.

Minimum commitment between 7-12 months

Food, accommodation and a small monthly stipend provided during placement. Volunteers arrange and pay for own travel and insurance.

All volunteers must attend one week's training before start of placement

Apply 6-12 months in advance, depending on project

Information leaflets; monthly *PBI Project Bulletin*

PEACE CORPS

Peace Corps, 1990 K Street, NW, Room 9320, Washington, DC 20526, United States

Within the United States (800) 424 8580

Benin, Botswana, Burundi, Cameroon, Cape Verde, Central African Republic, Chad, Comoros, Congo, Côte d'Ivoire, Equatorial Guinea, Gabon, Gambia, Ghana, Guinea, Guinea-Bissau, Kenya, Lesotho, Madagascar, Malawi, Mali, Mauritania, Morocco, Mozambique, Namibia, Niger, Nigeria, Rwanda, São Tomé & Principe, Senegal, Seychelles, Sierra Leone, Swaziland, Tanzania, Togo, Tunisia, Uganda, Zaire, Zambia, Zimbabwe; Kazakhstan, Kyrghyzstan, Mongolia, Nepal, Sri Lanka, Turkmenistan, Uzbekistan; Anguilla, Antigua/Barbuda, Dominica, Grenada, Haiti, Jamaica, Montserrat, St Kitts/Nevis, St Lucia, St Vincent & Grenadines; Albania, Armenia, Belarus, Bulgaria, Czech Republic, Estonia, Hungary, Latvia, Lithuania, Malta, Moldova, Poland, Romania, Russia, Slovakia, Ukraine; People's Republic of China, Philippines, Thailand; Argentina, Belize, Bolivia, Chile, Costa Rica, Dominican Republic, Ecuador, El Salvador, Guatemala, Honduras, Nicaragua, Panama, Paraguay, Uruguay; Yemen; Cook Islands, Fiji, Kiribati, Marshall Islands, Micronesia, Papua New Guinea, Solomon Islands, Tonga, Tuvalu, Vanuatu, Western Samoa

Established in 1961 by John F Kennedy to promote world peace and mutual understanding between people in the United States and in developing countries, Peace Corps offers American men and women a chance to gain credentials, stretch themselves personally and help solve the world's pressing problems. More than 140,000 Americans have been Peace Corps volunteers, with some 6,000 serving at any given time in over 90 countries worldwide. Peace Corps assignments emphasise appropriate technology, cultural sensitivity and lasting skills transfer.

Volunteers work in a variety of fields, usually at the community level. These may include small business and cooperative development; agriculture; forestry and environment; fish culture; health and nutrition, including nursing, disease control, physical and occupational therapy, maternal and child health care; education, including secondary maths or science, teacher training, curriculum development, library science, English teaching, vocational and special education; engineering,

continued opposite

including water and sanitation projects, bridge and road construction, architecture and urban planning; and industrial arts: vocational education and on-the-job training in carpentry, masonry, electricity, mechanics, metalworking, cabinetmaking, plumbing and welding.

Applicants must be US citizens aged 18+; most people do not have the experience or maturity for successful service until they reach their 20s. Most assignments require 3-5 years' substantive work experience and/or a bachelor's degree; others may require a master's. Graduates in liberal arts fields must have relevant skills as selection is highly competitive. Those with a strong background in agriculture, business management or skilled trades may qualify without a degree.
All applicants need flexibility, adaptability, social sensitivity, cultural awareness, creativity in problem-solving, perseverance, effective interpersonal skills and commitment. Knowledge of French, Spanish or other languages useful. Application procedure involves medical and legal screening. **B D PH W** many disabled people have served successfully.

Two years

During service, volunteers receive a monthly allowance for housing, food, clothing and incidentals. They also receive free medical and dental care, transportation to and from their overseas sites and 24 vacation days a year. Following service there is a readjustment allowance of approx $5,400.

8-12 week training programme prior to assignment covers intensive language, cultural and technical training. Periodic in-service workshops help volunteers in project planning, reinforce skills and teach new ones. Help with jobhunting provided for returned volunteers.

Apply one year in advance; application and screening process may take 9-12 months. As most training programmes start June-September it is best to apply September-March.

Peace Corps Today quarterly newspaper; information leaflets and booklets

THE RICHMOND FELLOWSHIP INTERNATIONAL

International Secretary, Richmond Fellowship International, The Coach House, 8 Addison Road, London W14 8DL

0171-603 2442   Fax 0171-602 0199

Mainly United States; possibly also Eastern Europe/developing countries

Founded in 1981, the largest international voluntary organisation working in the field of community mental health. Based on experience gained in the UK and elsewhere, it provides a form of social therapy - the therapeutic community - in which clients are helped to re-enter society through a carefully designed programme of group activities and individual counselling. There are now 29 affiliates worldwide providing psychiatric and drug rehabilitation services, and on-the-spot training.

Volunteers are needed to work within projects, side by side with the project staff, assisting with therapy and helping in day-to-day running. As well as assisting with the basic necessities of life, some volunteers also become involved in activities such as gardening, cooking, art, music, drama and sport. Also opportunities for administrative and financial workers. Senior volunteer positions may arise for consultants/trainers.

Ages 22+. Selection process identifies committed, capable and resilient volunteers. Applicants should be mature, have previous volunteer experience plus professional training in nursing, social work or psychology, particularly in the rehabilitation of mentally and emotionally disturbed adults or children, and have practical skills in cooking, home making, art or recreational activities. Applications are viewed creatively; candidates matched with the placement best suited to using their skills.

Twelve months

Volunteers expected to accept the obligations and responsibilities which apply to staff members. 48 hour shift week. Board, lodging, 28 days annual leave, stipend in local currency equivalent to £30 per week, full insurance cover, and return airfare in certain circumstances, provided.

Applicants interviewed in the UK at own expense; sometimes possible to arrange local interviews. Orientation may include placement on a UK project and one or more Richmond Fellowship College courses.

Recruitment all year

Annual Report

ST JOSEPH'S INDIAN SCHOOL

Stephanie Swanson, St Joseph's Indian School, PO Box 89, Chamberlain, SD 57325, United States

(1 605) 734 3486

South Dakota, United States

Founded in 1927, St Joseph's is a residential facility that provides for the spiritual, educational, emotional, and physical welfare of Native American children in need. The students attend school and live in one of 17 homes on campus, each housing 10-12 children and two houseparents in a family setting.

Opportunities for volunteers to work as houseparents, nurses, elementary, religious and special education teachers. Houseparents work a six days on, three days off rota, living in one of the houses for six days at a time. Approx 20 placements each year.

Ages 21+. All volunteers must have a high school or equivalent education, some posts require a college degree and/or a relevant qualification. Good communication, organisational and living skills essential; relevant prior experience preferred. **B D PH**

Minimum one year. 72-108 hour week on a rota basis.

Room and board provided for houseparents on working days; other volunteers find own accommodation. Insurance cover provided. Salary approx $14,155 per annum for houseparents, $16,500 per annum for other volunteers. No travel expenses paid.

Compulsory two week orientation programme provides introduction to the area, background to the school, the clientèle, and school policies. One week orientation before the start of each year.

Apply two months in advance

SCOTTISH CHURCHES WORLD EXCHANGE

The Volunteer Programme Coordinator, Scottish Churches World Exchange, 6A Randolph Place, Edinburgh EH3 7TE

0131-225 8115

Africa, Asia, Central America, Europe and the Middle East

An agency of the Scottish Churches, managed by a committee of representatives or observers from most of the major Christian denominations and a number of missionary societies

Placements are arranged with an overseas partner of one of the Scottish churches or agencies. Volunteers are placed according to their interests, skills and personality, and work on a project of their choice. Emphasis is placed on volunteers becoming part of the local church and community.

Ages 18+. Open only to candidates from Scottish churches or others in Scotland willing to work in a church-related post. Relevant skills and experience are welcome but not essential.

6-18 months, beginning August/September

Food, accommodation and pocket money provided by the host and World Exchange. Volunteers are expected to try and raise at least £1,500 towards the cost of their placement, which represents about one third of the real cost.

Compulsory preparation courses consist of four days at Easter and a week in early summer. On return, volunteers have a medical check, debriefing, and are encouraged to attend a weekend conference for returned volunteers.

Preliminary interviews held October-December; final selection days January and February

SERVICES FOR OPEN LEARNING

Services for Open Learning, North Devon Professional Centre, Vicarage Street, Barnstaple, Devon EX32 7HB

Barnstaple (01271) 327319

Croatia, the Czech Republic, Hungary, Romania, Slovakia

A registered educational charity set up in 1991 to recruit teachers for schools in Central and Eastern Europe.

Placements are available at schools in Croatia, the Czech Republic, Hungary, Romania and Slovakia to teach English as a foreign language and also business studies. Recruits approx 70 teachers each year.

Ages 21+. Experience not always necessary, but all applicants must have a degree or teaching certificate and at least a minimum TEFL qualification. TEFL experience essential for some positions. Knowledge of relevant language desirable. UK nationals only.

Contracts are for 10-12 months, beginning September or January

In general, teachers work approx 18 hours per week and are paid the equivalent of £50-£180 per month, depending on the country. Accommodation is provided, sometimes in return for a small fee. Schools provide full health care cover; in Romania this is supplemented by private insurance arranged by SOL. Participants pay own travel expenses, but are encouraged to seek sponsorship to cover this.

If required, SOL can arrange, at cost, an introductory TEFL course before appointment and further TEFL training during the working year. In-country induction programme held prior to starting work.

Apply by 10 February

SHATIL: SUPPORT PROJECT FOR VOLUNTARY ORGANIZATIONS

Volunteer Coordinator, SHATIL: Support Project for Voluntary Organizations, POB 53395, Jerusalem 91533, Israel

(972 2) 723597

New Israel Fund of Great Britain, Craven House, 121 Kingsway, London WC2B 6NX

Throughout Israel

Created in 1982 by the New Israel Fund, provides technical and organisational support for non-profit and social change efforts in Israel. Helps non-governmental organisations clarify goals, develop objectives, obtain *amuta* status, seek funding, establish priorities, coordinate with related agencies and increase visibility.

Can arrange volunteer work placements with various non-profit, social change organisations. Work may include teaching English and writing English language materials; organising events and projects; working with children or people with disabilities; legal or other special research projects. Type of work varies depending upon volunteer's individual language abilities and skills. Places approx 100 volunteers each year.

Ages 18+. Preference given to those with previous experience of Israel, especially if they have worked in the development or non-profit sector. Ability to communicate in Hebrew or Arabic essential. Qualifications and skills dependent on position: good writers, experienced teachers, community organisers, computer experts, medical or dental personnel are particularly sought.

Minimum 4 months commitment preferred

Working hours from 4 hours per week to full-time, depending on placement. Accommodation and meals can be provided in rural village placements. No wages, insurance or travel costs paid, unless travel is demanded by the job.

Training may be provided. Occasional study tours organised.

Ongoing recruitment

SKILLSHARE AFRICA

Cooperante Services Unit, Skillshare Africa, 3 Belvoir Street, Leicester LE1 6SL

Leicester (0116) 254 1862

Botswana, Lesotho, Mozambique and Swaziland

Established in 1990 after being part of International Voluntary Service, Skillshare Africa sends skilled and experienced people to work in support of development in southern Africa

Volunteers are recruited following requests from community groups, non-governmental organisations and government departments in the countries concerned. They contribute to every aspect of development including education, planning, construction, agriculture and health. Some 40-50 workers are recruited each year.

Ages 22-65. Applicants must have a recognised qualification and at least two years' work experience in an appropriate field. They must be committed to sharing their skills with others. All nationalities considered, provided they have right of re-entry into the EU.
B D PH W considered depending on conditions of work at the project.

Two years minimum

Volunteers are provided with housing and a salary in accordance with local levels. National Insurance contributions, medical insurance and travel costs also covered.

Orientation course provided. Opportunity to discuss posting and related matters with UK staff on return.

Apply 3-6 months in advance

SOUTH AMERICAN MISSIONARY SOCIETY

Personnel Secretary, South American Missionary Society, Allen Gardiner House, Pembury Road, Tunbridge Wells, Kent TN2 3QU

Tunbridge Wells (01892) 538647

Spain, Portugal; Argentina, Bolivia, Brazil, Chile, Paraguay, Peru, Uruguay

Founded in 1844, the Society exists to encourage and enable the spreading of the Gospel of the Lord Jesus Christ in Latin America and the Iberian Peninsula through partnership with Anglican and other churches, and to initiate and respond to opportunities by mutual sharing of prayer, personnel and resources, with the purpose of being a servant, partner and communication bridge in response to Christ's commission to live out the Gospel among all people

A variety of placements are available, including working with street children and orphanages in Brazil; practical involvement with local churches in Argentina; teaching at a church school in Paraguay or Chile; and working with local Christian groups on evangelical outreach programmes in Spain. There are also opportunities for medical students to visit South America as part of their medical elective placement period. Approx 20 volunteers recruited each year.

Ages 18+. Applicants must be committed Christians with the support and backing of their home church in Britain. They must also have a desire to extend their own personal experience in serving the national church. Knowledge of Spanish or Portuguese very useful.

6-12 months

Volunteers expected to contribute towards the cost of accommodation, which will be with other missionaries or a host family. They must also raise their own return airfare, medical and travel insurance and living expenses (but some help may be given towards obtaining sponsorship).

Orientation is recommended. Debriefing meeting provided on return.

Recruitment all year; apply 4-6 months in advance

Information leaflets; *Share* quarterly newsletter

SOUTHERN AFRICA RESOURCE CENTRE

The Secretary, Southern Africa Resource Centre (SARC), 6 West Street, Old Market, Bristol BS2 0BH

0117-941 1442

Beira, Mozambique.
Opportunities also in Bristol.

Set up in 1989 to educate the public in the southwest of England in the fields of art, culture, history and current affairs of southern Africa; and to manage and develop Bristol's link with Beira, a port on the coast of Mozambique

Opportunities for self-funded volunteers to participate in medical, architecture, administrative and possibly teaching placements in Beira. In Bristol there are also opportunities for volunteers to help with educational, cultural, commercial and social projects, administrative work; campaigning; press and public relations, and production of materials.

Ages 18+ (16+ in Bristol). Experience of campaigning and development preferred. For placements in Beira volunteers should be independent and confident, with appropriate experience, initiative and an interest in development issues. Knowledge of Portuguese also essential.

Three months minimum

Volunteers must be self-financing and cover their own travel, insurance, board and accommodation costs

All volunteers must attend orientation before beginning of placement

Recruitment all year

Information leaflets

UNITED NATIONS ASSOCIATION INTERNATIONAL SERVICE

Recruitment Administrator, United Nations Association International Service, Suite 3a, Hunter House, 57 Goodramgate, York YO1 2LS

York (01904) 647799   Fax (01904) 652353

Burkina Faso, Mali; Brazil, Bolivia; West Bank and Gaza

Works in partnership with other organisations to promote long-term development by providing skilled and experienced people to collaborate with locally organised initiatives. It works to promote understanding between people of different nations, cultures, religions and languages through a sharing of skills and exchanges of experiences, acting in response to requests for skills that are not available locally. Project workers pass on their skills to local people, strengthening their efforts to improve their situation, and leave behind them something of lasting value to the communities and organisations for which they work.

Recruits from a wide range of disciplines, such as nurses, midwives, agriculturalists, Human Rights researchers, documentalists, agroforesters, water specialists, livestock technicians, community development workers and primary health care advisers

Relevant qualifications, working experience and skills essential. Third World and community work experience an advantage. Knowledge of the relevant language or the ability to learn essential. Applicants must have an understanding of development issues in order to strengthen local development groups and help increase understanding between peoples. They also need to be adaptable to new ways of working and living. Selection takes place in the UK.

Two years minimum

Accommodation, living allowance in relation to local costs, travel and insurance provided. Class 2 Volunteer Development National Insurance contributions paid. 20 days leave per year.

Orientation course. Language training provided where necessary.

Recruitment all year

Annual Review; information leaflets; *Viva* magazine

UNITED NATIONS VOLUNTEERS

The Executive Coordinator, United Nations Volunteers, Palais des Nations, 1211 Geneva 10, Switzerland

(41 22) 788 2455   Fax (41 22) 788 2501   Internet: enquiries@UNV.CH

In the UK apply to United Nations Volunteers, VSO, 317 Putney Bridge Road, London SW15 2PN ✆ 0181-780 2266

UNV specialists and fieldworkers serve in 119 countries in Africa, the Asia-Pacific region, Arab States/Europe and in Latin America/Caribbean. Some two thirds are at work in 47 countries classified as least developed; 76% are themselves citizens of developing countries.

Its main activity is to programme, deliver and administer suitably qualified, experienced and motivated personnel for international technical cooperation and humanitarian work in developing countries.

With particular emphasis on facilitating community-based initiatives, the programme provides middle- and upper-level skills in a wide range of sectors such as agriculture, health, education, humanitarian relief and rehabilitation, the environment, small industry, and for UN operations to promote Human Rights and democracy. Specialists are drawn from 115 different professions and trades, from accountancy to zoology.

Ages 25-45+; retired people welcome to apply. Applicants must have a first degree and preferably a postgraduate award or equivalent technical qualifications. Two years' work experience required, several years preferable. Lengthy work experience may be substitutable for academic qualifications. Ability to work in English and/or French, Spanish, Arabic, Portuguese, Russian or relevant local language essential. Candidates must possess motivation to help others and share skills on a peer basis.

Two years, possibly renewable; shorter-term assignments can arise

Modest accommodation, settling-in allowance, monthly allowance intended to cover living costs, and outward and return travel provided. UNVs and their dependants insured against sickness and accidents; resettlement allowance payable on completion of the assignment.

Briefing may be provided in the UK, in Geneva, on arrival in the host country or by a combination of these

Recruitment all year

UNV News; UNV Spectrum provides update on roster of candidates

UNITED REFORMED CHURCH IN THE UNITED KINGDOM

The Secretary for International Church Relations, United Reformed Church, 86 Tavistock Place, London WC1H 9RT

0171-916 9020   Fax 0171-916 2021

Botswana, Madagascar, Zambia, Zimbabwe; Bangladesh, India; China, Hong Kong, Taiwan; Kiribati, Papua New Guinea, Solomon Islands, Tuvalu, Western Samoa; Jamaica; Germany, Hungary, Italy, Romania

One of the world family of Reformed Churches; meets requests from overseas partner churches for staff for their projects. Also involved in arranging short-term appointments for young people with partner churches in Europe, and in recruiting teachers of English for China.

Most requests are for lay missionaries to work as secondary teachers, theological educators, doctors, nurses, accountants and, occasionally, administrators. Opportunities in Europe as volunteers in church institutions and to teach conversational English; in China, for qualified and experienced teachers of English for tertiary institutions.

Ages 22+, 18+ for short-term volunteer placements. Unqualified volunteers are accepted for short-term opportunities in Europe; for other placements relevant qualifications, a few years of professional experience and a knowledge of relevant languages are required. Applicants should be members of the United Reformed Church or actively associated with it.

Two years minimum; six months minimum for short-term placements

For long-term placements accommodation and salary are in line with local workers and return travel is provided. For short-term opportunities volunteers meet their own travel costs and are provided with accommodation and minimal pocket money.

Compulsory preparation and orientation course for long-term appointments. Advice and help with re-integration given on return and, occasionally, specialist in-service and debriefing courses arranged. Short-term volunteers given preparation and advice.

Recruitment all year

Information leaflets

THE UNITED SOCIETY FOR THE PROPAGATION OF THE GOSPEL

Short-Term Experience Programmes Officer, Mission Personnel Team, United Society for the Propagation of the Gospel, Partnership House, 157 Waterloo Road, London SE1 8XA

0171-928 8681

Worldwide placements including Africa, Asia, Latin America and the UK

Founded in 1701, enables the Church of England to relate effectively to Anglican and associate churches throughout the world and to support the work of overseas churches by offering them personnel and funding

Operates Experience Exchange Programme (EEP), enabling UK Christians to learn from the insights and experiences of Christians in other countries. Volunteer placements, agreed by local Anglican bishops and Christian community project leaders, in schools, medical centres, social welfare and agricultural projects. Recruits 30 volunteers annually. Small number of personnel may also be required for work with the church overseas; 3 year renewable contract. Also British-based Root Group Programme (RGP), where 3 or 4 volunteers live together in a small community, usually an area experiencing social problems, using their individual gifts to serve the church and the wider community.

Ages 18+, EEP; 18-30, RGP. Applicants must be mature practising Christians with an interest and commitment in identifying with a local Christian community, adaptable to new situations, resourceful, sensitive to people and willing to suffer some hardship/loneliness. UK nationals only. No special qualifications or experience necessary. **B D PH W**

EEP 6-12 months, usually departing July-October. RGP June development weekend preceding 10 month placement, September-June.

EEP volunteers pay their own fares and insurance, and may be asked to contribute to board and lodging costs. Advice given on obtaining sponsorship. RGP self-supporting, preferably through part-time work but failing this, through social security benefits.

EEP 2 week training period, July, 24 hour personal debriefing and weekend group debriefing on return. RGP 3 week training period, September, 2 in-service training weekends and 5 day debriefing, June.

Apply September-May

Newsletter; *TransMission* paper; various leaflets and resource materials

UNIVERSITIES' EDUCATIONAL [FU]ND FOR PALESTINIANS (UNIPAL)

The Projects Officer, UNIPAL, 33A Islington Park Street, London N1 1QB

0171-226 7997

West Bank and Gaza Strip; Palestinian communities in Israel, the Lebanon and Jordan

Founded in 1972, UNIPAL is a small educational charity which aims to provide forms of help which will benefit not only individuals but also Palestinian communities and especially over 700,000 refugees still in camps. Palestinian teachers of English are brought to the UK for training; financial aid is given to Palestinian educational institutions that are helping deprived children and young people; and volunteers are sent to the Middle East to share their skills.

Strictly limited number of volunteers needed. Work involves providing English courses for Palestinian organisations, school children and teachers. There are also short-term summer opportunities helping in United Nations schools, children's homes and kindergartens.

Ages 22+ for long-term volunteers, 20+ for summer volunteers. Applicants should have sensitivity, tolerance, readiness to learn, political awareness, adaptability and a sense of responsibility. TEFL qualifications and previous relevant experience necessary for long-term volunteers. Background reading on the Middle East situation essential.

6-12 months; or 4-6 weeks for summer volunteers

Long-term volunteers receive accommodation, airfares, living allowance and medical insurance; summer volunteers receive accommodation and food but pay their own fares, insurance and personal expenses.

Interviews held and successful applicants are briefed on their placement

Recruitment all year. Selection and interviews for summer volunteers usually take place March-April.

UNIPAL News newsletter

VADHU

Narendra Rautela, Secretary, VADHU, Dogra Estate, Ganiadeoli, Ranikhet 263645, India

(91 5966) 2506

In or near Ranikhet, India

VADHU stands for Voluntary Organisation for the Development of the Hills of Uttarakahnd, a non-governmental, non-profit group aimed at creating a model of sustainable mountain development in the Ghatgar watershed area, near Ranikhet in the Himalayan foothills, 4,000-6,700 feet above sea level. This includes an agricultural programme; establishing measures to improve soil and moisture conservation; horticulture, vegetable and fodder production; energy conservation; and appropriate technology for villages.

Volunteers with relevant skills are required to assist in various activities related to watershed management, and in the administration of the project. There are also opportunities for unskilled volunteers to work in plant nurseries, planting seedlings and levelling the land. A maximum of four skilled and twenty unskilled volunteers are needed each year.

Ages 18-40. All volunteers must be prepared to work hard and learn from others. They should have a belief in basic human values and be ready to experience a different culture and respect it. Those wishing to take up skilled positions must have relevant experience in various aspects of watershed management. Working knowledge of English essential; Hindi desirable. **B D PH** must be able to manage in hilly terrain.

One month minimum

Food and accommodation provided. Cost £70 for skilled volunteers; £80 per month for unskilled. As the area is rural, volunteers should expect very basic living conditions. Volunteers pay own travel and insurance costs.

All volunteers must attend orientation course

Apply at least six months in advance

VIATORES CHRISTI

Viatores Christi, 38 Upper Gardiner Street, Dublin 2, Ireland

(353 1) 872 8027   Fax (353 1) 874 5731

Ethiopia, Ghana, Kenya, Liberia, Malawi, Nigeria, Sierra Leone, South Africa, Tanzania, Zambia, Zimbabwe; India; Grenada, Haiti, Jamaica, Trinidad; Argentina, Brazil, Chile, Venezuela. There are usually some volunteers involved in areas of need in Europe and North America.

A lay missionary association founded in 1960, dedicated to the active involvement of Catholic laity in the missionary work of the Church, with the task of recruiting, training and helping to place laity overseas in areas of need. It has the object of furthering the Church's work, of bringing Christ to people everywhere, and sharing skills in the process.

Most frequent requests are for teachers; medical personnel including doctors, nurses and laboratory technicians; social workers; catechists; agriculturists; and mechanics, carpenters, builders, electricians and engineers. Some volunteers work as full-time pastoral, development or youth workers. Volunteers fulfil a specific task, usually in which they have training or experience, passing on their skills so that local people will be able to continue when they leave.

Ages 21+; training can be given before this age. Relevant skills and experience preferred. Volunteers should be concerned, caring and practising Catholics with a desire to share in Christ's mission and spread the Gospel. They should be open to learn, adaptable, in good health, have a sense of humour, and suited to the work to be done. Whether single or married, applicants should be free of commitments, and should be resident in Ireland in order to attend training course.

One year minimum

Conditions depend on the requesting agency. Insurance, travel and usually board and lodging provided. Advice given on sponsorship.

Emphasis placed on the preparation programme, which comprises Christian formation, orientation and practical experience. Part-time orientation course lasts 9-12 months, depending on the individual's readiness and availability of suitable post. As a debriefing service, residential weekends and seminars are held; home involvement invited.

Recruitment all year

International newsletter; *Annual Report*

VINCENTIAN SERVICE CORPS

The Director, Vincentian Service Corps, 7800 Natural Bridge Road, St Louis, Missouri 63121, United States

(1 314) 382 2800 ext 249

In the UK apply to Coordinator, Vincentian Volunteers, St Michael's, 40 George Leigh Street, Ancoats, Manchester M4 5DG ✆ 0161-236 9360

Midwestern United States: San Antonio, St Louis, Chicago, Indianapolis and rural areas of Arkansas

A lay volunteer programme sponsored by the Daughters of Charity for men and women who want to serve the poor, live in community and experience a simple lifestyle.

Placements are generally in the fields of social services, education, health care and parish ministry, such as working as pastoral care staff in hospitals; nurses in clinics; teachers at schools; care providers for emotionally disturbed teenagers and people with physical handicaps; staff for transitional housing for the homeless; and parish staff working to meet the needs of inner city poor

Ages 18+. Applicants must have a real desire to serve the poor, flexibility, a sense of identity, a sense of humour, an openness to living in community and a willingness to explore personal and spiritual growth through service. All nationalities accepted; fluent English required, and Spanish is useful in some areas.

One year minimum, beginning August

Accommodation provided, plus $100 per month stipend and $80 per month to cover food costs. Costs of health insurance and of travel to and from St Louis to the placement site covered.

Compulsory one-week orientation course held in St Louis in August

Apply before 15 June

VSC News newsletter for current and former volunteers

VISIONS IN ACTION

Visions in Action, 3637 Fulton Street NW, Washington DC 20007, United States

(1 202) 625 7403

Burkina Faso, Kenya, Somalia, South Africa, Tanzania, Uganda, Zimbabwe; Dominican Republic
Possible future expansion to Brazil, Egypt, Mexico

An international not-for-profit organisation founded in 1988 out of the conviction that much can be learned from and contributed to the developing world, by working as part of a community of volunteers committed to social and economic justice

Opportunities for volunteers to be placed in non-profit development organisations working in the fields of business, health care, housing, environment, women's issues, family planning, youth work, research, journalism and Human Rights. Some 50-80 volunteers recruited each year.

Ages 20+. Volunteers must be committed to social justice and improving the lives of the world's poor; they should have a degree or equivalent experience and speak English, French or Spanish depending on placement. **B D PH W**

One year minimum; six months for volunteers in South Africa. Programmes throughout the year.

Participants are responsible for all travel and living expenses. Advice given on fundraising. Cost from US$3,400-US$3,800 covers accommodation, health and emergency evacuation insurance and US$50-US$100 pocket money per month. Accommodation is in a single or double room in a Visions group house.

Compulsory one month travelling orientation course with intensive language training

Apply 3 months in advance

Information leaflets; *The Visions in Action Fundraising Guide*

THE VOLUNTEER MISSIONARY MOVEMENT

The Regional Director, Volunteer Missionary Movement, Comboni House, London Road, Sunningdale, Ascot, Berkshire SL5 0JY

Ascot (01344) 875380

The Regional Director, VMM Scotland, Gillis College, 113 Whitehouse Loan, Edinburgh EH9 1BB

0131-452 8559

The Regional Director, VMM Ireland, High Park, Grace Park Road, Drumcondra, Dublin 9, Ireland

(353 1) 376565

Southern and eastern Africa: Bophutatswana, Kenya, Sierra Leone, South Africa, Tanzania, Uganda, Zambia, Zimbabwe

Founded in 1969 following the Second Vatican Council, VMM is an ecumenical movement within the Catholic Church which recruits, prepares and sends Christian volunteers with a skill or profession to work as lay missionaries in Catholic or other Christian mission projects linked with local churches. It is also involved in long-term development projects, mission awareness and development education in the UK.

Skilled volunteers are required to work in schools, hospitals, rural health centres, technical institutions and community development projects, where the aim is to help people help themselves. Work may be teaching, medical, administrative, pastoral, technical or agricultural. There are opportunities for experienced mechanics, builders, carpenters, plumbers, agriculturists, administrators, accountants, teachers of all subjects, nurses, midwives, doctors, laboratory technicians, pharmacists, physiotherapists and community development workers. Most volunteers work in rural areas which may be isolated, with limited social amenities. Recruits approx 40 volunteers annually.

Ages 21+. Applicants must have a Christian commitment, a concern for people and a desire to serve overseas motivated by a Christian faith.

continued overleaf

They need to be adaptable, stable and patient, capable of working independently, good at improvisation, with a sense of humour. Professional or technical qualifications required, plus at least 2 years' post-qualification experience in own trade or profession. Married couples without school-age children are accepted provided both are suitably qualified and available for work. All nationalities considered; applicants must speak good English and be willing to learn the basics of the local African language.

Two years minimum

Basic board and lodging, small allowance in local currency and return airfare provided. Volunteers contribute £134 towards insurance.

Successful applicants attend weekend introductory course. Compulsory 5 week residential preparatory course arranged; volunteers contribute £75 towards cost. Open house for returned volunteers; weekends and retreats organised.

Recruitment all year. Application process can take several months before final acceptance; delays may also be experienced in obtaining work permits.

Newsletter; information leaflets; *VMM Spirit and Lifestyle* booklet setting out the Movement's role in the Church.

VOLUNTEERS FOR LATVIA

Jana Teteris, Project Director, Volunteers For Latvia, World Federation of Free Latvians, Elizabetes Iela 63-3, Riga, LV1050, Latvia

(371 2) 227210

Inta Skinkis, Program Director USA, Volunteers For Latvia, American Latvian Association, PO Box 4578, 400 Hurley Avenue, Rockville, MD 20850, United States

(1 301) 340 8174

Throughout Latvia, mainly outside Riga, but also in other large towns

Established in 1990, Volunteers For Latvia is a joint project of the American Latvian Association and the World Federation of Free Latvians, which encourage Latvians and their supporters to assist in the rebuilding of an independent, democratic republic of Latvia

Volunteers are required to teach English, mainly to pupils in secondary schools; they may also be required to help teach the teachers themselves. Approx 15 placements available each year.

Ages approx 25-70. Applicants must be native English speakers with a degree in any discipline and a TEFL qualification. At least two years' teaching experience preferred. Knowledge of Russian or Latvian an asset; willingness to learn essential. Volunteers need to be independent, self-reliant individuals with cultural sensitivity and a sense of humour.

One academic year, August-June

Volunteers work a 21 hour week in return for accommodation and a local salary of approx Lat 60 per month (approx Lat 0.85 to £1). Return travel costs paid, but volunteers must arrange and pay for their own insurance.

Orientation course, including language training, held before beginning of placement

Apply by May for the following academic year

VSO

Enquiries Unit, VSO, 317 Putney Bridge Road, London SW15 2PN

0181-780 2266

Egypt, Gambia, Ghana, Guinea-Bissau, Kenya, Malawi, Mozambique, Namibia, Nigeria, São Tomé & Principe, Sierra Leone, South Africa, Tanzania, Uganda, Zambia, Zimbabwe;
Bangladesh, Bhutan, Maldives, Nepal, Pakistan, Sri Lanka;
Anguilla, Antigua, Dominica, Grenada, Montserrat, St Kitts, St Lucia, St Vincent, Turks and Caicos;
Cambodia, People's Republic of China, Indonesia, Laos, Thailand;
Belize, Guyana;
Fiji, Kiribati, Papua New Guinea, Philippines, Solomon Islands, Tonga, Tuvalu, Vanuatu

An independent organisation founded in 1958 with the aim of transferring practical experience, skills and expertise to developing countries. VSO enables men and women to work alongside people in poorer countries in order to share skills, build capabilities and promote international understanding and action in the pursuit of a more equitable world. Volunteers with relevant skills or qualifications are sent at the specific request of governments and local employers overseas, so that local counterparts can carry on the work once the volunteer's term of service expires. Volunteers are only sent to schemes which demonstrably help the appropriate community concerned, and all requests are evaluated against firmly established project criteria. There are more than 1,500 volunteers overseas at any one time working on projects in 50 developing countries.

The majority of requests are in the following fields:
Primary, secondary and tertiary education: TEFL, teacher training, librarianship, special education, home economics, commerce and science.
Health: midwives, doctors, physiotherapists, health visitors, community nurses, pharmacists, dentists, laboratory technicians, occupational/ speech therapists and nutritionists.
Technical trades, crafts and engineering: carpenters, bricklayers, joiners, plumbers, electricians, building instructors, mechanics, marine/civil engineers, technicians and technical teachers.

continued opposite

Agriculture: livestock and crop specialists, foresters, agricultural engineers, horticulturists, animal health and production specialists, fisheries experts and agricultural science teachers.
Social, community and business development: advisors to help set up small business, establish craft workshops and cottage industries, community social workers and instructors working with disabled people, town planners and architects, communications experts, systems analysts, journalists and solicitors.

Ages 20-70. Relevant qualifications essential, plus at least 2 years' relevant work experience. Applicants should have a genuine desire to assist in the long-term development of the developing world. They should be in good health, adaptable, prepared for life in a completely different culture, resilient in the face of frustrations, tolerant, have a sense of humour and a desire to combat all forms of exploitation. Couples without dependent children welcome, provided both partners have skills or qualifications acceptable to the programme and can be posted together. Volunteers should be living in the UK with unrestricted right of re-entry. **B D PH W**

Two years minimum

Accommodation provided by the host country. Volunteers live and work as members of the community, alongside their colleagues on similar pay. Airfare and other travel expenses, National Insurance contributions and payments to a specially arranged endowment plan plus medical insurance provided. A further grant is paid on return.

Compulsory course arranged in which volunteers learn to adapt their skills to the needs of the host country, with briefing on the country, health care and any special training they may need by nationals and returned volunteers. Debriefing and advice on resettlement provided on return.

Recruitment all year; most volunteers are sent out in September and January. There is an average of 6-8 months between receipt of application and departure.

Orbit quarterly magazine; *Annual Review*; information literature

WORLD ASSEMBLY OF YOUTH

Ms Maj-Britt Dahl, Administrative Associate, World Assembly of Youth (WAY), Ved Bellahøj 4, 2700 Brønshøj, Denmark

(45) 31 60 77 70

Brønshøj, Denmark

Founded in 1949, WAY is an international coordinating body of national youth councils and organisations. WAY recognises the Universal Declaration of Human Rights as the basis of its action and services, and works for the promotion of youth and youth organisations. Publishes youth related newsletters and organises workshops, seminars and training courses.

Offers two internships each year. Interns are responsible to the Secretary General of WAY; work primarily involves the writing, designing and carrying out of projects and workshops on a variety of youth related subjects

Ages 20-30. Applicants must have proven experience in youth work and an interest in development and international issues. They need to be self-motivated, able to work with little supervision, resourceful, flexible, in good health and accustomed to dealing with people from diverse cultures. They must be able to speak, read and write fluent English; French and Spanish also desirable. Preference given to applicants recommended by WAY member organisations. All nationalities accepted, with the exception of Danish residents.

Six months minimum

Interns work approx 40 hours per week. Accommodation provided in small apartment, possibly sharing with one other intern. US$500 paid as a scholarship at end of each month. Travel to and from Denmark is reimbursed. Interns are covered by the Danish social welfare system for all emergency and most general health needs.

Apply at any time

Information leaflets

SECTION V

PROFESSIONAL RECRUITMENT

BRITISH RED CROSS

Overseas Personnel, British Red Cross, 9 Grosvenor Crescent, London SW1X 7EJ

0171-235 5454

Mainly Africa, Asia and Eastern Europe/former Soviet Union

Founded in 1870, an independent voluntary organisation and part of a worldwide non-political, non-religious movement based on the fundamental principles of humanitarianism, neutrality and impartiality. As part of the International Red Cross, it has a statutory obligation to work for the improvement of health, the prevention of disease and the mitigation of suffering throughout the world.

Recruits qualified and experienced professionals to work with the International Red Cross overseas. Vacancies arise for senior managers; community and institutional development specialists; surgeons and anaesthetists; public health, operating theatre and surgical ward nurses; accountants and finance delegates; relief and logistics specialists; water/sanitation engineers; warehouse/workshop managers; information/press officers; other opportunities sometimes arise. Around 200 people are recruited each year.

Ages 25+. Applicants must be British residents or nationals, with relevant professional experience and qualifications. Previous experience of working in a developing country usually required.

Contracts are from 3-24 months

Salaries range from £15,000-£26,000 per year. Local daily allowance, accommodation, flights, excess baggage costs and insurance provided. Family status is possible on contracts of at least 12 months.

One week residential training course provided as part of briefing and induction package. Professional and personal debriefing.

Apply in writing to above address, enclosing cv

Red Cross News quarterly newsletter; *The Red Cross Then and Now*; Annual Review; International Red Cross publications concerning relief and development work

HEALTH UNLIMITED

The Administrator, Health Unlimited, 3 Stamford Street, London SE1 9NT

Africa, Asia, Latin America

Health Unlimited works in developing countries to improve the health of communities affected by conflict

Provides expert teams of medically qualified personnel to train trainers of community health workers and enable them to set up and run health systems at district and provincial level in developing countries. Some 10-15 people are recruited each year.

Maximum age limit 60. Only experienced, professionally qualified medical personnel or health educationalists are recruited. Applicants must have experience in developing countries, as well as a commitment, knowledge of development and sensitivity to the communities with whom they will be working. Knowledge of French or Spanish recommended.

1-2 years, depending on project

Personnel are paid at a rate of £600 per month for the first year, and £660 per month for the second year. Flights, insurance and accommodation provided.

Runs a 3 day Learning to Teach course twice a year in which recently enrolled team members may take part. Briefing provided to team members before they join a project, and debriefing on their return.

Apply in writing 6-12 months in advance.

Those unable to attend the Learning to Teach course can obtain a copy of the manual from the above address, price £6.50 plus postage

HELPAGE INTERNATIONAL

Personnel Department, HelpAge International, St James' Walk, London EC1R 0BE

0171-253 0253

Recruitment mainly for programmes in African countries, including Sudan, Tanzania and Mozambique; also in Cambodia

A network of 45 independent organisations working to improve the standard of living of poor, elderly people throughout the world. Through HelpAge International, member organisations can share their knowledge and experience, as well as drawing on a pool of financial and personnel resources. Members support or undertake work in the areas of health, disability, shelter, training, home-based care, income generation, refugees and emergency programmes.

Ophthalmologists and ophthalmic nurses are recruited to work alongside counterparts in programmes with a strong training element. Occasionally posts arise for social workers, occupational therapists etc, particularly those with a background of working with older people, as well as staff with skills in disaster and refugee situations.

Applicants should hold relevant qualifications, and have solid professional experience either in the UK or preferably in a developing country. Training experience is desirable as is the willingness to learn local languages. Applicants should be self-motivated, resourceful, adaptable to work in a different cultural and economic setting and able to communicate well at all levels.

1-2 years, depending on the post

Reasonable salary is offered, normally tax-free. Accommodation provided, and is of a basic but reasonable standard.

Comprehensive briefing and induction arranged before departure

Recruitment at different times of the year, depending on programme

Annual Report; Ageways; range of leaflets and other materials available

OVERSEAS DEVELOPMENT ADMINISTRATION

- Overseas Development Administration, Room AH354, Abercrombie House, Eaglesham Road, East Kilbride, Glasgow G75 8EA

- East Kilbride (01355) 844000

- Caribbean, Latin America, the Pacific, Asia and Africa

- Responsible for administering the British government's programme of aid to developing countries. Also assists in the recruitment of specialists for the field programmes of the United Nations and its specialised agencies such as FAO and the International Labour Office, as well as for its Junior Professional Officer Scheme.

- Vacancies occur on an *ad hoc* basis for graduates in natural science, education, engineering, accounting, law, medicine and veterinary science and are normally advertised in the national press and relevant professional journals

- Substantial postgraduate experience is normally required, but postgraduate study awards are also offered. **B D PH W** all overseas appointments are subject to medical clearance.

- Vacancies are usually 2-3 year contracts

- Recruitment all year. Enquiries stating brief personal details and requests for booklets should be sent to the above address, quoting reference number AH354/RDG.

- A number of useful free booklets such as *ODA Guide to Working Overseas for the Aid Programme*; *Organisations Concerned with Employment in Education*; *List of Non-Governmental Agencies*; *International Agencies and Other Bodies*; *Careers in the Geological Sciences*, and a booklet outlining the *Associate Professional Officers Scheme* are available on request.

OXFAM

Overseas Personnel Officer, Oxfam, 274 Banbury Road, Oxford OX2 7DZ

Oxford (01865) 311311

Africa, Asia, Eastern Europe, Latin America and the Caribbean, Middle East

Oxfam is a funding agency that exists primarily to provide finance for work to relieve and prevent suffering overseas, and to aid development. It does not itself normally carry out this work by sending expatriate personnel overseas, but prefers to operate by distributing money and resources through other organisations, agencies and local groups which have their own programmes in the field. It is therefore only occasionally possible for Oxfam to offer employment for work overseas.

Maintains a retrieval register of qualified people able to work overseas, mainly for emergency relief postings in the areas of health, water supply and sanitation, and logistics; or advisory posts, for example in primary health care programmes.

Vacancies are for people with specialist skills and qualifications, and previous relevant overseas experience. There is no demand for unqualified and unskilled staff. Full driving licence essential; language ability useful. Personnel must be fit and healthy, and prepared to live under what may be very difficult conditions, often in extreme climates.

The register includes those available to go overseas at short notice in response to an emergency, usually on 6 month contracts. Before joining the register applicants should ensure that they would be able to leave their present employment at short notice.

Oxfam meets all travel costs and pays a competitive salary. Depending on circumstances all accommodation and food costs are met or an allowance is allocated to cover them.

WORLD VISION UK

Overseas Recruitment Officer, World Vision UK, World Vision House, 599 Avebury Boulevard, Central Milton Keynes MK9 3PG

Milton Keynes (01908) 841005

Angola, Mali, Mauritania, Rwanda, Somalia, Sudan; Cambodia, Vietnam; CIS/Russia, Romania

Founded in 1950, part of the World Vision Partnership, an interdenominational Christian humanitarian organisation dedicated to serving God through childcare, emergency relief, community development, Christian leadership training and mission challenge. Operates in over 70 countries through local churches and community leaders in close cooperation with the United Nations and other international relief agencies.

World Vision seeks to employ local staff wherever possible and will only recruit staff to send overseas if it has not been possible to find a suitably-qualified person locally. They may recruit doctors, nurses, nutritionists, logisticians, vocational instructors, agriculturalists and income generation specialists.

Applicants must have Christian commitment, relevant skills, qualifications and experience, knowledge of French or Portuguese, and usually at least 3 years previous experience of working in the Third World. **B D PH**

One year minimum

Salary based on UK scales, board, lodging, travel and insurance provided

Orientation course provided

Quarterly magazine; *Annual Report;* leaflets giving information on various issues

All the essential advice and information you need to arrange a successful and enjoyable seasonal job is in the Central Bureau's information guide **WORKING HOLIDAYS**, acknowledged as *the* authoritative guide.

WORKING HOLIDAYS lists hundreds of employers offering over 99,000 temporary or seasonal jobs in Britain and 70 other countries. Whatever the job, in whatever country, **WORKING HOLIDAYS** gives very full details. Any age or nationality restrictions are noted, the period of work on offer, salary and terms, including whether travel, accommodation or insurance is included is listed, and application deadlines are given. But it doesn't stop there.

WORKING HOLIDAYS carries information on a wide range of other useful details: where and how to advertise for a job in a foreign newspaper, services of local youth information centres, useful publications to help you plan your visit, what work or residence permit you'll need and how to go about getting it, what medical precautions you should take, what insurance cover you should have, and what passports or visas will get you across borders. It lists addresses and telephone numbers of embassies, high

From picking pears in Australia to being an au pair in Greece; from excavating Inca remains in South America to restoring medieval castles in France; from teaching sports in the USA to cooking in Switzerland, **WORKING HOLIDAYS** has thousands of opportunities and a wealth of information to help you see the world.

commissions, youth and student travel offices, youth hostels, passport and tourist offices and other organisations to help you, tells you all about accommodation, insurance, health requirements, money and travel, and provides just about everything else you'll need not only to get a holiday job but to make the whole experience as fulfilling and trouble-free as possible.

Unlike some other guides, every piece of information in **WORKING HOLIDAYS** is checked each and every year, and updated against reports and other received information. Combine this with the latest in information technology we use to edit and produce the guide and you can be sure that the information you will be using to choose your holiday is right up to date.

WORKING HOLIDAYS has opportunities for those aged 12-70+, younger if accompanied; from 3 days up to a year; from Au pairs to Zoo staff; from Austria to Zimbabwe. It is available from all good bookshops or direct form the Central Bureau. For further information on the Bureau's publications and programmes contact the Information Desk on ✆ 0171-725 9402.

WORKING HOLIDAYS is published each November for the following year.

SECTION VI

SERVICE IN BRITAIN & IRELAND

ATD FOURTH WORLD

General Secretary, ATD Fourth World, 48 Addington Square, London SE5 7LB

Britain. For overseas opportunities see page 71

Supports the efforts of the poorest in overcoming poverty and taking an active role in their communities. Involved in grass roots projects, the approach is tailored to the particular requirements in each community. Works to three core objectives: to breakdown ostracism endured by the poor; enable the poorest to participate in and contribute to society as a whole; and develop a constructive public awareness of poverty. It is not aligned with any political or religious group.

Potential volunteers participate in a working weekend and then a 3 month induction programme in London or Surrey, where they live and work alongside full-time workers and undertake manual and office work, assist in projects with poor families and learn about ATD through discussions, books and videos. They also join in planning and evaluation meetings and are expected to write about their experiences. Accommodation provided and, after the second month, a small allowance. Can stay on as workers in Britain, become friends of ATD, encouraging the public to view the very poor as useful members of society, or become core workers abroad,

Ages 18+. No professional/academic requirements; everyone welcome. Applicants should have a genuine interest in learning from the experiences and hopes of very disadvantaged communities as a vital first step to building a future with them, and a willingness to work hard with others in a team.

Three months minimum

Accommodation provided; volunteers pay food expenses for first month; subsequent increments up to the minimum salary all workers receive after one year

Working weekend acts as selection period; 3 month induction programme in Britain followed by several weeks in France before joining a team. Intensive in-service training for new volunteers during the first two years.

Recruitment all year; applicants should enclose an A3 SAE

Emergence from Extreme Poverty, a book describing the nature of the work of the permanent volunteers on behalf of the poorest families in Europe

BEANNACHAR LTD

Elisabeth Phethean, Housemother, Beannachar, Banchory-Devenick, Aberdeen AB1 5YL

Aberdeen (01224) 861825/868605/861200

Outskirts of Aberdeen

Camphill community for further education and training, with the aims of providing meaningful work and a home for young adults with varying degrees of handicap or disturbance.

Volunteers are required to help care for students and work with them on a communal basis. Work involves gardening, cooking, cleaning, laundry, looking after animals, candle making and weaving. Volunteers are also expected to participate in other community activities such as folk dancing, drama, festivals, walking, swimming, games and outings.

Ages 19+. Volunteers should be enthusiastic, caring and willing to learn, with a sense of responsibility and initiative. No previous experience or qualifications necessary.

6-12+ months; some short-term summer placements available

Volunteers work a 6 day week and receive £20 per week pocket money, plus full board and lodging in the community. Students and staff live together in 2 large family units and a smaller, new, purpose-built house. Volunteers staying 12 months or more have return journey home paid.

Recruitment all year

CAMPHILL RUDOLF STEINER SCHOOLS

Central Office, Camphill Rudolf Steiner Schools, Murtle Estate, Bieldside, Aberdeen AB1 9EP

Aberdeen (01224) 867935

Outside Aberdeen, Scotland

Founded in 1939 by the late Dr Karl König, the Camphill schools offer residential schooling and therapy, based on the teachings of Rudolf Steiner, for children and young adults in need of special care. Members of staff and their families live with the 155 pupils in 16 separate house communities on the three small estates that comprise the Schools' grounds.

Co-workers are required to live with children in family units, helping with the care of children and the running of the house and garden, and of the estate. Approx 80 volunteers are recruited each year.

Ages 20-40. No previous experience or qualifications required, but applicants should have an open mind and an interest in children, community life, curative education and anthroposophy.

Twelve months minimum, beginning August, late October, early January and late April

Co-workers receive board and lodging plus £23 per week pocket money. There is one day off each week, otherwise no separation between on and off duty. Return travel costs to home country (within Europe) provided after 1 year.

Orientation course provided

Recruitment all year; apply at least 6 months in advance

THE CAMPHILL VILLAGE TRUST

The Secretary, Camphill Village Trust, Delrow House, Hilfield Lane, Aldenham, Watford, Hertfordshire WD2 8DJ

Watford (01923) 856006

Throughout the UK

A charity founded in 1955, aiming to provide a new and constructive way of life for mentally handicapped adults, assisting them to individual independence and social adjustment within the communities of the Trust. It guides them towards open employment while helping them to achieve full integration within society as a whole, by providing a home, work, further education and general care. The centres are based on Rudolf Steiner principles.

Volunteers are needed to work alongside the residents in every aspect of communal life at centres where the handicapped can establish themselves, work and lead a normal family life in a social background. There are three villages offering employment, two town houses for those in open employment, a college, and centres for agriculture, horticulture and assessment. Volunteers work in gardens and farms run on organic principles, craft workshops, bakeries, laundries, printing presses, and participate in the general life and chores of the community. Special emphasis is placed on social, cultural and recreational life.

Ages 20+. Applicants should have an interest and understanding in work with the mentally handicapped and be prepared to live in the same manner as the residents. Experience not essential, but an advantage. All nationalities considered. Good command of English necessary.

One year minimum, if possible

Board, lodging, and a small amount of pocket money provided; one day off per week

Recruitment all year

Annual report; *CVT News* regular magazine; information booklet

CAREFORCE

Philip McAleese, Careforce, 577 Kingston Road, London SW20 8SA

0181-543 8671

Throughout the UK and Irish Republic

Careforce serves evangelical churches and organisations by placing Christian volunteers where their help is most needed. Enables volunteers to offer themselves to serve God in an area of need for 10-12 months and to share fully in the life of a Christian community.

Volunteer placements include serving with local churches; youth and schools work; evangelistic outreach; serving people who are homeless, have drug/alcohol related problems, have a physical disability, have learning difficulties, are from families facing difficulty or are elderly. Approx 120 placements arranged each year.

Ages 18-23. Applicants should be committed evangelical Christians, willing to be placed where they are most needed, to serve and to learn. No previous experience or qualifications necessary. British/Irish nationals only. **B D PH W**

10-12 months, beginning September

Volunteers work approx 40 hours per week. Full board and lodging with a family, in a flat or residential home provided, plus insurance cover and travel costs at beginning and end of placement. Volunteers receive £23 per week pocket money.

Two day course organised during first month of placement and halfway through the year

Applications accepted from September onwards. Initial interviews take place nationwide from January to August.

Information leaflets and annual newsletter

COMMUNITY SERVICE VOLUNTEERS

Volunteer Programme, Community Service Volunteers, 237 Pentonville Road, London N1 9NJ

0171-278 6601

Throughout the UK

A national volunteer agency inviting all young people to experience the challenge, excitement and reward of helping people in need. For over 30 years CSV has seen the unique contribution that volunteers make to the lives of those they help.

Over 3,000 volunteers are placed each year in some 700 projects. Volunteers are placed according to their interests, personality, experience and the needs of the project; work is usually with individuals or small groups, not in large institutions. Project examples include independent living projects which enable individuals or families with personal difficulties or disabilities to live in their own home; volunteers also work in group homes for people who may have a learning difficulty, who are leaving care, or who are recovering from mental illness, helping residents to lead their own lives as fully as possible. Some placements are in hostels for homeless young people; volunteers help with administrative tasks and housework, and spend time befriending residents, talking and listening to them and helping them.

Ages 16-35. Applicants should have enthusiasm, energy and a commitment to helping others. No academic qualifications or previous experience necessary. No one who applies is rejected. **B D PH W**

4-12 months

Volunteers are placed away from their home area. Full board, accommodation and £21 weekly allowance provided. 40 hour week. Overseas volunteers pay £440 placement fee.

Each placement is reviewed after one month, and CSV staff liaise with the volunteer and project organiser throughout the placement. One person on every project is assigned to the volunteer for support and regular supervision.

Recruitment all year; placements take 6-8 weeks to arrange

Annual Review; various information leaflets, brochures and newsletters

THE CORRYMEELA COMMUNITY

The Volunteer Coordinator, The Corrymeela Community, Ballycastle, Co Antrim, BT54 6QU

Ballycastle (0126 57) 62626

Northern Ireland

Founded in 1965, Corrymeela is an open village, comprising a house, cottages and youth village, supported by the Corrymeela Community, a group drawn from many different Christian traditions who work for reconciliation in Northern Ireland in conflict situations and promote a concern for peace and justice in the wider world. People under stress, such as those from problem areas, families of prisoners, the disabled, go to Corrymeela for a break or holiday; conferences and other activities challenge participants to look critically at contemporary issues.

Limited number of volunteers needed to participate in the programme work of the residential centre, working with the groups who use the centre and being the link during their stay. They should expect to be involved in the practical aspects of running the establishment, assisting with catering arrangements, preparing accommodation, and working in the kitchen, laundry or reception. Usually 10 long-term volunteers are recruited each year, 5 from Ireland, 5 from overseas.

Ages 18-30. Experience of community life and working with people helpful but not essential. Applicants must be fit and adaptable to cope with the demands and pressures of community life and a very busy programme, good at communicating with others and committed to the process of reconciliation. Open to all ages, backgrounds and traditions. All nationalities considered; good command of English essential.

One year, starting September or 6 months from March

Accommodation in twin bedrooms with all meals, £20 per week pocket money and emergency medical/dental cover provided. Each volunteer receives an agreed sum to help pay for travel home. Six days free per month; 1 week's holiday for every 3 months service.

Prospective volunteers spend a few days at Corrymeela before applying. One week induction period after acceptance. Weekly briefing and reflection programme with full-time coordinator. Great care taken in terms of staff support, external consultancy and pastoral access.

Apply December-February; interviews held in April

COTSWOLD COMMUNITY

John Whitwell, Principal, Cotswold Community, Ashton Keynes, Swindon, Wiltshire SN6 6QU

Cirencester (01285) 861239

North Wiltshire

Founded in 1967, the Cotswold Community is a village-type community catering for approximately 40 abused and emotionally disturbed boys between the ages of 9-18. The boys live in four separate groups and their therapy lasts 3-5 years.

Opportunities for volunteers in childcare and education. Volunteers are based in one of four group-living households caring for boys; or work in the education area, assisting in the classroom and spending a small amount of time in a household. Approx 6 placements each year.

Ages 20+. Volunteers should be hardworking, able to cope under pressure, have a sense of fun, enjoy working with children and an interest in the underlying causes of behaviour. Previous experience of looking after children required. Skills in music, art and outdoor education useful. All volunteers must speak English.

Four months minimum

Board and lodging, £22.50 per week pocket money, insurance and travel costs within the UK provided. Volunteers from overseas pay own travel costs.

2-3 day induction programme prior to placement for UK volunteers; induction for overseas volunteers on arrival. Staff support, supervision and training programme provided.

Apply at least two months in advance

THE CRYPT FOUNDATION

Mrs G Purvis, The CRYPT Foundation, Forum, Stirling Road, Chichester, West Sussex PO19 2EN

Nottingham and West Sussex, UK

Established in 1981, the CRYPT (Creative Young People Together) Foundation is a registered national charity providing small group homes for young people with disabilities, allowing them opportunities to further their artistic skills or interests

Approx 40 placements available each year for volunteers to act as personal care staff. Work may involve meeting the disabled person's personal needs such as washing, bathing, toileting, dressing and lifting; accompanying them to lectures and on other outings; assisting with domestic tasks such as cooking, cleaning and washing; and attending meetings, seminars and conferences as appropriate.

Ages 18-30. Experience not necessary, but volunteers should have a caring attitude and be prepared to work hard.

Four months minimum

Working hours are determined by the project coordinator, in consultation with the volunteer. In general, volunteers work 24 hours on-duty, followed by 24 hours off-duty, with alternate weekends free, sleeping in at the project on a rota basis (roughly 4 nights over 2 weeks). Board and accommodation provided, plus £20-£25 per week pocket money. Travel expenses within the UK may be covered, depending on length of time worked.

All volunteers must attend an orientation course before placement begins. Regular supervision and assessment sessions are held during placement.

Apply 3-6 months in advance. Overseas applicants should apply direct; UK applicants should apply through Community Service Volunteers, see page 169.

Information leaflets

EDINBURGH CYRENIANS

Director, Edinburgh Cyrenians, 20 Broughton Place, Edinburgh EH1 3RX

0131-556 4971

Edinburgh and West Lothian

Set up in June 1968 to develop self-help schemes for young homeless single people, the Edinburgh Cyrenian Trust runs a city community in central Edinburgh and a rural project on a small organic farm in West Lothian. Residents are a mix of young people referred by social workers, hospitals or other agencies.

Volunteers live and work alongside residents and other volunteers, sharing the jobs involved in running a large household, with particular responsibility for organising social activities, motivating people, attending weekly meetings, forming helpful relationships with community members and offering assistance and support to residents. Community life is challenging, difficult and stressful, but can also be extremely rewarding. Some 22 volunteers are recruited annually.

Ages 18-30. Applicants should have personal commitment, open-mindedness, willingness to learn, a sense of responsibility, energy, enthusiasm and a sense of humour. No previous experience or qualifications required. All nationalities accepted; working knowledge of English essential. **B D PH** unsuitable for wheelchairs.

6+ months

Volunteers work a 5 day week and receive full board accommodation in the community, with access to a flat away from the community on days off. £24 per week pocket money provided, plus £160 grant for 1 week's holiday after 3 months, £30 clothing allowance and £135 leaving grant after 6 months.

Regular training given and volunteers are supervised by non-residential social workers

Recruitment all year

Annual Report; information pack

GLASGOW SIMON COMMUNITY

Volunteer Coordinator, Glasgow Simon Community, 69 Dixon Road, Govanhill, Glasgow, G42 8AT

0141-423 0949

Glasgow, Scotland

Aims to offer time, friendship, practical help and supportive accommodation to men and women who have been homeless for some time

Volunteers contact and offer friendship and practical help to men and women who have experienced long-term homelessness, especially those who sleep rough. They work in small group homes alongside ex-homeless people, sharing in group living, giving and receiving support, and taking responsibility for money and medicines.

Ages 18+ Volunteers' attitudes are important; the community aims to accept people as they are, to live with them on an equal basis without patronising them. The work is demanding, so emotional stability and reasonable physical fitness are necessary.

Six months minimum

Volunteers work a 35 hour week on a rota basis with a maximum of 2 sleep-overs every 7 day period; separate living accommodation provided. A weekly personal allowance, holiday every three months and travel expenses provided.

Three week induction course, plus informal one-to-one training during the first month, with training visits to relevant agencies. Regular opportunities to participate in training events and attend conferences.

Recruitment all year; apply 3-6 months in advance

Learning to Care, Simon News, Annual Report

GREAT GEORGES PROJECT

The Duty Officer, Great Georges Project, The Blackie, Great George Street, Liverpool L1 5EW

0151-709 5109

Liverpool, UK

Founded in 1968, the Project, known locally as The Blackie, is a centre for experimental work in the arts, sports, games and education of today. Housed in a former church in an area typical of the modern inner-city - multi-racial, relatively poor, with a high crime rate and a high energy level - sometimes a lot of fun. Offers a wide range of cultural programmes, workshops and exhibitions, including pottery, sculpture, printing, film/video making, photography, painting, writing, outdoor plays, carpentry, puppetry, play structures, music, mime and dance. Open 7 days a week, 10.00-24.00.

Volunteers needed to work with children/adults in projects undertaken at the Project and in the local community, with endless opportunities to learn and create. The general work is shared as much as possible, with everyone doing some administration, cleaning, talking to visitors and playing games with the children. Recruits 100-150 volunteers annually.

Ages 18+. Applicants should have a good sense of humour, stamina, a readiness to learn, and a willingness to work hard and share any skills they may have. The children/young people who visit the Project are tough, intelligent, friendly and regard newcomers as a fair target for jokes, so the ability to exert discipline without being authoritarian is essential. No direct experience required. All nationalities considered. Good working knowledge of English needed.

1+ months, particularly at Christmas, Easter and summer

Accommodation in shared rooms at staff house; long-term volunteers may have own room. Vegetarian breakfast and evening meal provided; cooking on a rota basis. Those who can afford to, contribute approx £17.50 per week to cover food and housekeeping. Wages generally paid after six months. 12 hour day minimum, six day week, 1½ days off.

Orientation course includes a talk with films and a pack of literature

Recruitment all year

HOMES FOR HOMELESS PEOPLE

The Volunteer Recruitment Officer, Homes for Homeless People, 90-92 Bromham Road, Bedford, MK40 2QH

Bedford (01234) 210549

Throughout the UK

Founded in 1970, a national federation of local voluntary housing projects providing support and shared housing for the single homeless, who are amongst the most vulnerable and disadvantaged people in society, and whose housing needs are largely ignored. Encourages member groups to achieve a high standard of provision for their residents, and encourages residents to participate in decision-making. Provides a public information service and a volunteer recruitment and placement service.

Volunteers required to help operate homeless accommodation projects, living alongside and working for the benefit of homeless people. The work is challenging, rewarding and ideally suited to those aiming for a career in a caring profession. Some 30 volunteers recruited annually.

Ages 18-35. All nationalities considered. Fluent English essential. Applicants should have honesty, self-assurance, commonsense, the ability to mix with people from all walks of life, a sense of humour and a commitment to helping homeless people. Basic DIY skills and some experience of living away from home helpful.

6-12 months

Terms and conditions of work vary according to the project. Board, lodging, travel costs on joining and leaving the project and £30-£50 per week pocket money usually provided.

Briefing depends on individual project; all projects are encouraged to provide training, supervision and support There is usually a 2 week trial period for volunteers.

Recruitment all year

No Home of Their Own and *You Can't Put People in Little Boxes* leaflets

INDEPENDENT LIVING SCHEMES

Kenneth Smith & Dorothy Kendrick, Independent Living Schemes, Lewisham Social Services, Kingswear House, Dartmouth Road, Forest Hill, London SE23 3YE

0181-699 0111 ext 247/248   Fax 0181-291 5720

London Borough of Lewisham, south east London

Aims to enable severely disabled people (all wheelchair users) to lead the lifestyle of their choice, living in their own homes rather than in hospitals or residential care

Volunteer helpers carry out everyday tasks for the disabled person such as cooking, housework and shopping; assist with personal care including toileting, bathing and lifting; and share social, community and leisure activities

Ages 18-50. No experience necessary, just commonsense and a caring attitude. **B D PH** considered, depending on ability.

Six months minimum preferred

Rent-free accommodation sharing with other helpers is provided near to the scheme. Household bills, including council tax and local telephone calls are met and volunteers receive a weekly allowance of £20 pocket money and £35 for food. In addition, £15 per month is provided for clothing and leisure. Travel expenses paid within the UK at beginning and end of placement. One week's paid leave after 4 months.

Training given on project. Supervision and advice available from ILS team social workers and support/project worker.

Recruitment all year. Write, telephone or fax for application form and information pack.

JESUIT VOLUNTEER COMMUNITY (BRITAIN)

- The Promotion & Recruitment Coordinator, JVC Britain, St Wilfred's Enterprise Centre, Royce Road, Hulme, Manchester M15 5BJ

- 0161-226 6717

- Birmingham, Glasgow, Liverpool, Manchester, UK

- Established in 1987, recruits full-time volunteers for community placements in Britain

- Volunteers work alongside the homeless, victims of crime, people with learning difficulties, at advice centres and on local community projects. Some 25-30 volunteers are placed each year.

- Ages 18-35. No experience necessary. Applicants must be committed Christians, prepared to live according to the four JVC values of working for social justice, living in community, living simply and growing spiritually. **B D PH W**

- One year minimum, starting August

- Accommodation, £70 per week allowance and some travel costs provided

- Compulsory orientation programme at beginning of placement. Development programme throughout the year involves community weekend; spirituality weekend; social justice weekend; six day individually guided retreat; evaluation at year end.

- Apply January-June

L'ARCHE LIMITED

The General Secretary, L'Arche, 10 Briggate, Silsden, Keighley, West Yorkshire BD20 9JT

Keighley (01535) 656186

Bognor Regis, Brecon, Edinburgh, Inverness, Kent, Lambeth, Liverpool
Some opportunities also exist to serve with L'Arche overseas

An international federation of communities in which handicapped people and those who help them live, work and share their lives together. Founded in 1964 in northern France, there are now some 100 communities worldwide. L'Arche believe that each person, whether handicapped or not, has a unique and mysterious value; handicapped people are complete human beings and as such have the right to life, care, education and work. They also believe that those with less capacity for autonomy are capable of great love, and are loved by God in a special way. L'Arche was founded on a deep belief in the teachings of the Gospels and the simple, spiritual life is considered very important to L'Arche communities. L'Arche is a registered charity in the UK.

Assistants are required to share their lives with handicapped people, living and working as members of L'Arche communities. Some 60-70 assistants are recruited each year.

Ages 18-50. No previous experience necessary, but applicants must have a commitment to living in community and be interested in caring for disabled people. Communities are Christian based, but welcome people of all faiths, or none.

Twelve months minimum

Full board lodging, pocket money and insurance (employers' liability and personal) provided. Applicants pay own travel and personal expenses.

All placements involve a trial period of a week or weekend, with an exit interview at the end of the placement

Apply as far in advance as possible; no deadline

UK Newsletter; Letters of L'Arche quarterly journal; various books, leaflets, video and audio cassettes describing the history, philosophy and life of L'Arche communities.

LAND USE VOLUNTEERS

The Volunteer Coordinator, Land Use Volunteers, Horticultural Therapy, Goulds Ground, Vallis Way, Frome, Somerset BA11 3DW

Frome (01373) 464782

England and Wales

The Society for Horticultural Therapy is a non-profitmaking company founded in 1978 to help disabled and handicapped people enjoy and benefit from gardening, horticulture and agriculture. Land Use Volunteers, its volunteer service, is one of a wide range of practical services offered to disabled people and those who work with them.

Volunteers are needed to work with handicapped, disabled and disadvantaged people, living and working on rehabilitation projects on the basis of a common interest in plants and animals, to enable land use activities work more effectively. Past projects have included developing a small hospital market garden whilst working with psychiatric patients and care staff; working with adult mentally handicapped residents at a home farm, breeding rare domestic animals and organic growing; training clients and other care staff in simple horticultural tasks; and working with ex-drug addicts and offenders in planting and gardening. Also work with the physically handicapped, the hearing impaired, the blind, the elderly and disturbed young people.

Ages 18+. Applicants must have qualifications, skills and basic experience in agriculture, horticulture, forestry or any related environmental discipline and a willingness to transmit their skills to others. They should also be self-confident, adaptable and able to fit into a small community. Experience of working with people who have disabilities an advantage. **B D PH W**

6-12 months

Full board and lodging provided on or off site, plus at least £20 pocket money per week and initial travel expenses to project. One week vacation every four weeks, by arrangement with project management.

Recruitment all year

Annual Review; information leaflets; occasional papers; *Growth Point* newsletter; *Gardening is for Everyone* ideas for gardening with the handicapped; *Able to Garden*, practical guide for the disabled and elderly

LEONARD CHESHIRE FOUNDATION

Personnel Secretary, The Leonard Cheshire Foundation, Leonard Cheshire House, 26-29 Maunsel Street, London SW1P 2QN

0171-828 1822

Throughout the UK, though there are no Homes in Central London

A charitable trust founded in 1948, which now has some 260 Homes in 50 countries including over 80 in the UK. It has no boundaries of sex, creed or race, concerned only with the care of people with disabilities. The common aim of all Cheshire Homes is to provide care and shelter in an atmosphere as close as possible to that of a family home; residents are encouraged to lead the most active life their disabilities permit and to participate in the running of the Home and decisions affecting it.

Volunteers are needed in many Homes to assist with the general care of residents who require help in personal matters, including washing, dressing, toileting and feeding, as well as with hobbies, letter writing, driving, going on outings or holidays and other recreational activities. Recruits some 100 volunteers annually.

Ages 18-30. Applicants must have an interest in and a desire to help the handicapped; the work is hard and requires understanding and dedication. Previous experience useful but not essential. Preference generally given to those planning to take up medical or social work as a career. Volunteers must be adaptable, dedicated, hard working, punctual and willing to undertake a wide variety of tasks.

3-12 months

Volunteers work a 37½ hour, 5 day week. Board, lodging and at least £27 per week pocket money provided. Travel costs paid by volunteer.

Recruitment all year. More jobs available in summer than winter.

Annual Report; information leaflets

LOCH ARTHUR VILLAGE COMMUNITY

- Admissions Officer, Loch Arthur Village Community, Camphill Village Trust, Beeswing, Dumfries DG2 8JQ

- Kirkgunzeon (0138 776) 687

- Dumfriesshire, Scotland

- A Camphill village community providing a home, work, further education and general care for approx 30 handicapped adults. The community consists of 6 houses, a farm, a vegetable garden, craft workshops and a 500 acre estate.

- Volunteers are needed to live and work alongside residents in every aspect of life, including bathing, dressing and other personal tasks. Main areas of work are on the farm and in the garden, houses and workshops. Volunteers are also encouraged to take part in the community's cultural, recreational and social activities.

- Ages 18+. Volunteers should be open, caring, enthusiastic and willing to help wherever they are needed. No previous experience or qualifications necessary.

- Twelve month commitment preferred. Some short-term placements available in summer, minimum stay 6 weeks.

- Full board accommodation provided in the community, plus pocket money

- Ongoing instruction is given by experienced co-workers, plus formal introductory course sessions on a regular basis

- Recruitment all year; apply at least 2 months in advance

LOTHLORIEN (ROKPA TRUST)

Project Manager, Lothlorien (Rokpa Trust), Corsock, Castle Douglas, Kirkudbrightshire DG7 3DR

Castle Douglas (016444) 644

South west Scotland

Established in 1978, Lothlorien consists of a large log cabin set in 17 acres of grounds containing vegetable gardens, woodland, fields, workshops and outbuildings. It functions as a supportive community with everyone encouraged to participate in its daily running.
The guiding principals of the community are hospitality, care and respect for the person, and a belief that the potential of the individual can be encouraged through communal life, to which all have a contribution to make. There is accommodation for fourteen people, including four volunteers.

Volunteers live and work alongside people who may have had a crisis in their lives through mental illness, stress, other mental, physical or emotional problems. Together with the permanent staff volunteers make up a core group who are responsible for day to day management and providing a continuity of support to residents.

Ages 21+. Volunteers are sought with a caring, flexible and gregarious attitude. No previous experience or qualifications are necessary, but those with special skills are encouraged to use them where appropriate and to involve other residents in their activities.

Six months minimum

Board and lodging provided, and volunteers receive £25 per week pocket money. Two weeks leave within six month period.

Training and supervision provided

Recruitment all year

NANSEN SOCIETY (UK) LTD

Volunteer Organiser, Nansen Society (UK) Ltd, Redcastle Station, Muir-of-Ord, Ross-shire IV6 7RX

Muir-of-Ord (01463) 871255   Fax (01463) 870258

Scottish Highlands

A non-governmental organisation and registered charity, motivated in its aims by the humanitarian and adventurous deeds of the explorer Fridtjof Nansen. Much of its work is concerned with helping young people with emotional and behavioural difficulties to gain greater control over their own lives and contribute more positively to others. Runs a youth training project at Redcastle Station and, linked to this, a permaculture project at a farm 6 miles away.

Volunteers are required to live and work with youth trainees. Responsibilities may include work on the farm or nature trail; restoration and general maintenance work; or teaching office skills, library skills, car mechanics, domestic work and basic life skills such as reading and writing. There may also be duties related to the general administration of the project and meetings with external bodies.

Ages 21+. Previous experience desirable, for example in teaching young people with special needs, outdoor education, farmwork or conservation. Good spoken English essential. Applicants should be able to motivate young people and fit in with the community.

1+ months

Full board accommodation provided, plus £25 per week pocket money for those staying longer than 3 months. Volunteers pay own travel and insurance costs.

Regular meetings held to discuss activities, share experiences and plan future action

Recruitment all year

PARADISE COMMUNITY

The Principal, Paradise Community, Paradise House, Painswick, Gloucestershire GL6 6TN

Painswick (01452) 812376

In the Gloucestershire Cotswolds, between Stroud and Cheltenham

Founded in 1976, aims to provide long-term homes for people in need of special care and to create training, employment and leisure activities within a therapeutic environment, based on the principles of Rudolf Steiner. Comprises some 50 people of all ages including about 30 mentally handicapped adults. It has a smallholding and vegetable garden run on bio-dynamic lines, as well as a variety of crafts workshops.

Volunteers are needed to look after small groups of mentally handicapped people in a family atmosphere, to train them to do useful, meaningful tasks, look after their needs and give them the education and opportunities they require and deserve. Volunteers assist in the running of craft workshops, classes, the house, garden and farm, and the provision of leisure activities. 6-12 volunteers are recruited annually.

Ages 18-25. No special skills or experience required; enthusiasm is considered the main qualification. Applicants should also have a generosity of spirit, be physically and mentally fit and willing to work hard. All nationalities considered, but good spoken English is essential.

6-12 months

Accommodation in single or shared rooms, all meals, £20 per week pocket money plus £8 holiday money per week and work clothes, where required, provided. Hours variable, with one day off per week, 2 weeks holiday in the first 6 months (around Christmas and Easter). Further holidays according to length of stay.

First 4 weeks considered a trial period. Introductory training concurrent with the work.

Recruitment all year

Information leaflet

ST CHRISTOPHER'S HOSPICE

Andrew Knight, Chief Nurse, St Christopher's Hospice, 51-59 Lawrie Park Road, Sydenham, London SE26 6DZ

0181-778 9252

London, UK

Established in September 1967, St Christopher's Hospice provides in-patient and home care for terminally ill patients with cancer, AIDS and motor neurone disease. It also has a separate facility caring for the frail elderly.

Placements for 16 volunteers a year to work as nursing auxiliaries in wards and in nursing home

Ages 17-60. Nursing or paramedical qualifications desirable. Applicants who have experienced bereavement or loss preferred, as volunteers must have an understanding of the dying process and the maturity to be able to work alongside professional carers in the care of the dying. They should also be able to show a sense of commitment and an understanding of where a volunteer placement will fit within their chosen career path.

2-8 week summer programme runs from June to end September; Christmas programme runs 2+ weeks from mid December

Board and lodging provided in return for 37 hour week. Volunteers pay own travel costs.

Volunteers are mentored and supervised throughout placement. Debriefing held on departure.

Apply in March for summer programme; in November for Christmas programme

Information leaflets

SHARE DISCOVERY 80 LTD

Norma Heap, Share Holiday Village, Smiths Strand, Lisnaskea, Co Fermanagh, BT92 0EQ

Lisnaskea (013657) 22122

Lisnaskea, Northern Ireland

A residential activity centre for handicapped and able-bodied people, situated on a 30 acre site on the shores of Upper Lough Erne, Co Fermanagh

Twelve placements available each year for volunteers to act as companions to disabled guests needing assistance during their stay

Ages 18-45. Experience not essential. Applicants need to be enthusiastic and caring, with good spoken English.

3-12 months

Volunteers work a 40 hour week in return for board, lodging and £10 per week pocket money. Public liability insurance cover provided. Volunteers arrange and pay for own travel costs.

Orientation course available

Recruitment all year

THE SIMON COMMUNITY

The Community Leaders, The Simon Community, PO Box 1187, London NW5 4HW

0171-485 6639

London and Kent

Founded in 1963, committed to caring and campaigning for and with the homeless and rootless. Catholic founded and inspired, ecumenical in action with members of all faiths and none. Residents are men and women, young and old, who have been rejected by society and without support have slipped through the net of the welfare state. A night shelter, community houses and a farmhouse comprise a tier system enabling residents find the appropriate level of support.

Volunteers live and work with residents, helping them obtain medical care and social security, referral, fundraising and campaigning, cooking, administration, going out with tea and sandwiches to make contact with homeless people and helping at a night shelter. Non-residential openings for regular part-time volunteers for specific functions such as driving or street work. Emotionally demanding work, dealing with problems including alcoholism, drug addiction and psychiatric disorders; of particular interest to those seriously considering social work.

Ages 19+. Applicants should have a commitment to, and perception of, the Community's aims and philosophy, a willingness to learn and adapt, the ability to relate and respond to people, and must be caring, mature and stable enough to take the burden of other people's problems while retaining their own balance. Volunteers should be capable of taking initiatives within a team framework, learning to cope with crises; a sense of humour is an asset. Qualifications or experience not essential. All nationalities accepted; good command of English necessary.

Three months minimum, 6 months or more preferred

Workers live alongside residents, sharing the same facilities/conditions; accommodation can be basic. Pocket money £20 per week. Average 16 hour day; 1 day per week free. Fourteen days leave after 3 months.

Volunteers are required to do a weekend's orientation before a decision is taken whether to accept or not. Training is given within the project.

Recruitment all year; apply 1 month in advance

Information leaflets; *Caring on Skid Row; No Fixed Abode; The Untouchables*

SIMON COMMUNITY (IRELAND)

The Recruitment Coordinator, Simon Community (National Office), PO Box 1022, Dublin 1, Ireland

(353 1) 671 1606

Cork, Dublin, Dundalk and Galway

A voluntary body offering support and accommodation to the long-term homeless at night shelters and residential long-stay houses in Cork, Dublin, Dundalk and Galway. Full-time work in Simon is demanding and involves a very full commitment to people who will be difficult and who will challenge the volunteer's motivation and feelings. It does not suit everyone, yet for those whom it does it can be a very rewarding and enriching experience.

Volunteers are required to work full-time on a residential basis, living-in and sharing food with residents, taking responsibility for household chores and working to create an atmosphere of trust, acceptance and friendship by talking and listening, and befriending residents.

Ages 18-35, older applicants considered. Applicants should be mature, responsible individuals with an understanding of, and empathy for homeless people. Tolerance and an ability to get on with people and work as part of a team are also essential. No experience or qualifications necessary. All nationalities welcome; good standard of spoken English essential.

3+ months; first month is probationary period

Volunteers work 3 days on and 2 days off, with 2 weeks holiday entitlement every 3 months. Full board and lodging on the project provided, plus a flat away from the project on days off. Volunteers receive an allowance of IR£34 per week; insurance provided, but not travel costs.

Training on-site is given by project leaders. Workshops on relevant topics take place throughout the year.

Recruitment all year

STALLCOMBE HOUSE LTD

Maureen Wright, Stallcombe House, Sanctuary Lane, Woodbury Salterton, Devon EX5 1EX

Woodbury (01395) 232373

Devon, UK

Founded in 1981, Stallcombe House is a 55 acre working farm community for adults with a mental disability. An integral part of the nationwide programme to close long-stay mental handicap hospitals and integrate the former patients into the wider community, Stallcombe believes that residents should have similar opportunities to those who are not handicapped and a quality of life that enables them to reach their full potential. Initially funded by the health authority and social services, today Stallcombe is run independently with support from the DSS and local social services.

Full time volunteers are needed to help run the household and care for residents, work in the garden and help on the organic farm. Approx 6 volunteers are recruited each year.

Ages 18+. No experience necessary; volunteers must be flexible, willing to learn, have a go at new jobs, be able to make contact with residents and have a sense of humour. Interpersonal and practical skills useful; English essential. **D PH**

Six months minimum

Board, lodging, insurance and £25 pocket money per week provided. Volunteers pay own travel expenses. Two days free each week, plus two days holiday after each month. Volunteers work a 38 hour week on the same rota as staff.

An induction course and debriefing are provided

Apply 6-12 months in advance

SUE RYDER FOUNDATION

The Administration Officer, Sue Ryder Foundation, Sue Ryder Home, Cavendish, Sudbury, Suffolk CO10 8AY

Glemsford (01787) 280252

England and Scotland

A charity founded in 1952 with over 80 homes throughout the world, primarily for the disabled and incurable, but also admitting those who, on discharge from hospital, still need care and attention. The aim is to provide residents with a family sense of being at home, each with something to contribute to the common good. Seeks to render personal service to those in need and to give affection to those who are unloved, regardless of age, race or creed. The homes are a living memorial to the millions who gave their lives during two world wars in defence of human values, and to the countless others who are suffering and dying today as a result of persecution.

Volunteers are needed at headquarters and sometimes in other homes. Work includes helping with patients, routine office work, assisting in the kitchen, garden, museum, coffee and gift shop at headquarters, general maintenance and other essential work arising. Experienced volunteers also needed for secretarial work and nursing.

Ages 16+. Applicants should be flexible and adaptable. A keen interest in caring work is desirable. Qualifications or experience not essential, but an advantage; preference given to students or graduates. Doctor's certificate required. All nationalities considered; good standard of English required.

Two months minimum

Board, lodging and £10 per week pocket money provided

Two week trial period. On the job instruction provided.

Recruitment all year; larger number of volunteers required in summer

THE TIME FOR GOD SCHEME

The Director, The Time For God Scheme, 2 Chester House, Pages Lane, London N10 1PR

0181-883 1504

Throughout the UK

Aims to offer young people the chance to explore their Christian faith and themselves through voluntary service in a supportive framework. An independent charity, governed by the Anglican, Baptist, Catholic, Congregational, Methodist and United Reformed Churches, the Church Army and the National YMCA Councils for England and Scotland.

Volunteers work in community centres, care homes, churches, hostels for the homeless, YMCAs and outdoor pursuits centres. Work can involve arranging activities for youth groups or residents; being good listeners at a community drop-in or lunch clubs for elderly people; visiting people and building up relationships; helping care for disabled children; and helping with typing and other administration. Some work in cities, others in rural and suburban areas. All projects are Christian based. Recruits approx 250 volunteers each year. **B D PH W**

Ages 17-25; overseas volunteers 18+. Volunteers need to be committed Christians or genuinely searching for a Christian faith, have a concern for others, willing to accept the challenge of Christian service, wishing to be involved in God's work in the world and normally recommended by a local church. Experience not necessary. Those with voluntary work experience can be placed in appropriately challenging placements.

6-12 months; 12 months minimum for volunteers from overseas.

Full board and lodging in private house, staff quarters or self-catering flat and £22 per week pocket money provided. Return fare paid for initial visit and every 3 months of service. 40 hour week, 1 week's leave after 3 months. UK volunteers' home church invited to contribute £350 towards training; help given where this is not available. Overseas volunteers pay £550 to cover registration fee and training.

3-4 day preparation course; mid-service course; 2 day end of service gathering. Training programme seen as essential part of the service. All volunteers receive support, supervision and visits during the year.

Starting dates in September and January each year. UK volunteers should apply 6-32 weeks in advance; overseas volunteers 6-12 months.

Information leaflets; newssheet

VINCENTIAN SERVICE CORPS

Coordinator, Vincentian Volunteers, St. Michael's, 40 George Leigh Street, Ancoats, Manchester M4 5DG

0161-236 9360

London, Manchester

A lay volunteer programme sponsored by the Daughters of Charity for men and women who want to serve the poor, live in community and experience a simple lifestyle.

Projects include caring for homeless and elderly people, prison service and pastoral and youth retreat work.

Ages 18+. Applicants must have a real desire to serve the poor, flexibility, a sense of identity, a sense of humour, an openness to living in community and a willingness to explore personal and spiritual growth through service. All nationalities accepted; fluent English required.

One year minimum, beginning August

Board and accommodation provided, plus £30 per week stipend. Volunteers must cover own expenses.

One week induction course, followed by five training sessions during the year; placements terminate with a retreat.

Apply before April

Options Newsletter for current and former volunteers

If you are fed up with being packaged on holiday; if you want to improve your language skills and make lasting friendships; if exams are looming and your vocabulary is a bit limited; if you really want to get to know a country, its language and culture, then the Central Bureau guide **HOME FROM HOME** will provide you with all the information needed to discover a different way of life in a way not possible when visiting as a mere tourist.

Being welcomed into the home of a foreign family offers an excellent opportunity to immerse yourself in another culture. All the essential advice and information needed to arrange a successful and enjoyable homestay, exchange, term stay or home exchange is in **HOME FROM HOME**, which details over 100 bona fide organisations arranging stays and exchanges in 50 countries worldwide. Each organisation is profiled, giving information on its aims and activities; an important factor is to have the most compatible host family, so full details of matching are provided. Information is also given on those organisations that can arrange language courses during the homestay or exchange.

Say L O to L A when you have a home exchange with a family in the US. Swap John for Jean-Pierre on a 2 week Anglo-French exchange. And make your own Soviet union when you stay with a family in Moscow. **HOME FROM HOME** *has hundreds of opportunities and a wealth of information to help you discover a different way of life.*

Most host families are only too happy to include visitors in their activities, but where additional leisure or sport activities are available, **HOME FROM HOME** provides details on those too. The full costs of the stay or programme are given, including any agency fee, meals, travel and insurance. Where additional costs are involved, for example escorted travel or tuition fees, these are also indicated.

As well as full information on each homestay or exchange, **HOME FROM HOME** also gives practical advice on health, insurance requirements, visas, passports, travel, dealing with emergencies and guidelines for visitors as well as host families.

HOME FROM HOME has opportunities for those aged 8+; from 1 day to a whole year; from Austria to Uruguay; from Britain to Japan; from staying with a French family for two weeks to spending a year in school in Canada; from swapping your home in Britain for a holiday in one in the USA. For further information on the Bureau's publications and programmes contact the Information Desk on ✆ 0171-725 9402.

HOME FROM HOME is published biannually   Third edition   ISBN 0 900087 99 4   £8.99

SECTION VII

NON-RESIDENTIAL SERVICE

SHORT-TERM VOLUNTARY WORK

ACET

Volunteer Trainer, ACET, AIDS Care Education and Training, PO Box 3693, London SW15 2BQ

0181-780 0400

London

A national Christian charity set up in 1988 to provide practical care to people living at home with HIV/AIDS. Also works for AIDS prevention, providing AIDS education in schools and organising training and awareness initiatives.

Volunteers provide practical home care for those ill with HIV/AIDS, including tasks such as shopping, cooking, driving and housework. Some 12-15 volunteers recruited each year.

Ages 20-60+. No experience or qualifications necessary, just commonsense and a sympathetic attitude. All volunteers are Christian, and applicants must be part of a church which can provide them with support.

Commitment usually six weeks to three months

Flexible time commitment. Public and employer's liability insurance cover and travel expenses within London provided.

All volunteers must attend a training programme; these are held every two months

Ongoing recruitment

Annual Report, newsletters, factsheets, schools pack

ADFAM NATIONAL

Kathy Robson, Coordinator, ADFAM National, 5th Floor, Epworth House, 25 City Road, London EC1Y 1AA

0171-638 3700

London

Founded in 1984, the national charity for the families and friends of drug users. Provides help through a national telephone helpline, and through training people to work with families of drug users and/or to set up drug-related family support services.

Volunteers are required to work on the national telephone helpline offering confidential support and information to anyone worried about someone using drugs. Approx 15 volunteers are recruited each year.

Ages 21+. Volunteers should have an interest in caring for others and be prepared to offer emotional support rather than give advice.
No previous experience necessary, but volunteers need to be good listeners who are non-judgmental about other people's lifestyles.
Good command of English needed

6 months minimum

Volunteers work approx 3 hours per week. Employer's liability insurance cover and travel expenses up to £5 per session provided.

All volunteers must attend an eight week training course

No set deadline for applications. All prospective volunteers are interviewed to determine their suitability prior to acceptance onto training course and then as a volunteer.

Annual Report; information leaflets; quarterly newsletter

BOOK AID INTERNATIONAL

Book Aid International, 39-41 Coldharbour Lane, Camberwell, London SE5 9NR

0171-733 3577

Camberwell, south London

Founded in 1954, Book Aid International (formerly Ranfurly Library Service) is a registered charity which supports education, training and literacy in the developing world by sending over 500,000 books overseas every year in response to urgent requests. Each year over 1.5 million books are donated; unsuitable books are sold or recycled and funds are raised to buy books not available form donated stock.

Opportunities for library/warehouse volunteers, stamping, packing and shelving books. Office volunteers also needed, processing incoming mail, composing and typing letters, maintaining database and filing systems and dealing with routine telephone enquiries. Opportunities may arise in the fundraising department or in finance. Suitably qualified librarians may be offered the chance to select books to go overseas.

No specific age limits. No special skills or experience necessary, basic training provided. One year's general office administration and typing skills desirable for office volunteers; relevant experience or librarianship qualification essential for book selection. All volunteers must speak English, have a basic level of numeracy and literacy and the ability to work as part of a team. **D PH**

Three month commitment expected of part-time volunteers; two week placements also available

Most volunteers work 0900-1700, 1-2 days a week. Employer's liability insurance and travel costs within the London Travelcard area or equivalent provided.

Induction given

Ongoing recruitment

BRITISH DYSLEXIA ASSOCIATION

Helpline & Volunteer Coordinator, British Dyslexia Association, 98 London Road, Reading, Berkshire RG1 5AU

Reading (01734) 662677

Head office in Reading, 100 affiliated associations nationwide

Set up in 1972 to promote awareness of dyslexia/specific learning difficulty and to work locally and nationally to improve early identification, appropriate remediation and fair opportunities for all with this condition

Volunteers are needed to help with marketing, fundraising, general clerical work and staffing a telephone helpline. Those not local to Reading are referred to a local affiliated association. Approx 10 volunteers are recruited each year.

Ages 17+. Volunteers are recruited across a wide spectrum of experience, qualifications and ability. Applicants should be reliable, willing to learn, interested in the area in which they will be working, capable of working on their own initiative and of using discretion in confidential matters. **B D PH**

Six months minimum

Time commitment of at least one half day a week expected. Public/employer's liability insurance cover provided, and travel costs reimbursed.

Support and training provided

Ongoing recruitment

Annual Report; information leaflets

BRITISH LIMBLESS EX-SERVICE MEN'S ASSOCIATION

R R Holland, General Secretary, British Limbless Ex-Service Men's Association (BLESMA), 185-187 High Road, Chadwell Heath, Essex RM6 6NA

0181-590 1124

72 branches throughout England, Scotland and Wales

Founded in 1932, a national charity catering specifically for limbless serving and ex-service men and women, and also accepts responsibility for the dependants and widows of its members. It provides permanent and respite care and accommodation at two residential/nursing homes; offers a counselling and advice service; provides assistance in the form of grants or equipment; operates a welfare visiting service; organises rehabilitation programmes for amputees and helps to find suitable employment; provides limited funding for research and development into artificial limbs; and acts as consumer watchdog in respect of artificial limbs, wheelchairs and appliances.

Volunteers are needed to help run branches, organise social events and do fundraising

Ages 18-70. No specific experience or qualifications required, but some skills in administration, finance, welfare, counselling and care an advantage. Volunteers should be committed and dedicated, with an interest in disability and genuine empathy for limbless ex-service men. **PH**

No set minimum period, but long-term commitment appreciated

Hours worked are at the discretion of the volunteer, usually 2-4 hours per week. Public liability insurance cover and travel expenses provided.

Orientation can be arranged

Ongoing recruitment

Annual Report; *BLESMAG* quarterly newsletter

CAT SURVIVAL TRUST / THE EARTH

Dr Terry Moore, Honorary Director, Cat Survival Trust/The Earth, The Centre, Codicote Road, Welwyn, Hertfordshire AL6 9TU

Welwyn (01438) 716873/716478   Fax (01438) 717535

Welwyn, Hertfordshire

The Cat Survival Trust is a registered charity formed in 1976 to work for the conservation of endangered species of wild cat, originally through a captive breeding programme. This programme has, however, been suspended until better techniques for introducing captive-bred animals to the wild have been developed. The emphasis has shifted to the conservation of cats in their natural habitat by purchasing land for reserves. One reserve has already been established in Argentina, and there are plans to extend it, and to establish reserves in other parts of the world. The Earth is a branch of the Trust which concerns itself with general conservation matters.

The Trust makes extensive use of voluntary help; there are no paid staff. Work is available in a wide range of areas including manual work such as building and gardening, office work, computer programming, secretarial work, environmental/scientific research, writing articles, fundraising and publicity. Approx 25-50 volunteers are needed.

Ages 17+. Precise skills and qualifications required would depend on the position applied for. Volunteers should have a concern for the environment, wildlife and animal welfare, and a desire to help find lasting solutions rather than temporary cures. Knowledge of Spanish useful.

Two weeks minimum commitment preferred

Only a limited amount of accommodation available. Employer's public liability insurance and local travel costs provided.

All volunteers attend an orientation course. Debriefing of work carried out plus advice on job search.

On-going recruitment; positions subject to availability

CHRISTIAN AID

Volunteers Coordinator, Christian Aid, PO Box 100, London SE1 7RT

0171-620 4444

London head office; church-based activities throughout the UK

Established in 1945 to respond to the needs of refugees in Europe during the Second World War, Christian Aid is now the official relief and development agency of 40 British and Irish churches. Works where the need is greatest in more than 70 countries through local churches and other organisations. Searches for creative ways to address the root causes of poverty, injustice and the denial of the most basic rights to life, and attaches great importance to education and campaigning in Britain.

In the London office, volunteers do general administrative work. There are also opportunities to volunteer locally through church-based groups, especially as fundraisers during Christian Aid Week.

Ages 16+. Volunteers should have general administrative skills and a knowledge of, and interest in overseas development issues. Knowledge of French, Spanish or Portuguese always useful but not essential. **B D**

One month minimum

Hours worked are at the discretion of the volunteer. Employer's liability cover, travel expenses and lunch allowance provided in London office.

Some training available if necessary

Ongoing recruitment

Report Back annual report; various information leaflets

COUNCIL FOR EDUCATION IN WORLD CITIZENSHIP

Patricia Rogers, Director, Council for Education in World Citizenship, Seymour Mews House, Seymour Mews, London W1H 9PE

0171-935 1752   Fax 0171-935 5548

London and throughout the UK

A non-political and non-sectarian organisation promoting such studies, teachings and activities as may best contribute to mutual understanding, peace and cooperation, and goodwill between all peoples

In the London headquarters, volunteers are needed to do library work; computing (database, wordprocessing, desktop publishing); researching/writing for educational material/activities; and general administrative work. All over the UK, there are opportunities for volunteers to work with groups of CEWC member schools and colleges, organising various activities including student workshops.

No specific age limits. Volunteers must have an interest in international issues and a commitment towards education for international understanding. No specific skills or experience required; these will depend on the particular task undertaken and some training may be available.

Three months minimum commitment preferred

Volunteers are expected to work at least one 5 hour day each week. Small lunch allowance provided. Local travel expenses and other agreed essential expenditure reimbursed.

Induction given

Ongoing recruitment

CRISIS

Helen Thorp, CRISIS, 7 Whitechapel Road, London E1 1DU

0171-377 0489

London

A grant-giving charitable trust, raising money and giving grants to projects working with homeless people. Also runs the CRISIS Open Christmas, which provides food and shelter for homeless people in London over the Christmas period.

Volunteers are needed to help with administration, computer work, wordprocessing, fundraising and public relations work in the London office. Extra volunteers are also needed to help run the Open Christmas project.

No specific age limits or requirements apart from enthusiasm and commitment. Relevant experience and skills always welcome. **B D PH**

Open-ended commitment

Hours worked are at the discretion of the volunteer. Public liability insurance cover and travel expenses provided.

Orientation and training provided

Ongoing recruitment

DAYCARE TRUST

Daycare Trust, Wesley House, 4 Wild Court, London WC2B 4AU

London

A registered charity established in 1986 to provide information on childcare services and to promote affordable, accessible, quality childcare that provides equal opportunities for all

Volunteers are needed to help with administrative and information work in the London office. Some 3-5 volunteer placements are available each year.

No specific age limits. Volunteers should have an interest in childcare issues, good English, plus typing and telephone skills. Administrative experience preferred. **B D PH W**

Two months minimum

Time commitment up to 35 hours per week. Travel expenses reimbursed within the London area.

Ongoing recruitment

Childcare Now quarterly magazine; range of information leaflets and publications

DIAL UK

D McGahon, Director, DIAL UK, Park Lodge, St Catherine's Hospital, Tickhill Road, Doncaster DN4 8QN

Doncaster (01302) 310123

Head office at Doncaster, South Yorkshire and 104 local disability advice centres throughout the UK

DIAL (Disability Information and Advice Line), established in 1981, is a network of information and advice services run by disabled people. Its aims are to provide free, independent and confidential advice for disabled people and any member of the public requesting information on matters relating to disability; to promote independence and encourage the full integration of people with disabilities into mainstream society; and to provide a quality service which responds to the changing needs of clients.

Volunteers are needed to undertake advice work and help with general administration. Approx 8 volunteers work at head office, with some 200 working across the network.

No specific age limits. Volunteers must have experience of disability, either through having a disability themselves or through caring for someone with a disability. Interviewing and information skills are helpful but not essential as training is given. **B D PH W** people with disabilities preferred.

One year commitment preferred due to training requirements

Public liability insurance cover and local travel expenses provided

Some orientation usually provided, although this depends on the centre

Ongoing recruitment

Information leaflets, *Annual Report*; list of local centres

FARM - AFRICA

Benjamin Janes, Fundraiser, FARM-Africa, 9-10 Southampton Place, London WC1A 2DA

0171-430 0440

Mainly London, but also in other parts of the country

FARM-Africa was founded in 1985 with the aim of helping small peasant farmers in Africa develop agricultural skills and techniques, increase food production and break the cycle of famine. Runs seven projects in East and South Africa.

Volunteers are needed to work in the areas of public relations and fundraising. This involves work on specific projects from the planning stage right through to completion.

Ages 18+. No specific experience or qualifications needed, just enthusiasm and a real interest in Africa and some understanding of development issues. The ability to communicate the organisation's message on a variety of levels, particularly on the telephone, and to enjoy the work is also important. **B PH**

Three months minimum, starting February/March

Hours negotiable. Employer's liability insurance cover and some travel expenses provided.

One-to-one training

Ongoing recruitment, but applications in November/December preferred

Newsletter

FRIENDS OF THE EARTH

Volunteer Coordinator, Friends of the Earth, 26-28 Underwood Street, London N1 7JQ

0171-490 1555

London head office, regional offices in Sheffield, Bristol, Birmingham, Brighton, Belfast, Cardiff and Luton; network of 250 local groups throughout England, Wales and Northern Ireland

Founded in 1971, the UK's leading environmental pressure group campaigning on a wide range of environmental issues to bring about changes in policy and practice and raise public awareness. Its network of local groups work with local communities on issues of environmental importance. Part of FoE International, the largest international network of national environmental groups in the world.

Approx 50 volunteers work in London and regional offices mainly carrying out administrative support work. Also some opportunities for volunteers with specialist abilities such as research or fundraising skills. Those interested in gaining experience of environmental campaigning at a local level can get involved by joining their nearest local group.

No specific age limits. Volunteers in the London and regional offices must be genuinely interested and committed to what Friends of the Earth does; they should have basic administrative skills, a flexible approach to work and be capable of working effectively on their own initiative and as part of a small team. Local groups require people who are interested and enthusiastic about environmental issues and want to get involved in protecting the environment in their local area. **B D PH**

2-3 months minimum preferred for London and regional offices

In London and regional offices most volunteers work a 3 day week. Travel expenses up to £5 are reimbursed and a lunch allowance can be claimed depending on hours worked. Within local groups there is no formal volunteer setup; the amount of time volunteers devote to campaigning is down to their own level of commitment.

To apply for volunteer work at London or regional offices send large SAE for further details/application form. To find out about volunteering with a local group call number above for details of nearest group.

Wide range of leaflets and publications on environmental issues

GREENPEACE UK

Fraser Dyer, Volunteers Manager, Greenpeace UK, Canonbury Villas, London N1 2PN

0171-354 5100

London head office; 250 local support groups nationwide

Greenpeace was formed by a group of North American activists in 1971 and the UK office was established in 1977. It is an international environmental pressure group which actively campaigns for a nuclear-free future, to stop pollution of the natural world and to protect wildlife. Campaigns have a common purpose: to preserve or recreate an environment in which living things, including people, can survive without threat to their lives and health.

In the London office volunteers do general administrative work, such as dealing with general enquiries; or they may work in areas in which they have specific skills and/or interests. Occasionally they assist in research, information technology, translation and other projects.
In local support groups volunteers organise fundraising initiatives such as street collections and sponsored events; they may also help with campaigns by lobbying MPs, gathering signatures for petitions and publicising campaign issues.

Volunteers must be committed to the aims of Greenpeace and interested in environmental issues. They must also be able to perform routine administrative tasks and respect confidentiality at all times.
B D PH W

Three months minimum

Regular time commitment of at least one day a week expected. Employer's liability insurance cover and out-of-pocket expenses up to £7.50 per day provided.

Some training and support provided

All prospective volunteers must complete a Volunteer Information Form to outline their skills and availability. There may be a large reserve list of volunteers, so a placement is not guaranteed.

Information leaflets

GUIDEPOSTS TRUST

Guideposts Trust, Two Rivers, Station Lane, Witney, Oxon OX8 6BH

Witney (01993) 772886

Watford and Ware, Hertfordshire

A charity which establishes and supports residential nursing homes, day care centres and similar projects for those with mental illness and learning difficulties seeking rehabilitation in the community.

Projects welcoming volunteer support include Watford Day Services Centre for people with mental illness and Ware Day Services Centre for people with learning difficulties. There is also a retail shop in Ware. Work involves acting as befriender to help people to integrate into the community, accompanying them on trips, teaching them new and everyday skills. Up to 20 volunteers recruited each year.

Ages 25-65. Previous experience of working with people with learning difficulties or mental health problems an advantage but not essential. Volunteers should be patient and committed to the work, with an empathetic and positive attitude. **B D PH W**

One year minimum commitment

Volunteers work 2-3 hours a week. Public liability insurance cover and local travel expenses provided.

All volunteers must attend orientation course before beginning work

Ongoing recruitment

IMPERIAL CANCER RESEARCH FUND

Mr John Cooper, Head of Retailing, Imperial Cancer Research Fund, 61 Lincoln's Inn Fields, London WC2A 3PX

470 high street retail units throughout England, Scotland and Wales

Founded in 1902, the Imperial Cancer Research Fund is dedicated to the prevention, treatment and cure of all forms of cancer, whilst relying almost entirely on voluntary contributions

Volunteers are needed to work in charity shops

Ages 18-65. Volunteers must be honest, loyal and dedicated. Previous experience in retail, accounts or sales preferred. **D PH**

No minimum commitment

Hours worked are at the discretion of the volunteer. Insurance cover provided, but volunteers pay their own travel costs.

Ongoing recruitment

MANIC DEPRESSION FELLOWSHIP

Michelle Rowett, Manic Depression Fellowship, 8-10 High Street, Kingston-upon-Thames, Surrey, KT1 1EY

0181-974 6550

Kingston-upon-Thames, Surrey

MDF was set up in 1983 to help people with manic depression, their relatives, friends and others who care through the establishment of self-help groups; to educate the public and caring professions through the provision of information; and to encourage research for the better treatment of manic depression

Volunteers support the work of the administrative staff in head office; this can involve telephone work, wordprocessing, preparing letters and filing

Ages 16-60. Volunteers should already have some basic office experience and skills, and be willing to undertake a variety of tasks as part of a team. They should also have an understanding of mental illness.

One month minimum

35 hour week. Travelcard expenses within London reimbursed.

Apply three months in advance

Annual Report' information leaflets

NATIONAL SOCIETY FOR THE PREVENTION OF CRUELTY TO CHILDREN (NSPCC)

Regional Appeals Department, NSPCC, 42 Curtain Road, London EC2A 3NH

0171-825 2655

Head office in London; regional offices and local groups throughout England, Wales and Northern Ireland

A voluntary organisation which exists to prevent child abuse and protect children at risk of neglect or abuse. Helps children overcome the effects of ill-treatment and protects them from further harm; provides advice and counselling through its National Child Protection Helpline and a network of over 100 child protection teams and projects who work directly with children and families. Dependent on public donations for 90% of its income.

Opportunities for part-time fundraisers to organise events and attract new members; also limited number of administrative posts in London and regional offices. Over 4,000 local groups, each of which raises funds to ensure that the NSPCC in their area can continue to provide services. Fundraisers may work alone, or in a new or existing group.

Ages 16+. Volunteers should have an enthusiasm for fundraising, be sympathetic to the aims of the NSPCC and have good interpersonal skills and speak English. Experience in fundraising, dealing with the media, running events and writing newsletters useful. Typing/basic office experience often required for administrative posts; willingness to learn and to start with basic tasks sometimes sufficient. **B D PH**

No set length of service

Hours according to availability of volunteer; administrative staff work approx 15 hours per week. General liability insurance provided; travel costs provided for administrative staff.

Induction programme available in most regions

Ongoing recruitment

NSPCC News quarterly newsletter; *NSPCC Promotional Catalogue*; *Annual Report*; *Annual Review*; *NSPCC Action* magazine; information sheets

OXFAM

The Personnel Officer, Management Services Division, Oxfam, Oxfam House, 274 Banbury Road, Oxford OX2 7DZ

Oxford (01865) 311311

Headquarters in Oxford, regional offices in Glasgow, Bradford, Manchester, Newcastle-upon-Tyne, Birmingham, Cambridge, Bristol, London, Southampton, Cardiff, Belfast and Dublin; over 900 Oxfam shops throughout the country

Founded in 1942, Oxfam works with poor people regardless of race or religion in their struggle against hunger, disease, exploitation and poverty in Africa, Asia, Latin America/Caribbean, and the Middle East, through relief, development, research overseas and public education at home. Oxfam is first and foremost a development agency and, although it still provides relief in times of crisis, its main concern is long-term sustainable development.

At the Oxford headquarters volunteers help with general administrative work. Throughout the country there are also opportunities to help with campaigning and fundraising; volunteers can also work in one of Oxfam's 900 shops throughout the country.

No particular experience or skills required; volunteers are placed in suitable positions according to their abilities. They should have an interest in development issues and some understanding of the charity environment. As well as contributing their time to Oxfam, they should also be willing to learn from the experience. **B D PH W**

Open-ended commitment

Time commitment is up to the individual volunteer. Accident insurance cover and out-of-pocket expenses provided.

Volunteers can attend a 3 day *Knowledge of Oxfam* course run by the training department

Ongoing recruitment. Those wishing to volunteer in campaigning or trading locally should get a list of regional offices from headquarters.

Annual Review; variety of publications, newsletters and other resource materials

QUIT

QUIT, Victory House, 170 Tottenham Court Road, London W1P 0HA

0171-388 5775

London

Established in 1926, QUIT is the UK's only charity whose main aim is to offer practical help to people who want to stop smoking. Runs a telephone helpline and offers down-to-earth advice about stopping smoking for good.

Volunteers are required to help with administration and fundraising. Some 2-5 volunteers are taken on each year.

Ages 18+. Applicants should have good administration and wordprocessing skills, have a professional attitude and be willing to work hard. **PH**

One month minimum

35 hour week. Travel expenses reimbursed.

Ongoing recruitment

Which Way to Quit Smoking - A Consumer's Guide

REACH

The Director, REACH, Bear Wharf, 27 Bankside, London SE1 9DP

0171-928 0452

Throughout Great Britain

A registered charity founded in 1979 by a small group of executives from the business and voluntary sectors, who reasoned that retirement should be looked upon as the beginning of a new way of life and the chance of continuing to be active in the community, and were concerned that the potential resources of retired professionals were not being deployed to advantage. Arranges part-time, expenses-only jobs for retired (or redundant) people with business or professional expertise who want to work as volunteers in charities. Although it is willing to help to define problems and develop proposals in assessing the required resources, REACH does not initiate projects on its own.

Retired professional people are matched to charitable organisations where there is a need for the volunteer's skills which cannot be met in any other way, and where the task makes use of the business or professional skills requested. Skills in high demand include finance, management, marketing and public relations. Also opportunities in the fields of arts, culture, environment, religion and sport. This job-finding service is offered free of charge to both volunteers and voluntary organisations. Some 700 volunteers are placed each year.

No age restrictions providing applicants can offer professional expertise gained during their working lives. They should have a desire to utilise their skills and experience for the benefit of the community, and adapt them according to the needs of the chosen charity. **B D PH W**

No limit on length of placement; volunteers work on average 2-3 days per week but this can vary from 1 day up to 5 days per week.

Applicants are asked to complete a registration form which includes details of their skills, the duration and amount of time they are willing to give, and geographical constraints. Work is usually part-time, and out-of-pocket expenses are paid.

After placement a 6 monthly follow up is carried out by letter

Recruitment all year; apply 2 months in advance

Annual Report; information leaflets; *To Shine in Use* video; *Reach Forward* newsletter

RICHMOND FELLOWSHIP

Personnel Department, Richmond Fellowship, 8 Addison Road, London W14 8DL

0171-603 6373

Throughout the UK

A registered charity and housing association which has worked in the field of mental health since 1959. Runs more than 50 community-based projects in the UK working with people of all ages, with headquarters in London. The projects include intensive rehabilitation programmes, supported housing projects, group homes and workshops for people with mental health problems, schizophrenia, addiction and emotional problems. Work in the projects focuses on helping residents to regain personal stability, the ability to make good relationships and to find and keep a job. The Richmond Fellowship also runs its own colleges and provides a comprehensive range of training options for its own staff and for people involved in mental health and human relations work.

Volunteers are needed to work within some of the projects, supervised by project staff, assisting the residents and helping in the day-to-day running of the house. As well as assisting with the basic necessities of life, some volunteers also become involved in activities such as gardening, cooking, art, music, drama and sport.

Ages 18+. Applicants should have the commitment to do what can be a very demanding but ultimately rewarding job, and the ability to relate sensitively and sensibly to the residents. Prior experience not essential, although previous knowledge of the mental health field is useful. More important is the genuine commitment and enthusiasm to become involved in a caring role. Skills in recreational activities an advantage.

Duration dependent on volunteer, although a reasonable time period is needed to become an effective part of the team

Volunteers are usually involved in a project in the locality in which they already live. Board and lodging not provided, and there is no volunteer wage. Reasonable expenses incurred during periods of work will be reimbursed subject to receipts. Volunteers are expected to accept the obligations and codes of practice that apply to staff members.

Recruitment all year. A list of projects is available; applicants should apply directly to the project(s) where they wish to work.

SURVIVAL INTERNATIONAL

Survival International, 11-15 Emerald Street, London WC1N 3QL

0171-242 1441

London

A worldwide movement founded in 1969 to support tribal peoples, standing for their right to decide their own future and helping them protect their lands, environment and way of life

Volunteers are needed to help with general clerical work in the London office. This may involve accounts/book-keeping, fundraising, picture library administration, helping on research projects, data entry, library administration, press and publicity work. Some 20-40 volunteers are recruited each year.

Ages 16+. Volunteers are allocated work according to their experience, skills and abilities. They should be conscientious, hardworking and reliable, with an interest in the work of Survival International.

Three months minimum commitment preferred

Time commitment of at least one day a week preferred. Travel costs within the London area reimbursed.

Ongoing recruitment

Biannual *Survival Newsletter*; various books, reports and other documentation on tribal peoples and the issues affecting them

THE TERRENCE HIGGINS TRUST

Volunteer Coordinator, The Terrence Higgins Trust, 52-54 Grays Inn Road, London WC1X 8JU

0171-831 0330

Greater London

A registered charity set up in 1983 to inform, advise and help on AIDS and HIV infection. The Trust currently involves over 1,300 people, the vast majority of whom are volunteers. They provide help, advice, information, support and training not only to people with AIDS and HIV infection, but to anyone concerned about this health crisis.

Volunteers are required to work as buddies, people who make a commitment to befriend someone with AIDS, contacting them at regular periods to talk, listen and help with practical tasks. Buddies may also act as mediators or advocates, helping the person with AIDS to access resources in the community. They are not nurses or carers, but friends. Also needs volunteers to help provide a variety of other services, including practical home support (driving, plumbing, electrics, DIY, gardening, interpreting and hairdressing); counselling; a helpline; welfare, housing and legal advice; health education and information.

Ages 20+. All volunteers must have a commitment to the aims and activities of the Trust. Buddies do not need any previous experience or qualifications, but they must have a non-judgmental, non-discriminatory attitude and a respect for confidentiality. Experience and qualifications may be required for other volunteer opportunities.

One year minimum commitment

The Trust provides travel and lunch expenses where necessary as well as personal accident insurance

After interview and induction training day those considered suitable to be buddies take part in an intensive residential training weekend which covers the issues which affect a buddy's work. Buddies also required to attend follow-up training sessions as well as monthly support groups.

Apply at any time

Annual Report, *Information for Volunteers* booklet, *Could you be a friend to someone with AIDS?* information leaflet

TOURISM CONCERN

Tricia Barnett, Tourism Concern, Southlands College, Wimbledon Parkside, London SW19 5NN

0181-944 0464

South London

A membership network set up in 1989 to bring together British people with an active concern for tourism's impact on community and environment, both in the UK and worldwide. Aims to raise the issues of the impacts of tourism on people at the receiving end, especially in Third World countries.

A limited number of volunteers - approx 3 per year - are needed to work in the London office, helping with tasks such as library work, wordprocessing, graphics, design, translation and fundraising.

Ages 23+. Volunteers need to have a keen interest in tourism issues and in working for an organisation that campaigns for just, participatory and sustainable tourism. In general they will need to be fairly well-travelled in order to have a good awareness of the issues. They must have skills relevant to the work involved. Fluent English essential; knowledge of other languages useful. **PH**

Two months minimum commitment preferred

40 hour week. Volunteers must cover their own travel costs.

Half-day orientation for all volunteers

Ongoing recruitment; apply 3 months in advance

In Focus quarterly magazine

VICTIM SUPPORT

Victim Support, Cranmer House, 39 Brixton Road, London SW9 6DZ

0171-735 9166

Throughout England, Wales, Northern Ireland; similar organisations in Scotland and Ireland

An independent charity founded in 1979 and committed to providing victims of crime with appropriate and sufficient recognition, support and information to assist them in dealing with the crimes which they have experienced; and to ensuring that the rights of victims of crime are acknowledged and advanced in criminal justice and social policy.

Trained local volunteer visitors contact people following a crime to offer free, confidential support and advice. Court-based volunteers in the witness service offer support to victims or witnesses called to give evidence in the Crown Court. Volunteers are also needed to act as committee members, fundraisers or office assistants, contributing to a range of work which keeps schemes and witness services running.

Ages 18-75. Volunteers should have a caring, mature and supportive attitude, willing to help victims of crime and their families come to terms with the emotional and practical problems which follow. Knowledge of community languages helpful. It is important to be able to communicate effectively on a 1:1 basis and to demonstrate support. References and a police check are required before volunteers can begin basic training. **B D PH W** welcome, but not all offices accessible.

Training course spread over several weeks; commitment to a reasonable period of service expected

Minimum commitment for volunteer visitors of 2 hours a week; of witness service volunteers, 1 working day per fortnight. Employer's liability cover provided and any out-of-pocket expenses reimbursed.

Volunteers undergo an approved basic training course, followed by a period of supervised visiting. A coordinator is available to discuss cases and any concerns. Strict duty of confidentiality applies; volunteers may not discuss cases with anyone outside the organisation.

Apply to above address or direct to local scheme (address in telephone directory). Allow sufficient time for references and police check.

Annual Report; information leaflets

WAR ON WANT

War on Want, Fenner Brockway House, 37-39 Great Guildford Street, London SE1 0ES

0171-620 1111

London head office and over 50 local support groups countrywide

Founded in 1951, War on Want is an international aid agency actively campaigning against injustice and oppression in developing countries and for increasing awareness in the UK of the causes of world poverty. Funds long-term and emergency relief in famine areas torn by military struggle, where little international aid is sent.

Volunteers are needed in the London office to do general administrative and secretarial work. There is also a network of local groups in Britain where those interested can find out more about the issues and help with fundraising.

Ages 16+. Administrative/secretarial experience helpful but not essential. More important is a desire to gain experience and a commitment to the work of War on Want. **D PH**

Six weeks minimum commitment preferred

Regular commitment of 7-21 hours per week preferred, depending on the circumstances of the volunteer. Accident insurance cover, reasonable travel expenses and lunch expenses up to £2 per day provided.

Ongoing recruitment

Annual Report; members' newsletter; various information sheets

WOMANKIND WORLDWIDE

Womankind Worldwide, 122 Whitechapel High Street, London E1 7PT

London

A small charity established in 1989 to fund innovative activities aimed at overcoming poverty and want. Provides opportunities to improve levels of health and education, and encourages women to have a greater say in their local community.

A limited number of volunteers - approx two per year - are needed to provide administrative help in the London office

Ages 21+. Volunteers must be computer-literate, numerate with general office experience and good verbal and written communication skills. They should be willing to help and work as part of a team. As well as fluent English, a knowledge of French, Spanish and/or Portuguese is useful.

Three months minimum commitment preferred

Volunteers work two to three days per week. Employer's liability insurance cover provided. A £2 lunch allowance is paid and local travel expenses are reimbursed up to a maximum of a one-day Travelcard for each day worked.

Ongoing recruitment

THE WOODLAND TRUST

The Woodland Trust, Autumn Park, Dysart Road, Grantham, Lincolnshire NG31 6LL

Grantham (01476) 74297

England, Scotland, Wales

The Woodland Trust is Britain's largest conservation organisation concerned solely with the acquisition and management of woodland. The Trust protects Britain's heritage of native and broad leaved trees by acquiring existing woodland and open land on which to plant trees for the future, and by managing those woods in perpetuity. This ownership ensures that the woods are open to all for quiet, informal, recreation, and they remain integral parts of familiar landscapes providing habitats for wildlife benefit.

Opportunities for woodland conservation include tree planting, path and weed clearance and working as a volunteer warden. Volunteers are also required to help with local fundraising campaigns, act as speakers to inform the public about Woodland Trust and develop new ways to raise funds in order to purchase threatened woodland.

Volunteers should have an enthusiasm for woodland conservation and be committed to complete a project. All volunteers must have good interpersonal skills; experience in fundraising or woodland management useful but not essential, providing applicants are willing and capable to take on board new skills quickly. Volunteer speakers should have good communication and public presentation skills as well as experience of working with the public.

Length of service according to project; projects run throughout the year

Hours according to projects. Accident and public liability insurance provided; travel expenses depending on project.

Compulsory briefing and, where appropriate, training provided

Ongoing recruitment

WORLD DEVELOPMENT MOVEMENT

Resources Manager, World Development Movement, 25 Beehive Place, London SW9 7QR

0171-737 6215

London head office; 150 local groups and 100 lobby teams countrywide

The World Development Movement is Britain's leading campaigning organisation on Third World issues. Unshackled by charity law, its campaigns create political changes that directly benefit the world's poorest people.

In the London office, volunteers are needed to help with routine administrative work such as mailings, photocopying, wordprocessing, data entry, telephone reception work or book-keeping. A network of 150 local groups are involved in campaigning and publicity at a local level, recruiting members and raising money; also 100 lobby teams get together to campaign and lobby locally.

No experience necessary, but particular skills, knowledge or experience are always welcome and an effort will be made to use them where possible. **B D PH W**

Open-ended commitment

Time commitment is down to the individual volunteer; the office is open 0930-1730 Monday-Friday; occasionally volunteers are needed in the evenings or at weekends. Return travel/Travelcard expenses reimbursed. Lunch expenses up to £2 reimbursed for those working at least three hours a day.

Volunteers are welcome to attend fortnightly staff meetings and team meetings

Ongoing recruitment. Applicants complete volunteer form and are contacted when suitable work is available.

Annual Report; information leaflets

SHORT-TERM VOLUNTARY WORK

This guide's primary aim is to provide information and advice on medium-term (6-12 months) and long-term (1-2+ years) volunteer opportunities. However, you may be unable to commit yourself for such periods of time, not yet have the necessary skills/qualifications required on many longer-term placements, or if you have never undertaken voluntary work before, particularly outside your own country, you may wish to participate in a short-term project to gain experience. The options for short-term voluntary work are discussed in **SECTION I**, and further opportunities are detailed under **UNDERSTANDING DEVELOPMENT** and in the previous pages under **NON-RESIDENTIAL SERVICE**..

Outline details of short-term voluntary projects, ranging in length from a weekend to six weeks, are given below. Comprehensive information on short-term voluntary placements in over 50 countries worldwide is given in the annual guide *Working Holidays*, see under **INFORMATION RESOURCES**.

International workcamps are a form of short-term voluntary service providing an opportunity for people of different national, cultural and religious backgrounds to live and work together on a common project providing a constructive service to the community. By bringing together a variety of skills, talents and experiences, volunteers not only provide a service to others but also receive an opportunity for personal growth and greater awareness of their responsibility to the society in which they live and work. Workcamp participants have an opportunity to learn about the history, culture and social conditions of the host country and to partake in the community life.

Workcamps generally run for periods of 2-4 weeks, April-October; some organisations also arrange camps at Christmas, Easter and at other times throughout the year. Workcamp participants need to be mature enough not to require supervision and should be prepared to take responsibility for the successful running of the projects, group recreation activities and discussions. The minimum age is 17/18, with the exception of a number of youth projects, with a minimum age of 13.

The type of work undertaken varies considerably depending on both the area and the country in which the camp is being held. The work can include building, gardening and decorating, providing roads and water supplies to rural villages or constructing adventure playgrounds, and is within the capacity of normally fit volunteers. Virtually all workcamp organisers will consider volunteers with disabilities providing the nature of the work allows their active participation. Any manual work undertaken is usually for 7-8 hours a day, 5 or 6 days a week. Workcamps can also involve community or conservation projects with work other than that of a manual nature. A few camps have shorter working hours and an organised study programme concerned with social problems or dealing with wider international issues.

Accommodation is provided in a variety of buildings such as schools, community centres or hostels, and may sometimes be under canvas. Living conditions and sanitation vary considerably and can be very basic; in some cases running water may not be readily available. Food is generally provided, although it is often self-catering, with volunteers preparing and cooking their own meals, sometimes on a rota basis. In many camps meals will be vegetarian.

Most workcamps consist of 10-30 volunteers from several countries. English is in common use as the working language, especially in Europe; the other principal working language is French. A knowledge of the host country's language is sometimes essential, especially for community work.

Workcamp applicants will generally pay a registration fee and arrange and pay for their own travel and possibly insurance. Most workcamp organisers operate on an exchange basis with organisers in other countries. In some cases, especially with regard to workcamps in eastern Europe, the registration fee is higher in order to support the cost of the exchange. Volunteers may occasionally be expected to make a contribution towards the cost of their board and lodging, and should take pocket money to cover basic needs. Although many organisations provide insurance cover for their volunteer, this is often solely against third party risks and accidents. Volunteers are advised to obtain precise details on this and, where necessary, take out individual policies against illness, disablement and loss or damage to personal belongings. In addition to the compulsory vaccinations required for foreign travel, anyone joining a manual workcamp programme is strongly advised to have an anti-tetanus injection.

It is quite usual for workcamp organisations to arrange day or weekend orientation seminars prior to volunteers going abroad. In some cases, especially for workcamps held in east European or Third World countries, attendance at these seminars is essential. Prospective volunteers will be able to learn a lot about aspects of voluntary work in the relevant countries as well as gaining background information on politics, culture and the way of life.

The following organisations run workcamps in the UK and also recruit volunteers for workcamps run by partner organisations overseas.

International Voluntary Service, Old Hall, East Bergholt, Colchester, Essex CO7 6TQ, the British branch of Service Civil International, a network of workcamp organisers promoting international reconciliation through work projects.

Concordia (Youth Service Volunteers) Ltd, 8 Brunswick Place, Hove, Sussex BN3 1ET ✆ Brighton (01273) 772086 aims to bring together the youth of all nations to promote a better understanding of their ideas, beliefs and ways of living.

Quaker International Social Projects, Friends House, Euston Road, London NW1 2BJ ✆ 0171-387 3601 aims to promote cooperation and understanding through non-violent methods; to support community initiatives; to enable people from different cultures to live together; to facilitate personal growth, the acquisition of skills and a sense of personal responsibility. Applicants for workcamps abroad must be over 18 with previous workcamp or voluntary service experience.

United Nations Association International Youth Service, Temple of Peace, Cathays Park, Cardiff CF1 3AP ✆ Cardiff (01222) 223088 aims to assist in community development by acting as a means to stimulate new ideas and projects, encouraging the concept of voluntary work as a force in the common search for peace, equality, democracy and social justice.

Volunteering in the 90s consists of two booklets listing organisations running workcamps. Book 1 covers Africa & Asia; book 2 covers Europe & North America. Published, with the support of UNESCO, by the Coordinating Committee for International Voluntary Service, 1 rue Miollis, 75732 Paris Cedex 15, France, cost £1 or 5 IRCs for each volume.

International workcamps are generally concerned with community and social schemes, but short-term voluntary work may also be undertaken on archaeological, conservation or environmental projects.

Archaeology Sitting in the bottom of a trench for hours on end, carefully brushing away decades of deposits is not everyone's idea of fun, but involvement in a project that may discover important finds of Palaeolithic, Bronze Age or Roman habitation has its particular rewards. Learning from the archaeological past is to seek to understand the Earth's history and discover how humans, plants and animals have adapted to change over millions of years.
As well as investigation into ancient monuments, archaeological projects also study landscapes, buildings and the evidence left behind by previous environments. You may be studying the life of reindeer hunters in France; working on Roman, Anglo-Saxon or medieval sites in Britain; or uncovering the skeletons of bison killed thousands of years ago by Native Americans. Many projects welcome complete beginners, but in some cases a more formal interest in history or a knowledge of archaeological techniques may be required. Experience is best first acquired on sites in your own country, after which you will find it easier to be accepted onto an excavation overseas. Archaeological

work can be hard and may continue in all weathers, so prepare yourself accordingly. Any relevant skills should be made clear when applying; those with graphic, topographic or photographic skills are often particularly welcome.

Wages and/or travelling expenses may be offered to more experienced volunteers; beginners usually pay a participation fee. Basic accommodation is normally provided, but you may need to take a tent and/or cooking equipment. The minimum age is usually 18; those under 18 may be welcome provided they have a letter giving parental consent or are accompanied by a participating adult. Work may be available almost all year round, but owing to the nature of the work, projects are most often undertaken in the summer season. Participants are advised to have an anti-tetanus injection beforehand.

The Council for British Archaeology, Bowes Morrell House, 111 Walmgate, York YO1 2UA ✆ York (01904) 671417 Fax (01904) 671384 operates a British archaeological information service, which gives details on how volunteers can assist in excavations. *CBA Briefing*, a supplement to *British Archaeological News* lists sites requiring volunteer helpers, giving details of location, type and accommodation. Available through membership (£18 for individuals, £10 for students).

Archaeology Abroad, 31-34 Gordon Square, London WC1H 0PY provides information on opportunities for archaeological fieldwork and excavations outside Britain; full details are given in 3 bulletins a year.

The Archaeological Institute of America, 675 Commonwealth Avenue, Boston, MA 02215, United States publishes the annual *Archaeological Fieldwork Opportunities Bulletin*, cost US$10.50 + $3 postage, which lists sites throughout the world where excavation and research are being carried out. Details are given of staff and volunteers needed at each site. Also lists field schools which provide practical training.

Conservation work The Earth is 4,600 million years old; over the last 150 years we have come ever closer to upsetting the planet's ecological balance. Earth's human inhabitants have raided the planet for fuels, used the land, sea and air as rubbish tips and caused the extinction of over 500 species of animals. If you care about the future of planet Earth and would like to make some contribution, no matter how small, towards its health and management, then a variety of conservation projects offer the opportunity for you to put your concerns to practical use.

Work can be undertaken on a wide variety of tasks: carrying out surveys to determine current population levels, habits or optimum environment of different species; building trails through forests and nature reserves; cleaning polluted rivers, ponds and lakes; stabilising sand dunes; or acting as environmental interpreter in a nature centre.

There are also plenty of opportunities to preserve the built environment, including the restoration of railways, canals and other aspects of our industrial heritage; renovating churches, castles, stately homes and gardens; rebuilding abandoned hamlets; carrying out coppicing and hedge laying and building drystone walls.

Relevant skills are welcome, but not essential, and many projects will include training on particular aspects of conservation work. All tasks involve work which could not be achieved without volunteer assistance. The projects are normally undertaken during the summer months, though opportunities exist at other times, and sometimes all year round. Basic accommodation is provided in church or village halls, schools, farm buildings or hostels, depending on the situation. Food is usually provided on a self-catering basis, with volunteers taking it in turns to cook. Volunteers contribute towards the cost of food and pay their own travel costs. Work can be strenuous; all volunteers should be fit and are strongly advised to have an anti-tetanus injection before joining any project.

The organisations listed below arrange short-term conservation projects. Some of them have a local group network, where, for example, volunteers can get involved in weekend conservation projects taking place in their locality.

The British Trust for Conservation Volunteers, 36 St Mary's Street, Wallingford, Oxfordshire OX10 0EU ✆ Wallingford (01491) 839766 is a charity promoting practical conservation work by volunteers and organises numerous working holidays throughout England, Wales and Northern Ireland. BTCV also cooperate with a number of conservation organisations overseas during the summer to offer places for volunteers on international projects.

The Scottish Conservation Projects Trust, Balallan House, 24 Allan Park, Stirling FK8 2QG ✆ Stirling (01786) 479697 is a charity promoting the involvement of volunteers working to improve the quality of Scotland's environment. Projects are organised throughout Scotland, including the Western Isles, Orkney and Shetland.

National Trust Working Holidays, PO Box 538, Melksham, Wiltshire SN12 8SU ✆ Melksham (01225) 790290 offer the opportunity to carry out conservation work on National Trust properties throughout England, Wales and Northern Ireland, including houses and gardens, parks and estates, mountains, moors, coastlines, farms and nature reserves.

National Trust for Scotland Thistle Camps, 5 Charlotte Square, Edinburgh EH2 4DU ✆ 0131-226 5922 ext 257 are residential work projects organised by the National Trust for Scotland where volunteers can help in the conservation and practical management of properties in the care of the Trust.

Earthwatch Europe, Belsyre Court, 57 Woodstock Road, Oxford OX2 6HU ✆ Oxford (01865) 516366 aims to support field research in a wide range of disciplines including archaeology, ornithology, animal behaviour, nature conservation and ecology, giving support to researchers as a grant and in the form of volunteer assistance. Members can take part in expeditions running worldwide, but are expected to share the cost of the expedition and pay their own travel expenses.

SECTION VIII

INDEX

REPORT FORM

COUNTRIES INDEX

AFRICA
66, 67, 68, 69, 70, 71, 72, 73, 77, 83, 85, 86, 87, 88, 89, 90, 92, 94, 95, 98, 99, 102, 103, 105, 106, 107, 110, 111, 113, 119, 120, 121, 122, 123, 124, 126, 127, 130, 134, 137, 139, 140, 141, 142, 143, 146, 148, 149, 152, 156, 157, 158, 159, 160, 161

Angola 72, 83, 92, 120, 122, 161
Benin 120, 130
Bophutatswana 149
Botswana 122, 130, 137, 142
Burkina Faso 71, 122, 140, 148
Burundi 92, 120, 130
Cameroon 70, 120, 130
Cape Verde 130
Central African Republic 71, 130
Chad 83, 120, 122, 123, 130
Comoros 130
Congo 120, 130
Côte d'Ivoire 71, 130
Djibouti 120
Eritrea 127
Egypt 73, 121, 122, 148, 152
Equatorial Guinea 120, 130
Ethiopia 83, 92, 99, 103, 120, 123, 146
Gabon 130
Gambia 130, 152
Ghana 120, 126, 130, 146, 152
Guinea 120, 130
Guinea-Bissau 130, 152
Kenya 67, 70, 85, 92, 94, 99, 102, 119, 120, 122, 123, 124, 126, 130, 146, 148, 149, 152
Lesotho 119, 122, 130, 137
Liberia 120, 146
Madagascar 71, 85, 120, 123, 130, 142
Malawi 120, 127, 130, 146, 152
Mali 120, 130, 140, 161
Mauritania 120, 130, 161
Mauritius 71
Morocco 130
Mozambique 83, 87, 92, 99, 120, 122, 127, 130, 137, 139, 152, 158
Namibia 110, 123, 127, 130, 152
Niger 130
Nigeria 122, 130, 146, 152
Rwanda 92, 99, 120, 130, 161
São Tomé & Principe 130, 152
Senegal 71, 130
Seychelles 130
Sierra Leone 88, 102, 103, 130, 146, 149, 152
Somalia 83, 92, 99, 120, 148, 161
South Africa 94, 102, 119, 120, 122, 127, 146, 148, 149, 152
Sudan 70, 87, 99, 120, 122, 158, 161
Swaziland 127, 130, 137
Tanzania 66, 87, 92, 94, 103, 105, 120, 123, 127, 130, 146, 148, 149, 152, 158
Togo 103, 130
Tunisia 130
Uganda 70, 85, 92, 94, 99, 102, 103, 119, 120, 122, 123, 130, 148, 149, 152
Zaire 70, 72, 87, 92, 99, 120, 122, 130
Zambia 66, 120, 122, 127, 130, 142, 146, 149, 152
Zimbabwe 66, 94, 99, 110, 120, 122, 127, 130, 142, 146, 148, 149, 152

ASIA
66, 70, 72, 75, 77, 78, 83, 85, 86, 90, 92, 94, 95, 98, 102, 104, 106, 107, 108, 111, 112, 114, 116, 117, 120, 122, 126, 127, 128, 130, 134, 141, 142, 143, 145, 146, 152, 156, 157, 159, 160

Afghanistan 114, 120, 127
Bangladesh 72, 92, 120, 122, 127, 142, 152
Bhutan 127, 152
India 66, 72, 78, 83, 85, 102, 104, 108, 112, 116, 120, 122, 126, 127, 142, 145, 146

Kazakhstan 130
Kyrghyzstan 130
Maldives 127, 152
Mongolia 127, 130
Nepal 72, 75, 112, 126, 127, 130, 152
Pakistan 70, 112, 114, 126, 127, 152
Sri Lanka 72, 117, 120, 127, 128, 130, 152
Tajikistan 120
Turkmensitan 130
Uzbekistan 130

CARIBBEAN
71, 72, 73, 77, 85, 89, 98, 99, 106, 110, 120, 122, 127, 131, 141, 142, 146, 148, 152, 159, 160

Anguilla 130, 152
Antigua/Barbuda 130, 152
Dominica 130, 152
Dominican Republic 85, 99, 110, 130, 148
Grenada 130, 146, 152
Haiti 71, 73, 85, 110, 120, 122, 130, 146
Jamaica 72, 122, 130, 142, 146
Montserrat 130, 152
Puerto Rico 73
St Kitts/Nevis 85, 130, 152
St Lucia 126, 130, 152
St Vincent & Grenadines 130, 152
Trinidad 72, 146
Turks & Caicos 152
Virgin Islands 73

CENTRAL & EASTERN EUROPE
72, 73, 77, 94, 96, 99, 107, 114, 120, 122, 126, 130, 132, 135, 142, 151, 156, 160, 161

Albania 72, 96, 120, 130
Armenia 120, 130
Azerbaijan 120
Belarus 130
Bosnia Herzegovina 120

Bulgaria 96, 114, 130
Croatia 120, 122, 135
Czech Republic 96, 130, 135
Estonia 96, 130
Former Yugoslavia 120
Hungary 96, 130, 135, 142
Latvia 96, 130, 151
Lithuania 96, 130
Macedonia 96
Moldova 130
Poland 73, 96, 114, 130
Romania 99, 114, 120, 126, 130, 135, 142, 161
Russia 94, 96, 122, 130, 161
Slovakia 96, 130, 135
Ukraine 114, 130

EUROPE
69, 71, 72, 73, 79, 90, 94, 100, 104, 119, 120, 124, 134, 138, 139, 141, 142, 146, 154, 164-225

Belgium 71, 72, 120
Denmark 154
France 69, 71, 72, 73, 94, 120, 124
Germany 69, 71, 73, 79, 142
Great Britain 69, 71, 90, 104, 119, 124, 139, 143, 164-169, 171-186, 188, 190-193, 196-225
Ireland 73, 168, 189, 214
Italy 69, 72, 142
Luxembourg 71
Malta 130
Netherlands 71, 73, 124
Northern Ireland 73, 170, 187, 208, 213, 214, 221
Portugal 94, 138
Spain 69, 71, 94, 120, 138
Sweden 100
Switzerland 71, 73, 104

FAR EAST
69, 71, 72, 73, 76, 83, 87, 89, 92, 99, 120, 122, 124, 126, 127, 130, 142, 152, 158, 161

Burma *120*
Cambodia *87, 92, 120, 122, 127, 152, 158, 161*
China (People's Republic) *73, 99, 120, 122, 127, 130, 142, 152*
Hong Kong *120, 127, 142*
Indonesia *83, 122, 127, 152*
Japan *69, 99, 124*
Laos *92, 99, 120, 122, 127, 152*
Malaysia *127*
Singapore *124*
Taiwan *71, 142*
Thailand *71, 72, 87, 99, 120, 126, 127, 130, 152*
Tibet *120*
Vietnam *76, 99, 120, 122, 127, 161*

MIDDLE EAST

73, 90, 110, 120, 121, 122, 125, 130, 134, 136, 140, 141, 144, 160

Iraq *120*
Israel *73, 125, 136, 144*
Jordan *121, 122, 144*
Lebanon *120, 121, 144*
Occupied Territories *120, 121*
Palestinian Authority *120*
West Bank/Gaza Strip *140, 144*
Yemen *110, 120, 130*

NORTH & CENTRAL AMERICA

69, 71, 72, 73, 74, 80, 81, 82, 84, 85, 91, 99, 101, 104, 109, 110, 115, 118, 120, 122, 124, 126, 127, 128, 130, 132, 133, 134, 146, 147, 148

Canada *71, 101, 122*
Costa Rica *85, 130*
Cuba *120*
El Salvador *72, 73, 85, 110, 120, 122, 127, 130*
Guatemala *71, 85, 120, 127, 127, 128, 130*
Honduras *71, 73, 85, 99, 110, 130*
Mexico *73, 85, 104, 127, 148*
Nicaragua *72, 73, 74, 85, 99, 110, 118, 120, 122, 127, 130*
Panama *120, 131*
United States *69, 71, 73, 80, 81, 82, 84, 85, 91, 109, 115, 122, 124, 126, 132, 133, 147*

PACIFIC

71, 77, 85, 86, 99, 120, 122, 127, 130, 141, 142, 152, 159

Cook Islands *127, 130*
Fiji *127, 130, 152*
Kiribati *127, 130, 142, 152*
Marshall Islands *127, 130*
Micronesia, Federated States *127, 130*
Palau *127*
Papua New Guinea *120, 127, 130, 142, 152*
Philippines *71, 85, 99, 120, 122, 127, 130, 152*
Solomon Islands *127, 130, 142, 152*
Tonga *127, 130, 152*
Tuvalu *127, 130, 142, 152*
Vanuatu *127, 130, 152*
Western Samoa *127, 130, 142*

SOUTH / LATIN AMERICA

70, 72, 73, 83, 85, 94, 95, 98, 99, 103, 106, 110, 111, 113, 118, 120, 122, 127, 128, 130, 138, 140, 141, 143, 146, 148, 152, 157, 159, 160

Argentina *118, 130, 138, 146*
Belize *130, 152*
Bolivia *73, 85, 94, 99, 103, 118, 120, 122, 130, 138, 140*
Brazil *72, 83, 85, 103, 118, 120, 122, 138, 140, 146, 148*
Chile *70, 73, 85, 130, 138, 146*
Colombia *85, 103, 120, 128*
Ecuador *73, 83, 110, 118, 130*
Falkland Islands *70*
Guyana *152*
Paraguay *103, 130, 138*
Peru *83, 85, 94, 99, 110, 118, 120, 138*
Uruguay *73, 130, 138*
Venezuela *85, 147*

PROJECTS INDEX

AGRICULTURE, HORTICULTURE & FISHERIES
68, 72-74, 85, 88, 92, 94, 99, 110, 113, 117, 122, 127, 130, 137, 140, 141, 143, 145, 146, 149, 152, 161, 180, 201

CONSERVATION, ENVIRONMENT & FORESTRY
73, 88, 92, 108, 110, 127, 130, 140, 141, 148, 152, 159, 223

ANIMAL HUSBANDRY & HEALTH
117, 140, 152, 159, 201, 224

BUILDING & CONSTRUCTION
68, 70, 87, 88, 92, 101, 105, 113, 117, 118, 130, 137, 146, 149, 152, 201

ENGINEERING & TECHNICAL SERVICES
68, 70, 72, 87, 92, 95, 99, 110, 112, 113, 117, 120, 122, 123, 124, 127, 130, 146, 149, 152, 159

ARCHITECTURE & PLANNING
130, 137, 139, 152

WATER TECHNOLOGY
92, 122, 126, 130, 140, 156, 160

COMMUNITY WORK / COMMUNITY DEVELOPMENT
68, 73-75, 79, 80-85, 87, 89, 92, 95, 98, 100-102, 107-109, 112, 113, 115, 116, 122, 125, 132, 134, 136, 140, 143, 146, 148, 149, 152, 156, 164-167, 169, 170, 171, 173, 175, 178, 179, 182, 183, 185, 188, 189, 190, 217, 219

SOCIAL PROJECTS
68-73, 83-85, 88, 91, 92, 96, 113, 115, 116, 122, 127, 128, 139, 141, 143, 146-148, 152, 158, 168, 169, 172, 174, 176-178, 180, 181, 188, 190-193, 196, 197, 210, 217, 219, 221

CRAFTS & SMALL INDUSTRIES
73, 77, 85, 110, 130, 141, 152

ACCOUNTANCY & LAW
92, 94, 95, 120, 132, 136, 141, 142, 149, 152, 156, 159, 216

MANAGEMENT & ADMINISTRATION
68, 77, 92, 94-96, 99, 117, 120, 122, 123, 127, 130, 132, 139, 142, 145, 148, 149, 152, 156, 161, 191, 198-209, 211-216, 218, 220, 222, 223, 225

MEDIA & COMMUNICATIONS
94, 110, 127, 139, 140, 148, 152, 154, 156, 201, 203-207, 209, 213-216, 218, 222, 224, 225

EDUCATION & VOCATIONAL TRAINING
67, 68, 69, 70, 72, 73, 74, 76, 83, 84, 85, 88, 89, 92, 94, 95, 96, 98, 99, 108, 110, 112, 113, 116, 117, 119, 122, 127, 130, 133, 135, 136, 137, 138, 139, 141, 142, 143, 144, 146, 147, 149, 151, 152, 159, 161

YOUTH WORK & CHILDCARE
67, 73, 79, 80, 84, 85, 101, 110, 112, 116, 133, 136, 138, 144, 147, 148, 154, 166, 168, 170, 171, 175, 184, 193

MEDICINE & HEALTHCARE
66, 68, 70, 72, 73, 74, 75, 78, 83, 85, 86, 87, 88, 89, 92, 94, 95, 96, 99, 103, 106, 107, 108, 110, 111, 112, 113, 114, 115, 117, 120, 121, 122, 126, 127, 130, 133, 137, 138, 139, 140, 141, 142, 143, 144, 145, 147, 148, 149, 152, 156, 157, 158, 159, 160, 161, 186, 191

PASTORAL & EVANGELICAL
70, 72, 90, 94, 113, 118, 122, 124, 142, 146, 147, 149, 168, 193

ORGANISATIONS INDEX

ACET 24, 196
Action Health 51, 66
ADFAM National 197
Africa Inland Mission 67
Air Travel Advisory Bureau 59
Amnesty International British Section 34
Appropriate Health Resources & Technologies Action Group (AHRTAG) 35
APSO 68
Archaeological Institute of America 229
Archaeology Abroad 229
Associate Missionaries of the Assumption 69
Associates of Mill Hill Missionaries 70
ATD Fourth World 71, 164

Baptist Missionary Society 72
Beannachar Ltd 165
Book Aid International 198
Brethren Volunteer Service 73
Bristol Link with Nicaragua 74
Britain-Nepal Medical Trust 75
Britain-Vietnam Friendship Society 76
British Dyslexia Association 199
British Executive Service Overseas 77
British Limbless Ex-Service Men's Association 200
British Red Cross 156
British Trust for Conservation Volunteers 230

CAFOD 35
Calcutta Rescue 78
Cambridge Cyrenians 22
Camphill am Bodensee 79
Camphill Rudolf Steiner Schools 166
Camphill Special Schools (Beaver Run) 80
Camphill Village Kimberton Hills 81
Camphill Village Trust 167
Camphill Village USA Inc 82
Campus Travel 59

Careforce 168
Cat Survival Trust/The Earth 201
Central Bureau for Educational Visits & Exchanges 40, 43
Centre for International Briefing 52
Centro Studi Terzo Mondo 83
Christian Aid 202
Christian Appalachian Project 84
Christian Foundation for Children & Aging 85
Christian Medical Fellowship 86
Christian Outreach 14, 87
Christian Service Centre 41, 44, 52
Christian Welfare & Social Relief Organisation 88
Christians Abroad 41, 45, 52, 57, 89
Church Missionary Society 90
Comhlàmh 57
Commonwealth Institute 35
Community for Creative Non-Violence 91
Community Service Volunteers (CSV) 30, 169
Concern/Concern Worldwide 92
Concordia (Youth Service Volunteers) 228
Contributions Agency 64
Coordinating Committee for International Voluntary Service (CCIVS) 41, 45, 228
Corrymeela Community 170
Cotswold Community 171
Council for British Archaeology 229
Council for Education in World Citizenship (CEWC) 36, 203
Council for International Educational Exchange 41
CRISIS 204
Crosslinks 94
CRYPT Foundation 172

Daycare Trust 205
DIAL UK 206
Dienst Over Grenzen 95

Directory of Social Change 41

Earthscan Publications 42
Earthwatch Europe 230
East European Partnership 29, 30, 96
Edinburgh Cyrenians 173
Education for Development 98
Expedition Advisory Centre 43

FARM-Africa 207
Food for the Hungry 99
Föreningen Staffansgården 100
Friends of the Earth 36, 208
Frontiers Foundation/Operation
    Beaver 101
Future in Our Hands Movement 102

German Leprosy Relief Association 103
Glasgow Simon Community 174
Great George's Project 175
Greenpeace UK 36, 209
Guide Association (UK) 104
Guideposts Trust 210

Health Unlimited 157
Health Projects Abroad 40, 105
Health Volunteers Overseas 106
HelpAge International 158
Help International 107
Homes for Homeless People 176

Imperial Cancer Research Fund 211
Independent Living Schemes 27, 177
Independent Schools Careers
    Organisation 43
India Development Group 108
Innisfree Village 109
Intermediate Technology Development
    Group 36
International Cooperation for
    Development 110
International Health Exchange 111
International Voluntary Service 228
Interserve 112
Irish Missionary Union 113
IT Publications 42

Jacob's Well Appeal 114
Jesuit Volunteer Community (Britain) 178
Jesuit Volunteer Corps (United States-
    Southwest) 115
Joint Assistance Centre 116

Key Travel 59
Kuperard (London) 44

L'Arche Limited 28, 179
Land Use Volunteers 180
Lanka Jathika Sarvodaya Sangamaya
    (Inc) 117
Latin America Bureau 37
Latin Link 118
Leonard Cheshire Foundation 181
Link Africa 119
Loch Arthur Village Community 182
Lothlorien (Rokpa Trust) 183

Manic Depression Fellowship 212
Médecins Sans Frontières 120
Medical Advisory Service to Travellers
    Abroad (MASTA) 63
Medical Aid for Palestinians 121
Mennonite Central Committee 122
Minority Rights Group 37
Mission Aviation Fellowship 123
Missions to Seamen 21, 124

Nansen Society (UK) Ltd 184
National Association of Volunteer
    Bureaux (NAVB) 46
National Council for Voluntary
    Organisations 41
National Social Service Board 46
National Society for the Prevention of
    Cruelty to Children (NSPCC) 213
National Trust for Scotland Thistle
    Camps 230
National Trust Working Holidays 230
Neve Shalom/Wahat Al-Salam 125
New Internationalist 42
North-South Travel 59
Northern Ireland Volunteer Development
    Agency 46

Options 126
Overseas Development
  Administration 159
Overseas Development Institute 37
Overseas Service Bureau 127
Oxfam 37, 160, 214
Oxfam Publishing 38, 42

Paradise Community 185
Passport Office 60
Peace Brigades International 128
Peace Corps 130
Population Concern 38

Quaker International Social Projects 228
QUIT 215

REACH 216
Returned Volunteer Action 40, 46, 53, 55, 58
Richmond Fellowship 217
Richmond Fellowship International 132

St Christopher's Hospice 186
St Joseph's Indian School 133
Scottish Churches World Exchange 134
Scottish Conservation Projects Trust 230
Scottish Council for Voluntary
  Organisations 47
Services for Open Learning 135
Share Discovery 80 Ltd 187
SHATIL: Support Project for Voluntary
  Organizations 136
Simon Community 188
Simon Community (Ireland) 189
Skillshare Africa 137
South American Missionary Society 138
Southern Africa Resource Centre 139
Southern Voices Project 55
STA Travel 59
Stallcombe House Ltd 190
Sue Ryder Foundation 191
Survival International 38, 218

Terrence Higgins Trust 219
Third World First 38

Time for God Scheme 192
Tools for Self Reliance 38
Tourism Concern 220
Trailfinders 59
Trotman & Company 43

UK Committee for UNICEF 39
UN Non-Governmental Liaison Service
  (NGLS) 43
United Nations Association International
  Service (UNAIS) 17, 25, 140
United Nations Association International
  Youth Service 228
United Nations Volunteers (UNV) 141
United Reformed Church in the United
  Kingdom 142
United Society for the Propagation of the
  Gospel 143
USIT 59
Universities' Educational Fund for
  Palestinians (UNIPAL) 144

Vacation Work 41
VADHU 145
Viatores Christi 146
Victim Support 221
Vincentian Service Corps 147, 193
Visions in Action 148
Volunteer Centre UK 22, 47
Volunteer Missionary Movement 53, 149
Volunteers for Latvia 151
VSO 27, 56, 152

Wales Council for Voluntary Action 47
War on Want 39, 222
WEXAS International 43
Womankind Worldwide 223
Woodland Trust 224
World Assembly of Youth 154
World Development Movement 39, 225
World Vision UK 161
Worldaware 39

Zed Books 42

REPORT FORM

Up-to-date reports enable us to improve the accuracy and standard of information in our guidebooks, and monitor the opportunities available. Your completion and return of this form, after a period of voluntary service, would therefore be much appreciated. Please return to the Information, Print & Design Unit, Central Bureau for Educational Visits & Exchanges, Seymour Mews, London W1H 9PE. **All reports will be treated in strict confidence.**

Name and address of volunteer-sending agency

When did you work for them, and for how long?

Country/area

Type of work involved

How efficient were the agency in arranging the placement?

How adequately were you occupied during the assignment?

Type of orientation or training provided

Do you think it was adequate?

PLEASE TURN OVER

What was the relationship between the organisation you were working for and the local people?

Do you think that volunteers are really needed on the project?

What sort of help or advice was given to you once the assignment had finished?

Would you recommend this volunteer opportunity?

Please feel free to send a covering letter with any further comments you may have

Name

Address

Age   Signed   Date